Shannon Foster

Solution-Focused Treatment
of Domestic Violence Offenders

Aurora McEwenØ

Solution-Focused Treatment of Domestic Violence Offenders

Accountability for Change

Mo Yee Lee

John Sebold

and

Adriana Uken

OXFORD

UNIVERSITY PRESS

2003

OXFORD
UNIVERSITY PRESS

Oxford   New York

Auckland   Bangkok   Buenos Aires   Cape Town   Chennai
Dar es Salaam   Delhi   Hong Kong   Istanbul   Karachi   Kolkata
Kuala Lumpur   Madrid   Melbourne   Mexico City   Mumbai   Nairobi
São Paulo   Shanghai   Taipei   Tokyo   Toronto

Copyright © 2003 by Oxford University Press, Inc.

Published by Oxford University Press, Inc.
198 Madison Avenue, New York, New York 10016

www.oup.com

Oxford is a registered trademark of Oxford University Press

Library of Congress Cataloging-in-Publication Data

Lee, Mo Yee.
  Solution-focused treatment of domestic violence offenders: accountability
for change / by Mo Yee Lee, John Sebold, Adriana Uken.
     p. cm.
  Includes bibliographical references and index.
  ISBN 978-0-19-514677-6
  1. Abusive men—Counseling of. 2. Abusive men—Rehabilitation. 3.
Group counseling. 4. Solution-focused therapy. I. Sebold, John. II.
Uken, Adriana. III. Title.
   HV6626 .L44 2003
    362.82'9286—dc21   2002006009

9 8 7 6 5 4 3 2

Printed in the United States of America
on acid-free paper

Foreword

In numerous presentations, workshops, and supervision and consultation sessions I conduct every year, I meet many practitioners who are rightly curious and yet skeptical whenever I talk about the work of Lee, Sebold, and Uken. Many practitioners wonder how a person with a history of serious problems such as domestic violence could be treated with an intervention model that is often described as being minimal. They question how such huge problems can be treated in a nonconfrontational, nonblaming, and respectful approach as the solution-focused model. Do these offenders with personality disorders and lifelong flaws and habits of resorting to violence not need to be reeducated and made aware of what harm they are inflicting to their loved ones?

Holding someone accountable for solutions is a much more compelling way to conceptualize what we do with our clients. It also challenges the traditional view of the helping relationship not only because solution-focused therapy is an infinitely more respectful way to work with a client with very serious problems but also because it is liberating and optimistic to believe that clients are in control of their future, regardless of what kind of past they have had. By insisting that clients behave differently and holding them accountable for doing so, the authors demand that clients change, but these demands are spoken in gentle tones, as the reader will find described in this book. When they insist that a client comes up with a goal in order to stay in the group and fulfill requirements of the mandate, the client must change. Rather than micromanaging how and what to do to make this change, the therapists guide the journey of this change process, but not the destination.

I have had many conversations with John Sebold and Adriana Uken over the years, and it is awe-inspiring to listen to them describe their clients with such a sense of respect, admiration for their creativity, and tender feelings for their small successes. From the first phone contact to the termination, the authors describe, in detailed, step-by-step guidelines, ways to engage often angry clients—from first meeting to the last session of completing the assignments. Their guidelines express their philosophy and belief about their clients and how they approach their work with them.

This ability to think "outside the box" generated their treatment model, which shows great promise for treating these serious problems from a nonpathology stance. I recommend this book as a pioneering work of a dedicated scholar and two innovative and creative practitioners.

Insoo Kim Berg
Milwaukee, Wisconsin
January 2002

Preface

We have previously used a psychoeducational and confrontational approach in our work with domestic violence offenders that attempted to hold participants responsible for their problems of violence. We, like many other therapists, deeply felt the frustration of not being able to facilitate positive changes in this group of participants, who are commonly labeled "involuntary," "defensive," "uncooperative," and "difficult." Inspired by the work of Insoo Kim Berg, Steve de Shazer, and their associates at the Brief Family Therapy Center in Milwaukee, we started to experiment with a treatment approach that holds people accountable for solutions rather than responsible for problems. We have been surprised by the many positive changes in our group participants.

This book is written for helping professionals working with domestic violence offenders, for psychologists, social workers, therapists, and graduate students who have an interest in solution-focused therapy or a strength perspective, as well as for professionals working with court-mandated participants. We provide a pragmatic, step-by-step guide from intake assessment to termination about how to capitalize on participants' strengths and goal accomplishment to assist their efforts to do something different and beneficial in their lives.

Chapter 1 discusses the current scene of treatment for domestic violence offenders and highlights the debate between "responsibility for problems" versus "accountability for solutions." We also describe the principles and assumptions of solution-focused group treatment with domestic violence offenders. Chapter 2 focuses on assessment of and initial contact with group participants. We discuss in detail a solution-focused perspective of assessment that is substantially different from traditional assessment of domestic violence offenders in that participants are viewed as assessors, and the emphasis of assessment is on strengths and exceptions as opposed to the history of the problems and the severity of violence. We explain the step-by-step process starting with the initial phone contact and showing how accountability for change is introduced in the assessment interview.

In chapter 3, we discuss eight group rules that are imperative in establishing helpful group norms that encourage beneficial behaviors and eliminate potentially unhelpful and distracting conversations and behaviors in participants. In addition, we discuss useful assignments and helpful ideas regarding working as a team.

Chapters 4, 5, and 6 are devoted to a detailed discussion of the different stages of the treatment process. We utilize goals to provide an immediate and relevant context for participants to discover strengths in themselves and viable solutions for their problems. Chapter 4 focuses on the process of goal setting. We discuss clinical challenges in assisting participants in developing useful goals and suggest techniques for helping participants when they struggle with setting goals. Chapter 5 moves beyond the goal-setting stage to describe the process of utilizing goals in the change process. When participants report positive changes as a result of their goal work, we discuss techniques that can amplify, reinforce, and expand those changes. We also provide detailed pragmatic suggestions to assist participants who report no change. Chapter 6 focuses on useful therapeutic techniques that help consolidate changes in the final sessions.

Our group treatment model is different from most traditional group models in that the group process is secondary to an individual's search for solutions, which is essentially an individual exercise. Nonetheless, the group process constitutes a major and positive force for change. In chapter 7, we discuss the ways we differentially utilize the group process in each stage of our work with domestic violence offenders.

In chapter 8, we share useful principles and therapeutic tools to engage participants in accomplishing positive changes in their lives. We discuss the art of not knowing, the importance of creating choice, the role of playfulness in change, and useful therapeutic dialogues and questions in the process. Chapter 9 is devoted to a discussion regarding common but challenging situations that we have encountered in providing group treatment for domestic violence offenders. Chapter 10 describes the outcome study of our program. We involved program participants and their spouses or partners in sharing with us changes in participants' relational behaviors and self-esteem, as well as their experiences and views of our treatment programs. We also used official arrest records to examine recidivism rates for participants. Chapter 11 offers some of our final thoughts about our program. We discuss potential modifications, useful application of this program to other participant populations, and the domestic violence system of care.

This book is an effort of collaboration, and the naming of authors is based on alphabetical order. It is also collaboration between professionals in the field and a researcher from the university. John Sebold and Adriana Uken, director and senior therapist, respectively, at Plumas County Mental Health Services, are the facilitators who developed and have run the solution-focused groups for domestic violence offenders since 1991. Mo

Yee Lee, an associate professor at Ohio State University, is a researcher and a solution-oriented therapist and is responsible for evaluating the treatment program.

Our thanks must go, first, to Insoo Kim Berg for starting us on the journey to write about what we do and for her persistent encouragement, chiding, and friendship. Also, we would not have been able to hold these groups without the support of the Plumas County District Attorney, James Reichle; the Plumas County Judges, Ira Kauffman and Garrett Olney; and the Chief Probation Officer, Tom Frady. They have allowed us to proceed with our groups in the face of opposition and the threat of outside influences who would have offered traditional treatment programs for domestic violence. Without their help and referrals of participants, our work would not have been possible. In addition, we are very grateful to the Plumas County Sheriff's Office, the District Attorney's office, the Victim Witness Program, and the Probation Department for providing yearly recidivism rates, even when the lists grew longer and longer. Our thanks also go to the Lois and Samuel Silberman Fund, the New York Community Trust, that partly supports our research through the Social Work Faculty Awards Program.

We deeply appreciate Insoo Kim Berg at the Brief Family Therapy Center, Tony Tripodi and Gilbert G. Greene at the Ohio State University, for reviewing our manuscript, Albert R. Roberts at Rutgers University for his insightful feedback and incessant encouragement, and to Marcia Keeman, whose New York newspaper editor perspective reminded us that writing is about the story and the reader. Finally, we are thankful to Oxford University Press, which helped us make this book a reality.

Adriana Uken is grateful for the support of her daughter, Lindsey Buis-Kelley, and her best friend, Daniel Blake English, for their continued encouragement and belief in this project.

John Sebold is appreciative of Karen Jaggard for her deep pool of steady, enduring, loving support and of Josh Jaggard Sebold for his insightful thoughts regarding writing and his Calvin and Hobbes perspective: "It's A wonderful life."

Mo Yee Lee is thankful for her mother, Sho Yean Chan, who has given her the greatest gift of life; Kwok Kwan Tam for sharing his passion; and her two children, Tze Hei and Hok Hei, for showing her how to laugh and be curious and playful.

We are thankful to find in each other friendship and are grateful that we can share, challenge, compliment, and look at the sky with wonder.

Finally, we are deeply indebted to the individuals who have participated in our domestic violence groups for the past 12 years, who have inspired and surprised us with their trust, willingness to work, and courage to change. They have renewed our faith in the meaning of our work, and given us hope in the power of change even with mandated clients. They have been our greatest teachers.

Contents

Solution-Focused Treatment
of Domestic Violence Offenders

1

Introduction
Accountability for Solutions

In the world of music every note is selected with regard to many variables such as rhythm, tone, and volume, and each note must harmonize with the surrounding notes. In jazz the composers are often the players themselves, creating new musical ideas in response to each other. To accomplish this the musicians must have an extensive knowledge of notes and how they relate to each other. They must be able to closely listen to and accurately respond to the notes of the other musicians with whom they are playing. They must also be able to play with, suggest, and expand new themes and ideas that are consistent with the themes established by other players. Our work is much the same except we use words instead of notes. Each word has value, purpose, and a role in creating the meanings that surround it. Thinking of words in this manner is both fascinating and challenging. It suggests that people who use conversation to facilitate change should be as serious about words as musicians are about notes.

For many years we thought of ourselves as therapists doing therapy, treating clients, patients, victims, and offenders. We sometimes labeled the people that we worked with as "antisocial," "borderline," "depressive," "aggressive," or "schizophrenic," as if these names provided an accurate and comprehensive description of the individual. The words we used to describe ourselves and the people we worked with implied that we did something to others as a result of our expert knowledge about them, their problems, and their deficits. These words often proved to be grossly simplistic and inaccurate. Even more problematically, they seemed to limit how we thought of people, in general creating a narrow point of view that resulted in seeing people as less capable. Consequently, we expected less of them.

As we began to change our way of thinking and behaving, many labels simply seemed to have little relation to the reality we were experiencing in our work. In the process of change, the strengths of domestic violence offenders seemed much more relevant than their deficits. The potential for change seemed to have no limits. We no longer see ourselves as experts who treat clients and patients who can be described by labels or defined by a category.

We have chosen to use words that create the fewest assumptions, particularly the fewest negative assumptions, about the people with whom we work. Throughout this book, we prefer the word "participants" to denote our group members because it accurately describes the role these persons are taking in relation to our work with them. They are participating with us to create new ideas, plans, and goals. We have chosen to refer to ourselves primarily as facilitators. We perceive our major tasks and functions in the group as facilitating useful goal development and accomplishment process in participants that contributes to positive changes in them.

This book presents a pragmatic, step-by-step, "how-to" description of what the facilitator can do in treatment to create positive changes in domestic violence offenders. It provides a guide from intake to termination, capitalizing on participants' strengths and goal accomplishment to encourage and assist their efforts to exclude violence from intimate relationships. Before we discuss the "nuts and bolts" of a solution-focused approach with domestic violence offenders, we would like to put our program in the broader context of treatment for domestic violence (see Appendix 1 for a detailed description of theories of domestic violence). In addition, we would like to share our assumptions and beliefs regarding the nature of change in human beings. We think this is important because solution-focused therapy is not just a set of therapeutic or interviewing techniques but also a way of thinking.

The following are excerpts of assignments written by several group participants. Toward the end of the program, we usually ask participants to write a page about what they have learned from the group. We learn a lot about our work with domestic violence offenders by listening to their voices.

Participant 1

"Why I think this program has some positive outcomes is because it is not demeaning you or shaming you. It makes you think about your life and where you want to be with yourself. What I got from the program is that everyone of us for one reason or another has something that we can change or improve in ourselves to become a better person. I feel better about myself, and my family has even noticed the difference in me. I have had more time to spend with my family on a happy note instead of a sour one. I really like going to the class not only to get away for my own time but to see all my fellow classmates and hear the good things they had to share. Sometimes, you run into an unfortunate situation. You pay the consequences and learn a lot. I knew that I am a good person, but with this class, I now know that other people think that I am a good person too! Best of luck to my classmates and hope they stay on track as I know I will."

Participant 2

"When I first started this class I was very doubtful that it would do any good for me. Now that I have finished my class I have realized, in some unexplainable way, I'm a lot calmer. I don't blow up at the littlest thing. I'm able to think before I react to the conflict without thinking it through, which caused a lot of problems. Now I think first, then react to the situation, and usually work things out a lot easier.

I've always had a problem being able to talk to my dad about what was bothering me. Now I'm able to talk to him, tell him my feeling and thoughts. Since I can sit down and talk to him and my stepmom, we have been able to start to become a family that can sit down and discuss everything. It's made all of us including my wife, kids, and father a lot closer together."

Participant 3

"When I first started this 8-week domestic violence program, I thought the group would be centered around why we were sent to the class. To my surprise, the class had nothing to do with why we were here. What do goals have to do with domestic violence?

"I've learned in this class that once you have worked on personal goals, and have the discipline to keep trying to better yourself, things seem to fall into place much easier.

"I think I've learned to look ahead at everyday life—to plan my days and try to stick to a schedule. Using my time more wisely, instead of being so unstructured, has been more productive for me. Therefore I feel better about myself, which leads to me being a happier person.

"I truly believe that I would very rarely lose my temper as long as I feel good about myself.

"Everybody makes their own destiny. By staying positive and productive and by treating people the way I would like to be treated is helpful. Having a few simple goals has helped me to stay focused and more productive, which makes me happy for myself. This all leads to controlling my emotions and making me a more patient person. By learning to have more patience, it makes me a mellower person. I can deal with problems big or small a lot more rationally. Therefore, I haven't lost my temper, which means no violence.

"If I can stick to my goals and can continue to have a positive attitude about myself, I'm sure I will not have a problem with domestic violence again."

The "Conventional" Approaches of Treatment Programs

Diverse responses have been instigated by society in an attempt to end domestic violence in intimate relationships, a problem that has plagued our society and deeply hurt our families and children. The early efforts of the battered women's movement in the 1970s to protect the victims and their children have been expanded to include legal sanction of domestic violence, as well as provision of treatment for offenders (Roberts & Kurst-Swanger, 2002; Schechter, 1982). Treatment programs for domestic violence offenders began as voluntary men's responses to the battered women's movement in an attempt to confront men's violence against women as a result of patriarchal beliefs. The first batterer program, EMERGE, was established in 1977 at the request of women working in Boston area shelters (Schechter, 1982). Currently, these treatment programs are incorporated as an integral part of the coordinated system response to domestic violence in which the courts routinely send domestic violence offenders to receive group treatment while on probation as an alternative option of serving sentences. Despite the proliferation of treatment programs across the nation, these programs are by no means monolithic in their theoretical and practice orientations. Most treatment programs are influenced by three major perspectives: the feminist perspective, the individual perspective, and the family systems perspective.

The Feminist Perspective

The feminist perspective focuses on sociocultural factors and a gender analysis of power. It maintains that male dominance and misogyny as based on patriarchal beliefs and social structure constitute the root of violence against women. The goals of pro-feminist treatment programs are to raise offenders' consciousness about sex role conditioning and to resocialize men to work toward equality for women and to take responsibility for their own abusive behavior (Mederos, 1999; Pence & Paymar, 1993). In other words, the goal of treatment is not only cessation of violence but also reeducation of offenders.

The Individual Perspective

Treatment programs that operate from an individual perspective identify the root cause of violence as grounded in the individual pathology and history of the offenders. Proponents of this perspective usually take a mental health perspective in treatment; offenders have mental health, substance abuse, and/or personality issues that must be addressed in order to stop violent behavior (e.g., Adams, 1988; Dutton, 1995; Hastings & Hamberger, 1988; Holtzworth-Munroe & Stuart, 1994; Kantor & Straus, 1987). In addition, clinical assessment is important to identify offenders' deep-rooted or unconscious motives for aggression. The goals of treatment include changing intrapsychic or behavioral patterns of offenders by identifying and resolving psychological trauma that leads to battering behavior, as well as teaching offenders effective ways to control and manage anger.

The Family Systems Perspective

The family systems approach views domestic violence from an interactional and relationship perspective. Violent behaviors are usually part of a pattern of escalating retributive strategies used by a couple to resolve differences (Lloyd, 1999; Margolin, 1979). The goal of treatment is to improve communication and conflict resolution skills between members of a couple so as to create healthy relationships. A family systems approach to treatment, however, receives tremendous criticism because it blatantly ignores or minimizes the gendered nature of violence and may put a victim in danger because of not addressing the power differential between the victim and the offender. While treating members of a couple together has rarely been used in programs for domestic violence offenders, many programs do focus on communication skills as part of the treatment curriculum. In addition, some proponents of a family systems approach to treatment have developed assessment frameworks and criteria for initiating couple work (e.g., Bograd & Mederos, 1999; Lipchik & Kubicki, 1996).

Currently, because of the predominance of individual and sociocultural factors in understanding the etiology of domestic violence, most treatment programs for domestic violence offenders are based on a cognitive-behavioral approach that mainly targets the individual factors (e.g., Rosenbaum & O'Leary, 1986; Saunders & Azar, 1989) and a feminist perspective that focuses on the sociocultural roots of domestic violence (e.g., Martin, 1976; Walker, 1984; Warrior, 1976; Pence & Paymar, 1993). Since the focus of understanding has been on individual and/or sociocultural pathologies, group approaches are also based on the assumption that domestic violence offenders have deficits in knowledge or skills that are necessary for avoiding battering (Geffner & Mantooth, 1999; Saunders & Azar, 1989). Building on such assumptions is a treatment orientation which holds that the behaviors of domestic violence offenders can and need to be changed through a reeducational process. Consequently, the core components of these treatment programs generally include direct education about violence, anger management, conflict containment, communication training, and stress management (Geffner & Mantooth, 1999; Russell, 1995) and raising awareness of patriarchal power and control (Pence & Paymar, 1993). The resulting psychoeducational programs usually focus on confronting participants so they will recognize and admit their violent behaviors, take full responsibility for their problems (Lindsey, McBride, & Platt, 1993; Pence & Paymar, 1993; Russell, 1995), learn new ways to manage their anger, and communicate effectively with their spouses (Geffner & Mantooth, 1999; Sonkin, 1995; Wexler, 1999).

The significant contributions of feminist-cognitive-behavioral group treatment approaches in the advancement of treatment for domestic violence offenders can never be overestimated. On the other hand, questions have been raised regarding the effectiveness of such programs from both a clinical and an outcome perspective. A major therapeutic hurdle when working with this population is the issue of motivation. Most domestic violence offenders are involuntary, court-mandated clients who are not self-motivated to receive treatment. Many practitioners who work with court-mandated domestic violence offenders are only too familiar with defensiveness, commonly manifested in constant evasiveness, silence, phony agreement, and vociferous counterarguments when participants are confronted with their problems of violence (Murphy & Baxter, 1997). Many participants stop attending the program altogether. According to a survey of program directors, nearly half of the treatment programs faced dropout rates of over 50% of the men accepted at intake (Gondolf, 1990). Cadsky, Hanson, Crawford, and Lalonde (1996) reported a 75% noncompletion rate of participants who were recommended for treatment at male batterer treatment programs in Canada.

In addition, some professionals have begun to raise doubts about how a focus on deficits, blame, and confrontation can be conducive to stopping violence or initiating positive changes in offenders (Edleson, 1996; Uken & Sebold, 1996). Because blaming is one of the main strategies used by offenders to intimidate victims and to justify their own abusive acts, using confrontation and assigning blame in treatment may re-create a similar and nonhelpful dynamic in abusive relationships. The effectiveness of a deficit perspective or a blaming stance in treatment is dubious if one looks at the characteristics of domestic violence offenders. The most consistent risk markers for violent males have been identified as having experienced and/or witnessed parental violence, frequent alcohol use, low assertiveness, and low self-esteem (Hotaling & Sugarman, 1986; Jenkins, 1990; Saunders, 1995). As a result, a high percentage of domestic violence offenders are likely to be insecure individuals at the margins of society who victimize others to boost their own low self-esteem. Studies on personality further indicate that many domestic violence offenders fit the profile of narcissistic or borderline personality disorder (Dutton, 1995; Hamberger & Hastings, 1990). It is well documented that persons who are narcissistic or borderline have a very fragile sense of self and do not, in general, respond well to confrontation and criticism (Kernis & Sun, 1994); such individuals may perceive and experience instruction and skill training as criticism and rejection. An important question to be raised is, "Will treatment approaches focusing on deficits, blame, and confrontation be helpful in changing the behaviors of offenders who have themselves witnessed and/or experienced violence and have a fragile sense of self?" (Lee, Greene, & Rheinscheld, 1999; Uken & Sebold, 1996).

Findings of empirical studies of the effectiveness of current treatment programs are not conclusive. Reviews of domestic violence offender treatment programs generally report recidivism rates ranging from 20% to 50% in the year after completion of the program (e.g., Edleson, 1996; Rosenfeld, 1992; Tolman & Bennett, 1990, Tolman & Edleson, 1995). On the other hand, the rates of early dropouts from these programs have been fairly high (Cadsky, Hanson, Crawford, & Lalonde, 1996; Edleson & Syers, 1990). The recidivism rate of the Duluth Domestic Abuse Intervention Program, on which the Duluth Model is based, was 40% (Shepard, 1992). The Duluth Model is the most widely used approach for treating domestic violence offenders that adopts a feminist-cognitive-behavioral perspective. Saunders (1996) also reported a recidivism rate of 45.9% for the feminist-cognitive-behavioral treatment models. Two recent experimental evaluations have found batterer treatment programs to be largely ineffective. In the Broward Experiment (Feder & Forde, 2000), court-mandated domestic violence offenders were randomly assigned to experimental or control conditions. Offenders in the control group were sentenced to 1-year probation with no treatment, and offenders in the experimental group received 26 group treatment sessions in addition to the 1-year probation. The study found no clear effects of the treatment program on offenders' attitudes, beliefs, and behaviors. In fact, offenders assigned to the treatment program were more likely to be rearrested than those in the control group unless they attended all group sessions. Davis, Taylor, and Maxwell (2000) conducted another experimental evaluation in Brooklyn, New York, in which offenders, who consented to receive treatment, were randomly assigned to either 39 hours of treatment (in 26 week or 8 week modules) or a community service program unrelated to domestic violence. Victims' reports of new violent incidents did not differ statistically across the experimental and control groups.

Helping professionals constantly search for effective ways to provide treatment for domestic violence offenders, although such a search is haunted by hope, promises, and controversies. Hanson (2002) suggests that the field of treatment of domestic violence offenders is political as well as empirical. "One does certain things not because they work, but because they are right—right, that is, in terms of the ultimate definitions of reality promulgated by the . . . experts" (Berger & Luckmann, 1966, p. 118). The inconclusive research and practice evaluations, on the other hand, can be an invitation for service providers to revisit the existing paradigm of treatment for domestic violence offenders.

Solution-Focused Treatment of Domestic Violence Offenders: Accountability for Solutions

Participants take ownership of their problem not by talking about or reaffirming the problem but by defining goals of therapy and constructing solutions.

A solution-focused approach holds domestic violence offenders accountable for building solutions rather than focusing on their problems and deficits. A solution-focused approach moves away from a skill-deficit perspective, educational, or social control model of treatment. Focusing on and emphasizing solutions, competencies, and strengths in offenders, however, must never be equated with minimizing the destructiveness of their violent behaviors. A solution-focused group treatment model does not deny or minimize aggressive or violent behaviors. Similar to other treatment programs, it acknowledges the role of offenders in instigating violence against victims and recognizes that treatment programs are part of a coordinated community response to domestic violence. In addition, the effectiveness of a solution-focused treatment program is contingent on the support of the legal system, which provides a strong sanction against violent behaviors. We also do not see a solution-focused approach as the ultimate panacea to treatment of domestic violence offenders. Instead, we perceive our program as part of the pluralistic, societal effort to develop pragmatic solutions to end the more immediate, visible violence in intimate relationships. In addition, a solution-focused approach considers it our central moral and ethical responsibility to respect victims and offenders by developing and using therapeutic techniques that effectively and quickly create changes in the offenders' lives, which include the cessation of violence in intimate relationships.

Building on a strengths perspective and using a time-limited approach, solution-focused group treatment for domestic violence offenders postulates that positive and long-lasting change can occur in a relatively brief period of time by focusing on "solution-talk" instead of "problem talk." Unlike the more traditional approaches, such an approach uses the language and symbols of "solution and strengths" as opposed to the language of "deficits and blame." Treatment focuses on identifying exceptions and solution behaviors, which are then amplified, supported, and reinforced through a systematic solution-building process.

Principles and Assumptions of Solution-Focused Group Treatment

Each person is a unique individual. Hence, psychotherapy should be formulated to meet the uniqueness of the individual's needs rather than tailoring the person to fit the Procrustean bed of a hypothetical theory of human behavior. (Milton Erickson, in Zeig, 1985, p. viii)

"How do people change?" is a question that has fascinated humans for many years, and probably will do so for many years to come. Most domestic violence offenders come to treatment because the courts mandate that they do so as part of the requirement to avoid being charged or to reduce punishment. Some may actually seek solutions for their violent behaviors. Our assumptions about how personal change occurs through therapeutic experience have immense influence on our treatment orientation.

A Focus on Solutions, Strengths, and Health

Participants have the answer.

We focus on what clients can do rather than on what they cannot do. Instead of discussing or exploring clients' problems or deficiencies, the focus is on clients' successes in dealing with their problems, and on how to notice and use them more often (Berg & Kelly, 2000; Berg & Miller, 1992). Focusing on solutions is neither a consequence of "naive" beliefs regarding participants' strengths nor simplistic "positive thinking." This approach is supported by repeated clinical observation about how participants discover solutions in a much quicker manner if the focus is on their abilities, strengths, and accomplishments (Berg & Dolan, 2001; Berg & Reuss, 1998). The focus on solution-talk to achieve change is also supported by a systems perspective (Bateson, 1979) and the role of language in creating reality (de Shazer, 1994).

A Systems Perspective

One basic assumption of a systems perspective is that change is constant. No domestic violence offender is always abusive. As such, every problem pattern includes some sort of exception to the rule (de Shazer, 1985). Such a view underlies our belief in the strengths and potential of participants (Berg & DeJong, 1996). Despite the multiple deficiencies or problems participants may perceive that they have, there are always times when they handle their life situations in a more satisfying way or in a different manner; there must be times when the individual is not aggressive or violent and uses other means to resolve conflicts and differences Greene, Uken, Sebold, & Rheinscheld, (Lee, 1997). These exceptions provide the clues for solutions (de Shazer, 1985) and represent the participant's "unnoticed" strengths and resources. The task for the therapist is to assist participants in noticing, amplifying, sustaining, and reinforcing these exceptions regardless of how small or infrequent they may be (Berg & Kelly, 2000). Once participants are engaged in nonproblem behavior, they are on the way to a solution-building process (Berg & DeJong, 1996).

Another major assumption of a systems perspective is that all parts of a system are interrelated and everything is connected. Change in one part of a system leads to change in other parts as well (Bateson, 1972; Becvar & Becvar, 1996; Keeney & Thomas, 1986). In other words, the focus is on circular rather than linear relationships among different parts of the system. As such, working with only one spouse in treatment can have helpful repercussions in the couple's relationship. In addition, solutions do not need to be directly related to the problem of violence for them to be effective in changing the problem pattern in offenders. The complex interrelatedness of different parts of systems also renders the effort to establish a causal understanding of problems essentially futile. It is almost impossible to precisely ascertain why a problem, namely, using violence in relationships, occurs in the first place. Without minimizing the importance of the participant's experience and perception of the history of the problem, solution-focused facilitators view what is going on in the present as more important than what caused the problem at the very beginning.

Language and Reality

We strongly believe that it is ethical and more effective to focus on the therapeutic, solution dialogues rather than on problem dialogues. There is a conscious effort on our part to stay focused on solution talk and de-emphasize problem talk. This conscious effort grows out of our concern about the role of language in creating reality. Solution-focused therapy views language as the medium through which personal meaning and understanding are expressed and socially constructed in conversation (de Shazer, 1991, 1994). Further, the meaning of something is always contingent on the contexts and the language within which it is described, categorized, and constructed by participants (Wittgenstein, 1958). Because the limits of reality that can be known and experienced by an individual are framed by the language available to describe it, and these meanings are inherently unstable and shifting, a key question for the facilitator to consider is how to use language in treatment to assist domestic violence offenders in describing and constructing a "beneficial" reality.

Because language is inherently powerful in creating and sustaining realities, the preferred language is the "conversation of change"—conversation that facilitates participants' efforts to create and sustain a solution reality (de Shazer, 1991; Walter & Peller, 1992). We prefer to use language that helps participants "get to the surface of their problems" (de Shazer, 1991). This dialogue avoids going "deep" into the problem but rather aims to construct meanings and solutions by describing goals, observable behaviors, and progressive lives in new, more beneficial ways (de Shazer, 1994; Miller, 1997). Pathology or problem talk sustains a problem reality through self-fulfilling prophecies and distracts group participants' and our attention from developing solutions (Miller, 1997). We similarly resist diagnoses or language that labels the participants' problem with violence as stable and unchanging (Berg & Miller, 1992; de Shazer, 1994). Pathologizing participants' claims of their problems and drilling on the "deep" causes may serve to further disempower participants. This is especially true for those offenders who are not accomplished persons or who lack regard for themselves. A pathological or deficit approach also focuses therapeutic effort on the problem of domestic violence rather than on what a life free of violence would be like.

A solution-focused approach to treatment with domestic violence offenders emphasizes solutions, strengths, and health. It is consistent with the empowerment-based and strengths-based approaches in human services, approaches that have gained increased prominence in the past decade (Rees, 1998; Saleebey, 1997). To empower participants and to use their strengths, therapists skillfully use the "language of empowerment" (Rappaport, 1985; Rees, 1998) and the "lexicon of strengths" (Saleebey, 1997) in creating a conversation of change.

Accountability for Solutions

A de-emphasis on problems and deficits and a focus on health and strengths does not mean that solution-focused group treatment is easy. We hold participants responsible for solutions instead of problems. By not focusing on participants' responsibility for problems or deficits, we are able to direct all therapeutic energy toward supporting participants' responsibility for building solutions. We believe that change requires hard work (Berg & Kelly, 2000). Solutions come neither easily nor effortlessly. DeJong and Berg (1996) describe a solution-building process that requires discipline and effort. Participants would not need treatment if they had a clear vision of the solution to their complaints and how to realize it. The "solution" as described by solution-focused therapy is established in the form of a goal that is to be determined and attained by the group participant. Berg and Miller (1992) described the characteristics of solutions and goals as being personally meaningful and important to the participant; small enough to be achieved; concrete, specific, and behavioral, so that indicators of success can be established and observed; positively stated, so that the goal represents the presence rather than the absence of something; realistic and achievable within the context of the participant's life; and perceived as involving hard work.

We believe that the formulation of a clear, specific, and attainable goal provides a context for group participants to identify, notice, rediscover, and reconnect with their strengths and resources.

Present and Future Orientation

Whereas the problems belong to something in the past, solutions and goals exist in the present and future. In order to hold group participants accountable for solutions, the focus of treatment is on assisting them in their present and future adjustment. Instead of delving into the past, which easily lends itself to discussing the history of the problem and, thereby, problem talk, we ask questions that will help participants to describe a future that does not contain the problem. We also help them to identify the first small step they can take to attain a future without the problem. Such descriptions help participants to be hopeful about their future and also help them discover for themselves specific directions for achieving positive changes in their lives.

Participants Define Their Goals: Solutions as Participants' Constructions

Influenced by social constructivism (Neimeyer & Mahoney, 1993; Rosen & Kuehlwein, 1996), we believe that solutions are not objective "realities" but private, local, meaning-making activities by an individual (Miller, 1997). The importance of and the meaning attached to a goal or solution are individually constructed in a collaborative process. Individuals' orientations to and definition of goals clearly have significant implications for their actions and how they experience life. Because the participant is the only "knower" of personal experiences and the sole "creator" of solutions, he or she defines the goals for treatment and remains the main instigator of change (Berg, 1994). Externally imposed therapeutic goals are often inappropriate or irrelevant to the needs of participants. In addition, participants are willing to work harder if they define the goal of therapy and perceive it as personally meaningful.

A Collaborative Therapeutic Relationship

A constructivist view of solutions has significant implications for the participant-facilitator relationship. Because participants are the only "knowers" and "experts" regarding their individual experiences, realities, and aspirations (Cantwell & Holmes, 1994), their stories, explanations, and narrations become the only valid data to work with in the treatment process. Their stories are no longer data to be filtered through formal treatment theories to help the facilitator arrive at a diagnosis and a treatment plan. Similarly, facilitators are no longer experts who know the right answer to participants' problems. The facilitator provides a therapeutic context for participants to construct and develop a personally meaningful goal. He or she enters the participants' perspective, adopting their frame of mind, listening to and understanding their goals, and looking for strengths instead of weaknesses or labels (Belenky, Clinchy, Goldberger, & Tarule, 1997). In place of a hierarchical therapist-client relationship is a more egalitarian and collaborative relationship. The offender takes the role of expert in determining and achieving goals that will lead to a life that does not contain violence. The group facilitator takes the role of expert in constructing a dialogue with the offender that focuses on change and solution.

A collaborative approach that respects participants' expertise and knowledge about themselves and their strengths helps to enhance their motivation to accomplish positive changes through treatment (Lee, Greene,

& Rheinscheld, 1999; Murphy & Baxter, 1997). Such an approach also aids the process of engagement in treatment because group participants feel listened to and valuable. The therapeutic challenges of engaging participants and enhancing their motivation are particularly important for court-mandated individuals, who are usually in treatment involuntarily.

Utilization: A Noninstructional, Noneducational Approach

Solution-focused therapists use whatever resources clients bring with them (de Shazer, 1985). The principle is one of utilizing clients' existing re-sources, skills, knowledge, beliefs, motivation, behavior, symptoms, social networks, circumstances, and personal idiosyncrasies to lead them to their desired outcomes (O'Hanlon & Wilk, 1987). Such a practice orientation is related to our belief in the presence of exceptions in every problem situation (de Shazer, 1985). Instead of attempting to teach our group participants something new and foreign based on our presumed notions of what is best for them, we focus on situations in which participants are already engaged in nonproblem behaviors. Utilizing and building on these exceptions is a more efficient and effective way for participants to develop solutions that are relevant to and viable in their unique life circumstances. In our expe-rience, participants are most invested in solutions that they themselves dis-cover or identify. The task for the facilitator is to elicit, trigger, reinforce, expand, and consolidate exceptions generated by the participant. We stay away from teaching group participants skills or intervening in their lives in ways that may fit our "model" of what is good but may not be appropriate or viable in their lives.

Tipping the First Domino: A Small Change

Consistent with the old saying "A journey of a thousand miles begins with one step," a solution-focused approach suggests that we must assist partic-ipants in describing the first small step they need to take if they are to accomplish their goal (Berg & Dolan, 2001). Having a vision of the ultimate solution without a clear idea of the first small step to achieve it may prove to be too distant and vague. In fact, we are concerned when a participant says, "My goal is to better communicate with my partner." This statement does not provide clear behavioral steps for him or her to take in reaching such a goal. Instead, we help the participant to "tip the first domino" in the process of change. In other words, it is of foremost importance for us to assist participants in making the first small step that will show them that they are moving in the right direction—the right direction as defined by them.

A focus on small change is also consistent with a "minimalist" ap-proach to therapy. We believe that small change is more possible and man-ageable, while consuming less energy. Participants are usually encouraged when they experience successes, even small ones. A minimalist approach to therapy is also suggested by Bateson (1972) and by Watzlawick, Weakland, and Fisch (1974). Based on a systems perspective, they are concerned about introducing any change that may disturb a person's equilibrium in unpredictable ways as a result of reiterating feedback. Repetitive attempts at the same unsuccessful solution are precisely what creates problems in the first place (Watzlawick et al., 1974). We believe that the best responses to domestic violence offenders' problems involve minimal, but personally meaningful, intervention by the facilitator into their lives. Participants should determine what constitutes acceptable solutions. The most important thing is for us to help participants identify the first small behavorial step toward desirable change.

About the Plumas Project

The domestic violence group treatment program is a solution-based, goal-directed program co-led by a female and a male therapist. The treatment model reflects an accumulation of practice experience, wisdom, and learning from errors since 1991, when we first experimented with using a solution-focused approach for treatment of domestic violence offenders. Treatment includes eight, group sessions (each lasting 1 hour) over a 3-month period. The group usually meets weekly for the first three sessions and then every other week for the remainder. Spacing out sessions toward the end allows participants to have more time to practice their solution-oriented behaviors.

The eight sessions can be conceptually divided into four phases. The major tasks for each phase are briefly described as follows:

Phase One: Introduction (Session 1)

- Establishing group rules and structure
- Establishing collaborative relationship
- Giving the goal task

Phase Two: Developing Useful Goals (Sessions 2, 3)

- Assisting participants in developing useful and well-formed goals
- Assisting participants in focusing on solutions, changes, exceptions, past successes
- Assisting participants who "get stuck" in developing a useful goal

Phase Three: Goal Utilization: Expanding the Solution Picture (Sessions 4, 5, 6)

- Reviewing positive changes

- Assisting participants in expanding, amplifying, and reinforcing their solution behaviors in their real-life context
- Assisting participants in making a connection between their behavior and positive outcomes
- Reinforcing and complimenting participants' positive changes

Phase Four: Consolidation and Celebration of Changes (Sessions 7, 8)

- Reviewing goals, evaluating progress, and making future plans
- Consolidating personally meaningful change descriptions and/or "new" identity
- Developing connection between participants' actions and positive outcomes
- Acknowledging and complimenting goal accomplishments
- Celebrating changes: ownership of goal accomplishments

Although each phase in the treatment process is characterized by recognizable therapeutic tasks and processes, it is imperative to keep in mind that change is a continuous, circular, and/or spiral process that fundamentally defies a clear-cut and linear categorization. An overlap of therapeutic tasks across phases is expected, and the choice of appropriate therapeutic tasks should be guided primarily by individual participants' unique situations and responses to treatment.

Conclusion

In our experience, adopting a solution-focused approach for treatment of domestic violence offenders requires more than learning and mastering a new set of therapeutic techniques. The process often represents a paradigm shift for helping professionals, who learn to establish a collaborative relationship in which they are willing and able to see, appreciate, and be curious about the hidden strengths, resources, and creativity of participants who usually appear to have more deficits and problems than resources. In this paradigm, the ability of the helping professionals to respect participants' strengths—sometimes more than participants respect themselves—constitutes the important first step for treatment to be successful. Such a paradigm shift may be easy or difficult for different practitioners. In the following chapters, we share our journey of cocreating solutions with domestic violence offenders.

2

The Solution-Focused
Assessment Interview

*Too often people who want to learn SFBT fall into the trap
of not being able to see that the difficulty is to stay on the
surface when the temptation to look behind and beneath is
at its strongest. (Correspondence with Steve de Shazer,
September 5, 2001)*

Assessment has always played an important role in the field of treatment of
domestic violence offenders for two broad purposes. Assessment usually
focuses on understanding the problem of domestic violence: the history of
the problem, risk factors that contribute to the problem, the effect of violence on self and others, and current symptoms. Comprehensive assessment
is thought to help offenders understand the reasons for their problem with
violence, which will help them gain insight into the problem and lead to
beneficial behavioral changes and the elimination of violence in intimate
relationships.

In addition, assessment takes on another level of significance, that is,
assessing and predicting the risk of severe violence in offenders. There are
obvious reasons for such a focus. Accurate assessment and prediction of the
risk of violence can help programs for offenders in selecting effective treatment, assist victims and their advocates in making realistic safety plans, and
help judges and prosecutors decide which offenders require closer and/or
restrained forms of supervision (Weisz, Tolman, & Saunders, 2000). In
other words, prediction of violence is important both for treating offenders
and for protecting victims. Professional accountability also plays a significant role in the call for predicting violence in offenders. The *Tarasoff* court
decision have made it clear that it is the legal duty of helping professionals
to exercise reasonable care to protect potential victims from a danger of
violence (McNeill, 1987).

In summary, conventional assessment focuses on obtaining a history
of the problem, identifying the effect of these problem, understanding current symptoms, making a diagnosis, and developing a treatment plan. The
therapist, who is assumed to be an expert who possesses domain-specific

knowledge of the problem, designs a treatment module that best fits the client's diagnosis. The implication is that a skilled therapist, when informed by an accurate assessment of the client and his or her problem, can formulate the "best" treatment plan that will alleviate the symptoms. Both the therapist and the client are interested in the "why" of the problem, believing that such understanding will help the client achieve insight, which in turn will lead to behavioral changes and elimination of the problem.

For example, consider a husband who is physically abusive toward his wife. In traditional programs, the task may be to assist the offender in developing insight into why he is being violent and to explore the history and extent of the violence. The root of violence is assumed to have both an individual and a sociocultural dimension. The therapist may educate the offender as to the pervasive nature of violence, raise his consciousness regarding how patriarchal beliefs contribute to violence, point out various forms that violence can take, and facilitate his personal exploration of how he was brought up, current marital relationship, life circumstances, and/or beliefs that may contribute to the problem of spouse abuse. The therapist will focus on teaching the husband how to handle his negative emotions in healthier and nonviolent ways. The assumption is that when an offender recognizes and takes responsibility for how he is being abusive, and for the effect the abuse has on those around him, he will change his reactions into nonviolent alternatives.

A closer examination of the characteristics of domestic violence assessment reveals the influence of a positivist paradigm that underlies its practices. A positivist paradigm emphasizes objective, rational, and linear thinking that implicates cause-and-effect relationships in explaining phenomena and solving problems (Katz, 1985). Accurate assessment in terms of a detailed understanding of the history of the problem of violence and how is it connected to the current symptoms is assumed to inform treatment choices and, therefore, is intimately related to successful treatment. Insight and identification of the problem are the first step, if not the road, to positive changes in clients. The focus on and belief in prediction in the field of domestic violence are also influenced by the reductionistic thinking of a positivist paradigm. If helping professionals can precisely (or microscopically) study domestic violence offenders and discover the fundamental principles or rules governing their behaviors, they will be able to accurately understand, predict, and treat the problem of violence in offenders.

A more fundamental assumption of a positivist paradigm is that the problem to be studied or treated exists independently as an objective entity outside the person who is making the observation or assessment or providing treatment. In other words, we can study the domestic violence offender as an independent entity and discover unifying patterns or traits that characterize this particular group of people. Such a belief underlies the importance of making clinical diagnoses; such diagnoses will inform professionals of the common characteristics of different types of domestic violence offenders, which can serve as a valid basis for determining treatment. Another implicit consequence of a positivist paradigm is the expert position assumed by therapists. Because a scientific way to understand and resolve human problems needs to be based on domain-specific expert and empirical knowledge, it has to be practiced by formally trained professionals who possess knowledge and expertise in assessing and solving human problems.

In this type of approach, there is a direct relation between the solution and the problem. The solution is to "attack" the problem of violence by developing insight into it, taking responsibility for the problem, and learning nonviolent ways to handle it. The therapist assumes the role of an expert who assesses the causes of the problem and derives a treatment plan that helps offenders learn better alternatives for handling their problems. The answer to changing the future lies in discovering and taking responsibility for past behaviors.

Issues and Concerns

There is no question that conventional assessment makes significant contributions to understanding the history and problem of domestic violence, as well as the characteristics of offenders. We, however, have concerns about the implications of conventional assessment for predicting violence, categorizing offenders, and providing treatment. Empirical evidence from studies of domestic violence offenders and clinical observations regarding treatment support our concerns.

Empirical Evidence

Current assessment efforts of domestic violence offenders focus on two main areas: (1) typology research that assesses and identifies personality tendencies and the potential psychopathology of domestic violence offenders that may contribute to violent behaviors or reoffense; and (2) assessment and prediction of risk of severe domestic violence. Existing knowledge regarding assessing domestic violence offenders is mostly informed by typology research (e.g., Dutton, 1998; Holtzworth-Munroe & Stuart, 1994); studies of risk markers (e.g., Saunders, 1995; Wilson & Daly, 1993); development of statistical or actuarial methods (e.g., Campbell, 1986; Kropp, Hart, Webster, & Eaves, 1999); and use of clinical judgment and survivors' prediction (de Becker, 1997; Hart, 1994; Weisz et al., 2000).

Typology literature generally assumes that domestic violence offenders and reoffenders have certain personality traits that differentiate them from others. Understanding these characteristics can help professionals to design appropriate treatment and predict the risk of severe violence or reoffense. The typology literature generally suggests that domestic violence offenders are likely to be antisocial or psychopathic (Dutton, 1998).

Roughly 25% of participants in domestic violence treatment programs belong to a generally violent or antisocial type (Holtzworth-Munroe & Stuart, 1994); this group of offenders is described as particularly dangerous, more likely to reoffend (Dutton, Bodnarchuk, Kropp, Hart, & Ogloff, 1997), and resistant to treatment (Wallace, Vitale, & Newman, 1999). The most severely violent type of male domestic offender also tends to be violent toward others and displays psychopathic tendencies (Gondolf, 1988). Some researchers propose that violent criminals tend to be unresponsive to intervention and counseling (Rice, 1997) and that psychopathic domestic violence offenders may warrant constraint in the form of jail or intensive supervision (Dutton, 1998; Jacobson & Gottman, 1998).

Studies of risk markers focus on identifying factors associated with severe violence. For instance, Saunders (1995) identified three risk markers that are consistently found in studies: generalized aggression, alcohol abuse, and abuse by parents. Using data from the 1985 National Family Violence Survey, Straus (1996) developed 18 factors, which include police involvement, drug abuse, extreme male dominance, abuse of a child, violence outside the family, and frequent verbal aggression. Using standardized instruments in the process of assessment to predict repeat domestic violence is still in the early stage of development. The Danger Assessment Instrument developed by Campbell (1986), which is widely used for predicting domestic homicide, correlates with the severity of the worst injury. Kropp and his associates (1999) developed the Spousal Arousal Risk Assessment (SARA) checklist. The instrument has known-group validity, although its ability to predict repeated violence has yet to be empirically tested. In addition, clinical judgment has traditionally been utilized for assessing responses to treatment and changes over time (Harris, Rice, & Quinsey, 1993; Milner & Campbell, 1995).

Conventional assessment identifies offender characteristics or types for determining treatment choices and predicting the future risk of violence. It also meets the expectation of courts and various professional bodies for treatment accountability. Despite a strong interest in assessment, accurate prediction of violent behavior is just out of our reach. Clinicians and researchers have generally noted the difficulties of accurate prediction despite deliberate efforts of assessment (Monahan, 1996). The ability of standardized instruments to accurately predict violence has yet to be tested. Identification of risk markers is extremely helpful in increasing our knowledge of factors associated with violence, although its utility in prediction is limited because many individuals who appear to be at risk for engaging in violent behavior do not actually do so.

More important, empirical evidence cautions against overgeneralization about high-risk domestic offenders based on assessment of offender types. Gondolf and White (2001) conducted a multisite evaluation study that included 840 male participants in batterer programs in Pittsburgh, Houston, Dallas, and Denver. Using the criteria for the Millon Clinical Multiaxial Inventory, Version III, the researchers grouped the personality profiles of 580 men who did not reassault their partners (394), reassaulted once (68), or repeatedly reassaulted (122) during a 15-month follow-up. Overall, evidence of psychopathic disorders was relatively low (9% of primary psychopathic disorder and 11% of secondary disorder). About 25% of the sample exhibited moderate personality dysfunction. The majority (60%) of the "repeated reassaulters" showed no serious personality dysfunction or psychopathology. There was no significant difference among the reassault types for personality dysfunction, psychopathic disorder, or personality type. The repeated offenders were significantly more likely to be younger, to have had substance use problems, to have severely abused their partners, to have been generally violent, to have been arrested for other criminal offenses, and to have dropped out of the treatment program within 3 months. On the other hand, the extent of difference in these problems was small (i.e., a difference of 10% or less) and not clinically significant (Gondolf & White, 2001).

This study was well designed and implemented by prominent researchers in the field of domestic violence. Its implications challenge some prevalent "beliefs" regarding domestic violence offenders, including the general perception that offenders are a distinctively pathological group. Based on rigorous assessment of personality profiles and psychopathologies, most offenders are not severely disturbed even among the group of "repeated reassaulters." In addition, the study's findings cautioned against using assessments based on personality dysfunction, psychopathic disorder, or personality type to predict future risk of violence. In other words, the differences between reoffenders and other participants are not substantial enough to help professionals predict or identify high-risk offenders (Gondolf & White, 2001).

Clinical Observations

Although conventional assessment makes a significant contribution to our understanding of who domestic violence offenders are, its value in predicting recurrence of offense is dubious (Gondolf & White, 2001). We are also concerned about the treatment implications of assessment of offender types.

Domestic Violence Offenders Are Not a Homogeneous Group

While typology research has significantly contributed to our understanding of common characteristics of offenders, it has also led to the assumption that the majority of offenders are more similar than different. When an offender presents with behaviors similar to a suggested profile, the tendency is to assume that the offender must in fact *be* the profile. We are concerned with the implications of such assumptions for treatment because they may cause an individual's unique features to be overlooked. If a behavior is viewed as representative of a particular type of offender, the situational and complex personal variables that may in fact be significant are ignored. Oftentimes, negative assumptions are made about the meaning of an offender's behavior; consequently, surface explanations may not be explored, and opportunities to assess for strengths may not be considered.

Problem Talk as Sustaining a Problem Reality

The emphasis on understanding the history, roots, and dynamics of the problem of domestic violence results in therapists and offenders spending an enormous amount of time and energy on therapeutic dialogues that focus on problem talk. While the benefit of understanding problems in order to find solutions is an empirical question yet to be answered by research evidence, we are concerned about the impact of problem talk on the offender because of the role of language in sustaining reality. Solution-focused therapy views language as the medium through which personal meaning and understanding are expressed and socially constructed by persons in conversation (de Shazer, 1991, 1994). Because language is inherently powerful in creating and sustaining realities, extended pathology or problem talk in assessment may have the unintended consequence of sustaining a problem reality and distracting offenders' and therapists' attention from developing solutions (Miller, 1997). We are especially cautious about making diagnoses or using language that labels the offender's violent behavior as stable and unchanging (Berg & Miller, 1992; de Shazer, 1994) because pathologizing such problems and drilling on their "deep" causes may further disempower the offender through a self-fulfilling prophecy. We believe that treatment should focus on identifying solutions that exist in the present and the future.

The Impossible Demand on Helping Professionals

Conventional models of assessment place an unrealistic demand on professionals who work in the area of domestic violence. The professional is expected to be able to determine the type, extent, and severity of the problem, as well as to properly apply a specific treatment that will remedy it. Ideally the professional should be able to accurately predict the likelihood of success for treating any given individual, as well as predict future violence based on past history and behavior. He or she must determine what type of treatment will stop the violence based on an accurate assessment of the offender's past, as well as attempt to predict what risks may be involved with each type of treatment. For example, would this offender benefit more from cognitive-behavioral approaches or from an educational model? Does this offender need powerful direct confrontation or long-term, persistent redirection? Does the offender need intensive individual therapy to address unresolved emotional problems, or does he need marital therapy? The implication is that a skilled professional who performs an accurate comprehensive assessment and establishes the correct treatment model for each particular offender should be able to get the offender to stop being violent.

On the other hand, research and clinical observations indicate that conventional models of assessment have not yet fulfilled their intention of connecting effective assessment with clear and specific treatments. Typical mental health clinicians lack consistency in applying a diagnosis, let alone in agreeing on specific treatments for any given individual. Helping professionals and researchers have emphasized the difficulty of accurately predicting future behaviors; professionals are not even particularly accurate in determining when people are being truthful. The desire for professional accountability and the recognition of indeterminacy in treatment present a constant dilemma for helping professionals, although we cannot fool ourselves into believing that we can accurately predict and take responsibility for the change process in other people.

Solution-Focused Assessment

Similar to conventional models of assessment, we agree that assessment constitutes a significant part of treatment that contributes to positive outcomes in domestic violence offenders. However, we view assessment from a rather different perspective. In conventional models, the therapist is the expert who conducts assessment and uses it to determine what treatment model fits each particular individual. In addition, assessment is based on formal knowledge of the problem of domestic violence. In sum, assessment is based on expert knowledge and is viewed as notably different and separate from the treatment process.

Solution-focused assessment involves a different set of assumptions and, thus, a different set of goals. In our program, treatment and assessment are closely intertwined and inseparable, with every effort made to activate a change process at the initial contact. More important, we believe that it is therapeutically more beneficial to view the participant, not the facilitator, as the assessor. In other words, solution-focused assessment is client-centered instead of professional-driven. Consequently, the process is differentiated by the establishment of a nonhierarchical dialogue with the participant and by maintaining a nonexpert stance. During assessment, the facilitator looks for client strengths and resources and uses compliments to develop a collaborative relationship. No attempt is made to control the participant. This approach is philosophically different from one that attempts to change behavior through education, control, or determining what the client needs to do from an "expert" point of view. Our view and practice of assessment are shaped by the following beliefs.

Staying on the Surface: Contextualized Understanding

As professionals who routinely make determinations regarding individuals' potential for harming themselves or others, we find that the immediate presentation of individuals—their intention, situational variables, and resources—is most important in determining their capacity to utilize our assistance. These "surface" issues are far more important than a diagnostic or more complex assessment in determining what will be helpful. We do not view individuals referred to us as part of a homogeneous group or as having established features that define them as offenders. Each person presents with features that are relevant at the moment, but these tend to change as individuals begin to define their situation differently and as they learn and change. The assessment process is designed to draw out people's strengths and unique personal features rather than identifying how individuals fit to a particular type of offender profile.

Effective solution-focused assessment requires the facilitator to stay on the surface, avoiding "deep" assumptions about why people are behaving as they are at any given moment and instead focusing on the potential value of any given presentation. It also requires that the facilitator help participants direct their energy in a manner that will lead to identifying and moving toward the goals they want to accomplish.

The Offender as Assessor: The Importance of Choice

In many respects we believe it is more useful for participants to be in the role of completing an assessment than it is for the facilitator. Participants evaluate and assess the program and determine if it will meet their needs. When the facilitator approaches the assessment from this perspective, the program becomes a choice for the participant, and as a result he or she is more likely to evaluate the program as one of a number of options. We know from experience that some individuals choose to avoid, delay, or ignore receiving treatment or serve jail time. Some prospective participants have previously made the decision to move from county to county or state to state as a way of "dealing" with court-ordered obligations.

When viewed from this perspective, assessment becomes a series of evaluations and choices that must be made by potential participants. Metaphorically, participants are offered the opportunity to step into deeper and deeper pools, first to commit to coming to the assessment, then to pay the fee, come to the group, choose a goal, do something different, and finally create meaning about what they have accomplished. In this model, the facilitator's role is to inform the participants regarding the expectations they must meet if they choose to attend the group.

The facilitator must understand the importance of emphasizing the group as an option or a choice, one that potential participants are welcome to accept or reject. The primary benefit of doing so is that participants become active partners in deciding what they believe is of value to them. This increases commitment to the process and shifts responsibility for change to the participants. As a result, they begin to evaluate how the process can be of benefit to them. When potential participants consider rejecting the group, they do so with the facilitator's recognition that they are capable of making a choice that will in some manner be helpful to them. This is particularly helpful to individuals who see authorities as controlling them because it allows them to make a decision to move toward what they really believe will be in their best interest. When participants consider the group as a choice between two or more options, it begins a long sequence of decisions through which they begin to take control of their lives.

Potential Participants' Perspective of the Treatment Program

Participants exhibit a wide range of attitudes toward our program. Some share a desire and willingness to do better in their lives. In our experience, a small number of offenders come for assessment with the hope of changing their behavior. They often are already making efforts to do something different. Other individuals come with the hope that the program will "fix" them and have not yet assumed responsibility to do something different in their lives. Many present as challenging or what is often described as "resistant," "hostile," or "difficult." Consistent with this presentation is the belief or statement that they were unfairly arrested and that the authorities are unreasonably trying to control their lives by taking away their rights. Initially, such individuals assume that we are closely aligned with the legal system and that we are not really interested in listening to and understanding them. They often anticipate that they will be humiliated and told that they are bad, abusive, and deficient in interpersonal skills. In some instances, they suspect that we believe they are not capable of making good decisions for themselves. Many individuals expect that the facilitator will assume the role of the expert and teach them how to do things differently, such as how to manage their anger more effectively.

In general, many potential participants arrive at the assessment with the expectation that they will be confronted, and they often are surprised when this does not occur. Prospective participants may experience varying levels of fear, anger, shame, or anxiety. We find most presentations to be consistent with people's natural response to the anticipation of being controlled. DeJong and Berg (2002) suggested that the natural responses to being coerced are defiance, resistance, and a desire to subvert the other's attempts at control. Human beings somehow sense that they are being robbed of their dignity when they permit themselves to be controlled. Some people feel compelled to tell their side of the story, which may reduce the initial anxiety and help them focus on other issues. Others may take the offensive and attack the "system" that ordered them to the assessment. They expect that the assessment will be an extension of a "coercive system" that will try to get them to further confess their faults and accept responsibility for the abuse. They are prepared for us to judge and blame them.

Setting Up the Assessment Interview: The First Phone Contact

The initial contact is the facilitator's first opportunity to begin a collaborative relationship with the client. The facilitator must set the stage for how the client will be treated. In this model it is important that the facilitator not assume the expert role or problem solve. Instead, he or she must trust that the potential participant has the skills to make helpful decisions and can be held accountable for doing so. The facilitator treats the prospective participant with respect and without judgment. Considering that some participants can present as hostile or demanding, and may perceive the facilitator as an extension of the court system, the initial contact can be very challenging. It is important to maintain a calm demeanor and not engage or react to the participant's aggressive presentation. The focus is on helping the participant discover what he or she wants and what the next step will be. In most cases, the next step is to set up an assessment appointment so that the individual can evaluate if the group will be beneficial. It is important for the facilitator to assume a neutral, unknowing position regarding the group. It is particularly important not to try to convince participants that they are obligated to take part in the program or that it is in their best interest to do so. At times individuals will attempt to initiate a discussion regarding their guilt, innocence, or motivations. We find it most helpful not to engage in this discussion and instead to help individuals determine what they want.

The first contact often comes in the form of a telephone call from a potential participant requesting to be signed up for the "domestic violence class." The initial contact typically occurs in the following manner:

Participant: Hello. I need to talk to someone about your domestic violence class.
Facilitator: OK. Have you been referred by the probation department?
P: No, the judge told me to call you.

It is important to obtain this information in order to let the referring agency know that the participant has signed up for the program.

F: OK, the first thing we need to do is make an appointment to set up an intake interview, so we can fill out some paperwork, and I can tell you about the group. Did the judge tell you that the group costs $200.00?

We want to let participants know about the cost right from the start, so that they can begin to consider how they will address this issue, and so that they are fully advised of this obligation. We find that paying a fee has a number of benefits, such as participants being held accountable for investing resources to attain help for themselves. This implies that they will experience a reciprocal benefit from the investment and increases the expectation that they will attain something useful from the experience.

P: Well, I don't have the money. I got laid off, and I don't have a job.

F: I'm sorry about your job. Our next group won't start for another 3 weeks. Do you think you could come up with the money before then?

For participants who state that they won't have the money at any time, we may ask, "What are you going to do?" We do not attempt to solve this problem for them. We assume that they have the skills to figure out this problem for themselves. In 11 years of doing these groups, this issue has never prohibited anyone from attending the group.

P: Well, I think I'll have a job by then, but the judge wants me in court next Wednesday to tell him I've signed up for the group.

Frequently participants will call to sign up for the program right before their next court date, even though they've been told to do so months and sometimes years previously. We do not confront them and ask them why they waited. We do whatever we can to help them get what they need.

F: That's fine. We can send notification to the judge as soon as you do the intake interview. Does next Monday at 4:00 P.M. work for you?

P: OK. Can I bring my wife? She really belongs in this program, too.

F: I'm sorry. This program is only for people who are court-ordered, but she is certainly welcome to see another therapist at our clinic.

Although participants often want their spouses to come, we do not see couples together in the group. In some cases both members of a couple have been mandated to attend our program, and we have directed them to separate groups. We have found that partners do better in the group if they attend separately.

The facilitator continues engaging the participant in a nonjudgmental and accepting manner, recognizing that the client is the expert of his or her own life. Participants often want to talk about what happened, how the "system" is screwed up, and to explain that they do not belong here, or that they acted in self-defense. The facilitator does not elicit or encourage this type of conversation in any way. Instead, the facilitator brings the discussion back to the issues at hand as soon as possible. One way to change the dialogue might be to say, "So, before you get into that, let me ask you . . . ," then to lead the dialogue into other items that need to be covered in the first phone contact. Quite often, the participant does not return to the original topic.

It takes some time for participants to trust that we are not interested in blame, and that they do not need to be defensive or offensive. We do not perceive their "story" as having a bearing on their future success; furthermore, we are not interested in judging them. Another reason for not engaging in the discussion about "what happened" is that we do not want to be put in a position of determining whether or not the story is true. We expect that those evaluations have been made by the legal system, and determining guilt or innocence is not the role or responsibility of the group facilitator. We believe that the task of the facilitator is to encourage change through a collaborative relationship with participants in as short a time as possible.

The Goals and Tasks of the Assessment Interview

Four major goals must be addressed during the solution-focused assessment. These are to (1) initiate a collaborative relationship, (2) build initiative for change, (3) plant seeds for immediate and future change efforts, and (4) define the expectations for the group. The goals of assessment can be listed sequentially, but from a practice perspective they mix and blend, and at times multiple goals are being addressed in a single brief conversation. It is also important to note that even though we are describing assessment as a separate phase of an overall process, it is in fact more or less a part of all interactions. Because people are forever changing, what is important or relevant to address at one point in time may no longer be of interest or important later. It is necessary to help participants reassess what is working and not working at all stages of the process.

Initiating a Collaborative Relationship

The assessment interview is often the first face-to-face contact with the prospective participant. It is important that the tone of interaction reflect the nature of the work that must be accomplished in future groups. The facilitator must actively introduce a collaborative process while at the same time defining what is expected of the participant. This is demonstrated by assuming a nonjudgmental attitude while also firming up the expectation that the participant will be expected to make a commitment to "do something different" in his or her life. A nonjudgmental approach does not imply that the facilitator never questions potential participants about their behavior, but rather that questions come from a position of genuine curiosity as opposed to coercion or pressuring for change. For example, questions that ask the potential participants to self-evaluate whether or not what they are doing is working are often part of this respectful positioning. The participant is treated with respect through listening carefully and using his or her own frame of reference or words to show that the facilitator is attending fully. The relationship is not based on a hierarchy, with the facilitator as a teacher and the participant as a student, or the facilitator as a doctor who diagnoses and treats the "patient." Both the facilitator and the participant are seen as competent in different areas; they learn from each other. The participant is viewed as the expert on his or her own life, and the facilitator is the expert in asking useful questions, helping individuals identify strengths and resources, helping them to generate a focus on what to do differently, and facilitating movement toward their goals. The participant is not viewed as a diagnosis, or the embodiment of the label "perpetrator," but rather as a whole person with strengths and weaknesses. Each person is seen as unique.

During the assessment interview, it is not necessary to use confrontation to challenge the potential participant's past or current behavior or perceptions. The goal is to begin a mutually satisfactory working relationship with the understanding that the participant will create new and different behaviors in the future.

Building Initiative for Change: Discovering Competency and Identifying Strengths

To build initiative for change during the assessment interview, it is extremely important to shift the focus to the competencies of the potential participant. The assumption in the solution-focused model is that all participants are competent in some areas of their lives, and in order to facilitate cooperation and the co-construction of a positive future, it is best to start with what has already worked for participants even if their apparent strengths seem unrelated to issues at hand. Recognizing that they already have tools, skills, and abilities enables them to have more hope about a positive future. Knowing about a person's strengths also helps challenge any preconceptions that might otherwise interfere with the facilitator's overall effectiveness and provides many resources to tap into during the group process.

The facilitator asks specific questions related to client strengths, such as "What are some of your recent successes?" "What have you done that you are proud of?" "What have you done that took a lot of hard work?" "Have you ever broken a habit that was hard to break?" "What kinds of things do people compliment you on?" These questions clearly give potential participants and the facilitator an opportunity to assess potential strengths and resources. They also allow for an assessment of the participants' level of receptivity to engage in a process that requires them to explore their own resources. This gives the facilitator an idea of how much support, encouragement, and structure participants may require in the group process. It also gives clues regarding the pace of the interaction that is acceptable to participants and the ideal balance between questions that require decision making and supportive statements and compliments.

Planting Seeds: Looking for Problem Exceptions

What the therapist knows, understands, or believes about a patient is frequently limited in character and often mistaken. (Milton Erickson, 1980, p. 349)

We assume that people are interested in doing the best they can, and we find it helpful as part of the assessment to explore their strengths from both a narrow and a broad perspective. As part of this assessment, it is important to discover an individual's receptivity and motivation to explore narrowly focused or broadly focused strengths and resources. Potential participants come to the assessment interview with different levels of investment in the problems that brought them to the attention of the legal authorities. Some are still actively involved and upset by the events and circumstances, and others are more disengaged. If they are angry, the anger may be directed at the authorities, the facilitator, family members, other individuals, or any combination of these. When this is the case, it is important for the facilitator to help them determine whether or not it is helpful to focus on their responses to the emotionally charged events or if it is more helpful to shift toward broader based exceptions to their current problems.

In general, when a potential participant is focused on problems directly related to the referral to the group, it is advantageous to ask him or her if it is helpful to talk about these events. At times, individuals will assume that they are supposed to talk about these events or feel compelled to talk about negative events even when they find that doing so is not helpful or may even be aggravating. If the latter is the case, the facilitator can help participants shift to potentially more useful territory by asking questions that help assess what they are doing that is working better. These questions can be open, such as "What is working better for you now?" or "What things are you doing that contribute to your life going better?" or "What little things are you doing that make life a little better?" or "How do you keep focused on what you have to do to make things better?"

For individuals who believe it is important to talk directly about the events that brought them to the assessment, we find it helpful to search for times when violent behavior could have occurred but did not. The purpose of doing so is threefold: It allows individuals the opportunity to consider what works and what does not; it moves to the foreground the fact that participants are not always violent; and it emphasizes that participants can assert control over their behavior. It is most helpful for the facilitator to gather detailed information regarding what the participants did differently in order not to be violent, how they accomplished this, when they did it, where it was done, who might have noticed, and so forth. These details help individuals pinpoint exactly how this change occurred and give them clues on how to do it again. The information gathered can empower participants to have confidence in being able to change their future, since they have had some success in the past.

Besides knowing what participants have done in the past that worked, it is sometimes valuable to discover what did not work. Many participants have invested considerable effort in trying to change their behavior prior to coming to the assessment. It is necessary to explore this possibility and give credit for this effort. Failing to do so implies that this behavior is not valuable or, worse, that it has not occurred. In our experience, what is noticed becomes reality, and what is unnoticed does not exist. The story of the three umpires provides a good reminder of this notion:

> The first umpire, being a man of small knowledge of how meanings are made, says, "I calls 'em as they are." The second umpire, knowing something about human perception and its limitations says, "I calls 'em as I see 'em." The third umpire, having studied at Cambridge with Wittgenstein himself, says, "Until I call 'em, they ain't." (Neal Postman, quoted by O'Hanlon & Wilk, 1987, p. 23)

Using questions to search for the participant's strengths creates the opportunity to identify potential compliments that can be given during the assessment or logged for future use. It is important to notice how the individual receives compliments and which compliments seem to resonate and have special meaning. In general, the impact of compliments should not be underestimated in developing a collaborative relationship during the assessment process. When the facilitator is genuinely impressed by the participant's accomplishments, the opportunity is created for the participant to see himself or herself as a competent person, and therefore as having the ability to create a positive future.

Specific questions are used to draw out successful life experiences that the potential participant may recognize as important achievements. This provides the opportunity for the participant to share successes. Such questions include "What are the achievements that you are most proud of having accomplished in your life?" "Have you ever stopped doing something that was difficult for you to stop?" or "Have you ever made an important change in your life that was difficult to make?" In our experience, individuals will often report that they have stopped using alcohol, cigarettes, or drugs. This creates the opportunity for the facilitator to respond with surprise, curiosity, and compliments, for example, "You did? Wow! How did you do that?" It is often advantageous to ask how confident participants are that they can continue to abstain from substances, how they will continue to build on this success. They might be asked how their children and spouse will be different when they abstain. These questions not only help both participants and the facilitator understand how the participants make changes in their life but also help potential participants recognize that they have important experience in changing their lives for the better. Pre-group change is a positive indicator for success in the group, and it can be used to build further changes.

When we have used these approaches to develop a collaborative relationship while demonstrating our belief in each person's competence, participants leave the assessment interview with both a sense of hope about their future and a sense that they can make changes that will benefit them and those around them. They leave with the awareness that the facilitator is not there to judge or condemn but to be a collaborator in discovering how to improve the quality of their lives. In addition, the participants begin to consider what future changes might look like, as they contemplate the goal work that will be required of them.

Defining the Expectations of the Group

Introduction to Group Format

One of the primary components of the assessment interview is to give the participant a detailed description of the program. The outline of the program is helpful in the following ways:

1. It informs participants as to what they can expect from the group. Most of the participants have never been in a group before and may express fear, hesitation, and anxiety about joining one. Knowing what is going to happen can alleviate anxiety.
2. It sets clear parameters about what is negotiable and what is not negotiable.
3. It informs participants about what will be required of them.

Group Logistics

Participants are told that the group will meet for 1 hour for eight sessions, and that attending the first session is mandatory. They are told that the first session will include an explanation of the group rules that will be operational for all eight sessions, as well as an introduction to developing an acceptable goal. The importance of attending groups and of being on time is emphasized by noting that participants will be allowed only one absence, with no exceptions. They are assured that if they miss more than one session, they must repeat the entire sequence. We explain that a lot of hard work needs to be done during a short amount of time and that missing more than one group is not negotiable. Participants are informed that they must arrive before the sign-in form is returned to the facilitator at the beginning of each group session. If they happen to be late and miss signing in on the sheet, they must use that session as their one absence. They are told that they will receive notification by mail 2 weeks prior to the group starting date, which will include the dates for all eight sessions. It is helpful to give as much notice as possible so that potential participants can schedule their lives around the groups. Participants are informed again about the fee and reminded that it must be paid in full prior to the first group.

Introduction to Goals and Homework Assignments

The final point of information given during the assessment interview is a description of what is expected of participants during the group process. Potential participants are told they must develop a goal to work on throughout the eight sessions. Introducing the concept of the goal usually results in confusion that often is not fully resolved until participants have actually watched or experienced the goal development process. Goals are described as something they choose to work on in order to improve their lives and a relationship in their lives. The goal must involve different behaviors, ones that can be noticed by significant others. The facilitator explains that the first three sessions will be devoted to helping participants develop and clarify goals; this will include helping them be as specific as possible regarding the behaviors that will help them reach their goals.

Once participants have established a workable goal, they will be expected to work on it between sessions and will be expected to report on their efforts. They are told that as they come into the group each week, the facilitators will be interested in what they did differently the previous week to work on their goal. We make it very clear that we will ask many questions about what they are doing regarding their goal. Potential participants are asked to begin thinking about what they might work on so that when the group starts, they will already have some ideas in mind, and perhaps will even have started working on a goal.

Once the concept of a goal has been explained, homework assignments are introduced. These assignments are described as one-page written responses to specific questions. Examples of assignments are given, such as "Tell us what you think are the small things that make a relationship work" or "Describe to us who had a positive influence in your life and why." The facilitator explains that we expect a full-page response to these question and are interested only in participants' thoughts and ideas, not their writing ability or style. Individuals who are illiterate are expected to elicit the help of someone who can write their ideas for them in their own words (see Appendix 2 for a complete list of assignments).

The facilitator needs to have a clear understanding of what aspects of the group process are negotiable and nonnegotiable. It is particularly important to be consistent in talking to all participants to avoid confusion and unnecessary conflict. The following lists serve as an effective guide.

Nonnegotiable and Negotiable Aspects of the Group

Nonnegotiable

They must attend the first group.

They must attend for at least seven out of eight group meetings.

They must be on time.

They must work on a goal.

They must do the homework assignments.

They must pay the fee.

Negotiable

They can choose any relationship to work on as a goal, as long as they have regular contact with the person during the 8 weeks of group time.

They can choose the specific behaviors that they believe will improve that relationship, given that the behaviors must be the presence of something rather than the absence of something.

They can choose how often they engage in these behaviors, as long as there is contact between each of the groups and progress is being made.

The final item of business during the assessment interview is to ask if there are any questions. Questions are rare at this point, since the program has been described as completely as possible. A participant sometimes asks when the group will start and is told the approximate date, if that is known. It is explained that we require at least 8 to 10 participants, and the beginning date will be determined by how quickly the referrals come in. Attending the program often interferes with people's lives, and they frequently have to take time off from work to attend. We set the group time as late in the day as possible, but nonetheless, it is difficult for some participants to get there. We do not attempt to make special arrangements, nor do we try to solve the issue of having to take time off from a job. We consider the participants accountable for figuring out how to get to the group and be on time.

Assessment of Special Populations

A number of individuals who are referred to our program have substance abuse issues or various psychiatric problems or have committed a wide variety of violent acts. Based on findings of our outcome study, between 1996 and 2002, 61.4% of our participants had substance abuse problems,

18.8% had Axis I psychiatric diagnoses, 25.5% had Axis II personality disorders, and 4.5% had brain injury (see chapter 10 for a detailed discussion). How do the facilitators use or not use, focus or not focus on, such information in the assessment process? In our program, we do not focus on exploring diagnoses in the assessment process or use diagnoses to determine treatment. We are more interested in assessing the "surface" behaviors of each individual participant that are relevant in his or her search for and accomplishment of personally meaningful goals in a group context.

Since individuals are expected to develop their own unique solutions from their own frame of reference, it is important to consider whether potential participants are capable of cooperating and developing solutions. It is also important to help potential participants assess their ability to manage their anger and frustration in a group process. The fact that a potential participant has multiple problems cannot compromise his or her responsibility to do the work that is required during and between groups. From an assessment standpoint, the question is, "What are the basic requirements that a participant must be able to meet to benefit from the group?"

From our perspective, participants must be able to (1) listen and respond to questions, (2) create a clear, well-defined goal, (3) describe work on their goal at each session, (4) evaluate their goal efforts, (5) manage their anger appropriately during and between sessions, (6) follow group rules, and (7) come to sessions clean and sober. We believe that, regardless of diagnosis, chemical dependency, or emotional control issues, we can help participants if they can satisfy these seven requirements. In our experience, most individuals referred meet these requirements or appear to have the potential to do so. As a result, we have never excluded an individual from the program at the assessment interview.

When a potential participant presents with questionable ability to meet one of the seven requirements, it is important to consider what, if anything, that person can do to increase his or her capacity to benefit from the group process. Some participants may require in-session adjustments such as extra time, simpler language, repetition, more clarification, or a slower pace. Others may need to return to previous treatments that were helpful to them or may benefit from seeking supportive services. It is the facilitator's responsibility to explore with the participant how such issues can be addressed. We never assume that a person cannot discover a way to successfully participate.

When a participant has alcohol or drug problems, mental illness, or "antisocial features," the assessment of his or her ability to use the group often extends into the group process. When this occurs, an individual may find it difficult or impossible to develop a clear goal, to come to group on time, to come without drinking, or to manage emotions effectively at group. These events offer the facilitator the opportunity to help the individual to evaluate what he or she needs to do differently. This type of assessment occurs in the group itself or, in some situations, must be scheduled as an additional session that occurs after or between groups. The focus of this type of assessment is on "surface" behaviors that can be observed in the group process. We prefer this type of assessment process, which values what the individual actually does and does not do, above and beyond our "clinical impression" or a "clinical diagnosis." Our clinical impression generally represents our clinical bias, whereas what the participant does and does not do is what really counts.

Alcohol and Drug Issues

Substance abuse is a serious concern, in that a significant percentage of mandated clients have substance abuse issues. In our program, 61.4% of participants had alcohol or substance abuse issues. Research also supports the notion that *chronic* alcohol abuse is a strong predictor of more violent behavior (Blount, Silverman, Sellers, & Seese 1994; Heyman, O'Leary, & Jouriles, 1995; Tolman & Bennett, 1990; Wesner, Patel, & Allen, 1991). Participants often tell us that either they or their partner was under the influence of alcohol or drugs when the domestic violence occurred.

Assessment offers an opportunity to help potential participants consider the impact of alcohol and drugs in their lives. Some individuals effectively use limited support and encouragement to make and sustain changes in this area. Others struggle in spite of tremendous resources and effort. The following guidelines keep the focus on what is realistic and potentially meaningful when addressing this issue at assessment: (1) We find it important to discover and support any and all efforts the participant is currently using that may help reduce or stop alcohol and drug use; (2) it is not helpful to argue with individuals about drug and alcohol use; (3) it is useful for participants to have a clear understanding of the group expectations related to drugs and alcohol; and (4) it is helpful for participants to fully understand that they will be held accountable for complying with the expectations.

During the assessment interview, all prospective participants are informed that we have zero tolerance for alcohol or drug use on the day of the group. We tell them that we want them to have the best opportunity to use the group to their benefit, and to do so they must, in our opinion, be clean and sober on the day of the group. We find that this statement is easily accepted as an honest, practical assessment by virtually all potential participants. We emphasize our resolve regarding this issue by stating that, if they are thought to be under the influence of drugs or alcohol, they will be asked to leave the group. This offers an opportunity for potential participants to make a commitment to change their behavior related to this issue. It also helps them assess whether such behavior may be creating negative consequences for them and their families. For many participants, agreeing not to drink on the day of the group is an important exception to their previous behavior. Not drinking on the day of the group represents another exception to their behavior and offers the opportunity for them to assess the difference it creates. This, combined with a focus on trying new and different nondrinking behaviors, often results in significant change.

Some individuals come to the assessment interview having stopped drinking and using drugs. They may note that drinking has only caused problems and that going to jail has given them new resolve and a desire to stop drinking. It is important for the facilitator to help these participants assess the advantages of not drinking and to expand their thoughts in this area. It is also important to note this behavior so that the facilitator can help participants reevaluate the impact and value of this change as it relates to them and the people they care about.

We do not exclude individuals from treatment due to alcohol or drug use if they are able to meet the basic expectations of the group. Change must begin at some place and some time. Waiting for individuals to walk in the "right door" at the right time to get the "right treatment" only delays the opportunity for something different to happen. This shift in approach is particularly important for individuals who have persistently refused to walk in the door that says "Drug and Alcohol Treatment Center." If individuals can become engaged in their goal work, they often abstain totally or greatly reduce their substance use because they find that it interferes with their goal efforts.

If, during the assessment interview, individuals inform us that they have quit using since the "incident," we use this as an opportunity to compliment them and to get information about how they did this. We may ask how confident they are that they can continue to abstain, and what difference the change is making in their relationships. We do not confront or lecture. We assume that friends, family members, employers, or the courts have already confronted them about their substance abuse problems, and we prefer not to do more of what has not worked in the past.

When the concept of a goal is introduced, potential participants sometimes state that they want to work on stopping drinking. When this occurs, they are informed that stopping a behavior is not an acceptable group goal, because stopping something is the absence of something, and the goal has to be something they will do rather than not do. We encourage them to continue their efforts in this area while helping them shift to doing something in addition to stopping drinking.

Tips for Addressing Drug and Alcohol Issues

Assess helpful efforts regarding reducing or stopping drug or alcohol use.

State clearly and unambiguously the group rules and consequences regarding drug or alcohol use.

Don't exclude participants because of history of drug or alcohol use.

Don't take responsibility for convincing participants to stop drug or alcohol use.

Psychiatric Problems

During the assessment interview, it may become obvious that an individual has symptoms that are typically associated with a mental health diagnosis. Because we work in a community mental health setting, we routinely apply mental health diagnoses. The majority of participants are diagnosed with relationship problems. There is also a preponderance of personality disorder diagnoses, including antisocial personality disorders and narcissistic and borderline personality disorders. Less frequently, an Axis I diagnosis, such as schizophrenia or bipolar disorder, is given. In general, we find diagnostic labels and categories to be limiting and poor predictors of potential participants' capacity to use the group. We do not use diagnosis to determine treatment or to exclude an individual from the program. We believe that people are not categories and that diagnosis does little to predict outcome (DeJong & Berg, 2002).

During the assessment interview we find it helpful to recognize an individual who is experiencing symptoms of a mental disorder because it can indicate that this participant may need extra help in seeking resources or help in the process of interacting effectively within the group. Again, the focus of assessment is on observable behaviors manifested in the group context and not on inferred behaviors based on a pregiven clinical diagnosis. When this appears to be the case, it is often helpful to directly or indirectly address the issue with the potential participant. Direct discussion is often most helpful with individuals who indicate that they have a particular symptom or are receiving medication to treat a particular symptom. Potential participants can then explore how they will deal with symptoms that might interfere with their group participation. In some instances, individuals will simply state that taking their medications is very important and that they intend to do so regularly. At other times they share or create a strategy they can use to focus their attention or formulate their thoughts in a group context.

It is also important for the facilitator to consider what, if any, modifications might be necessary or helpful to participants. We may have to be more patient with participants who have organic brain disorders, in that we may need to use simpler, more concrete language, but we have found that these individuals have the potential to change behaviors (see chapter 9 for a more in-depth discussion of this topic).

We treat all individuals as unique and base our questions on their responses. Individuals who need extra help are not necessarily those with psychiatric diagnoses. The findings of our outcome study showed that there was no significant difference in recidivism rates between individuals who had psychiatric disorders and those who did not. Increasingly, it is recognized that many individuals with mental health symptoms can be partners in developing plans to effectively participate in many areas from which they were previously excluded. The assessment process is an opportunity to invite individuals to participate in a process that includes their input and challenges them to use the resources that we assume they have.

Severity of Violence

We do not screen individuals out of the group based on the type, degree, or frequency of violent behavior. From a research perspective, such details are valuable in learning about offenders and for making decisions about public policy, but for our purposes they are not helpful. The individuals who are referred to us live in our community regardless of whether we treat them. We assume that unless proven otherwise, if the court deems these individuals safe to be in the community, they are acceptable in our program. Once in the group, participants are not treated differently based on the type or degree of violence they have committed.

Our referrals for the domestic violence program come from the courts, the probation department, and sometimes the parole board. The offenses for which people are referred include the entire range of domestic violence abuse. There are no typical domestic violence offenders, but the following examples provide a snapshot of two offenders: Jay was referred after shoving his wife into a couch while they were both intoxicated. His wife sustained bruises to her arm and leg. Jay spent 3 days in jail, was given 1 year of probation, and was referred to our program. Ricky, on the other hand, attacked his wife and her new boyfriend after watching through her bedroom window while they were having sex. He fractured his wife's nose and injured her eye socket, ear, and shoulder. He broke the boyfriend's jaw. He had no previous convictions and was sentenced to 1 year in jail and 3 years' probation. He was mandated to the group after his jail time was served. We accept referrals from the parole board for individuals who are required to do our program as a condition of parole. In general, we do not know, nor do we believe it is helpful to know, the nature of the offense that participants have committed. The vast majority of the offenders have spent time in the county jail, from several days to 2 years.

Our focus is on facilitating change in as short a time as possible in order to eliminate violence in the home. "Owning" or "taking responsibility" for problem behaviors is not helpful or necessary in order for participants to discover what will work in improving their relationships. Focusing on the problem behavior not only limits clients but also can limit our ability to facilitate change. Being aware of individuals' weaknesses and dysfunctional behaviors may impair our ability to see their strengths and resources. We consider it more useful to notice capabilities, resources, and strengths in order to believe in participants' ability to change. We consider it helpful for participants to notice their abilities and strengths so that they can believe in a more positive future as well.

Useful Attitudes and Behaviors in the Assessment Interview

Do take a position of respect and not knowing.

Do accept that the participant is the expert in his or her life.

Do discover what is worthy about the participant.

Do assess observable "surface" behaviors.

Do look for participant strengths and resources.

Do look for exceptions.

Do recognize the uniqueness of each person.

Don't confront.

Don't demand confessions.

Don't educate.

Don't demand conformity.

Don't solve problems.

Don't assume understanding or meaning based on clinical diagnosis.

3

Using Group Rules, Assignments, and a Team Approach

Group Rules

Group rules are handed out at the beginning of the first group session (see Appendix 3). They set the structure and limits for the eight sessions and establish what will and will not be accepted in the program. They are simple and straightforward. Many participants are concerned with fairness and with being taken advantage of by the "system." The rules indicate that everyone will be treated equally and fairly. They help the facilitators use time efficiently by eliminating many unhelpful or distracting conversations. Group rules are wonderful tools for keeping the group focused on change.

At the first group meeting, we ask participants to take turns reading the rules out loud. After each rule is read, we ask if there are any questions. Our purpose for reading the rules out loud is fourfold: (1) It offers an opportunity for participants to express disagreements or differences of opinion; (2) it communicates that the group process will involve participation and effort; (3) it confirms that each participant has had the opportunity to learn, understand, and if necessary challenge the "rules of game"; and (4) it helps us determine if anyone is illiterate.

Challenges to facilitators are most common during the first meeting. Open presentation of the rules allows participants to evaluate whether or not they will be treated with respect. This decreases challenges to facilitators. Because the rules are based on a commonsense approach to human interaction, most challenges are easily addressed with a brief discussion and explanation. The majority of participants find it easy to support the rules and find it difficult to go against the facilitators when one participant presents a challenge. All rules are explained matter-of-factly, with respect, and without confrontation or argument. We convey the practical and useful nature of the rules, emphasizing that they serve everyone's interest. We also note that the facilitators are accountable to the group and mention rules that have specific implications for the facilitators.

Rule 1. Attendance

There will be eight group sessions. You must inform us prior to the session if you will not be able to attend. You will still be responsible for any assignments due for the session you missed. If you miss more than one session, you will be terminated from the program. We are required to report your attendance to the probation office. We expect you to be on time. Arriving after the sign-in sheet has been passed around will constitute one miss.

We are very clear that we expect a time commitment from the participants. This rule communicates that the group is important and has value. It also conveys that their involvement has a purpose and that important work will be accomplished. We will not tolerate lateness or participants missing more than one session. Participants are told that a lot of hard work has to be accomplished in a short period of time, so it is important that they attend all sessions. We do not want them to miss anything that will be of value to them.

Rule 2. Violence

Violence of any sort is unacceptable. Any use of violence will result in termination from the program.

We let the group know, right from the beginning, that we take a very serious stand against violence and will not tolerate violence of any kind either inside or outside of the group. Normally there is little, if any, response to this rule. We explain that if any participants are violent, we must report it to the probation department, and they will be terminated from the group.

Rule 3. Confidentiality

Everything discussed in this group is confidential. If you break this rule, you will be terminated from the group.

We discuss this rule at length. We convey that participants issues are respected as private, and that we want the group to be a safe and confidential environment. We explain that participants should not tell spouses or friends who is in the group. We note that they may discuss what they are learning in the group but may not reveal information about other participants. We explain that some participants may share highly personal information and may become vulnerable in the group. We note our professional obligations regarding confidentiality and share examples of how we protect individuals' confidentiality. We specifically describe what information we are obligated to share, with whom, and under what circumstances. Often we explain how we would handle "bumping into them" in the community. We note that we will not respond to them unless they initiate an interaction, and we will protect their privacy if this occurs. Safety and respect are serious issues for our participants. Many participants have not had the experience of feeling safe or vulnerable in a group situation, and we work hard to offer them a safe, confidential environment.

Rule 4. Alcohol and drugs

You will be asked to leave the group if you are thought to be under the influence of drugs or alcohol. This means that any use of alcohol or drugs on the day of the group will lead to your being discharged from the group.

We make it completely clear that we expect participants to be fully present when they attend the meetings, and that any use of substances will not be tolerated. We also want participants to be aware of the consequences of breaking this rule. We explain that if we smell alcohol or sense that a participant has come to the group under the influence, we will ask him or her to step forward and leave the group for that day. If no one is willing to come forward, the whole group is dismissed, resulting in the scheduling of an additional meeting for all participants and the facilitators. We ask that all individuals be respectful of other participants, because everyone is potentially affected if this rule is broken. Since we initiated talking about participants' responsibility to each other and the manner in which everyone can be negatively affected, we have had very few violations of this rule.

Rule 5. Assignments

You will be expected to read and complete all written assignments. If for some reason you find it difficult to complete a task, it is your responsibility to ask for help.

Participants are expected to complete a number of assignments (see the list in Appendix 2). These assignments are designed to help participants think about certain subjects that may be a resource for them in their search for solutions. We explain that we are not interested in spelling or grammar but are interested only in their thoughts on these subjects. We ask participants to read or talk about their homework assignments during group sessions, and have found that this stimulates very useful group discussions.

Those participants who are illiterate are informed that they are accountable for finding someone to write their thoughts and ideas for them so that they can accomplish the required task.

Rule 6. Group discussion

Participants are expected to discuss and share their ideas and thoughts during the group. If you disagree with the facilitators

or other participants, you are encouraged to express that
response. However, all disagreements are to be handled with
respect for other people's opinions, ideas, and feelings.

The purpose of this rule is to let participants know that they and their opinions are important. We are interested in and value their input. This rule also conveys that we expect them to be invested and active in the group process. Participants report that they have learned a great deal from each other during group discussion. The underlying message is that everyone has the potential to contribute and that when we work together, we increase our potential. When discussing this rule, we stress that everyone must participate and note that often a shy person may offer important and unique perspectives that otherwise would go unnoticed. This often is followed by comments by participants about their own shyness and their willingness to do their best to comment. In some cases it results in a shy individual setting up a goal to be a regular contributor.

Rule 7. No blaming talk

We will not directly focus on the behavior of others, and we will
discourage you from doing so. We have found that the only
behavior you can change is your own.

This rule implies that participants are responsible for and will be held accountable for change. It helps to eliminate much problem talk and promotes efficient use of group time. It lets participants know that the group is not going to be a gripe or blame session but will focus on what they will be doing to create meaningful change in their lives.

Rule 8. Goals

You must have a goal by the end of the third session. The goal
must be something you choose to do differently that improves
your life and something that other people can notice and be
positively affected by. If you don't have a goal by the third
session, you will not be able to continue.

Initially some participants believe that simply attending the sessions will be sufficient for completing the group. This rule introduces the basic requirements of a goal without specifying the details. It informs participants that they will have to work in and outside of the group, and it implies that they can make a positive and important difference by planning and taking action. A goal must lead to a change that will improve the participant's life, and potentially a relationship, and the change must be apparent to other people.

Do's and Don'ts of Rules

Do go over the rules in the first group session.

Do keep rules simple.

Do allow time for discussion.

Don't let participants talk you into making exceptions.

Don't get into arguments or confrontations.

Assignments

We use two or three assignments during each series of eight group sessions. The first assignment is given at the end of session 4, followed by a discussion of the assignment during session 5 or 6. The final assignment is always given at session 7 and is discussed during the final session. If we use all three assignments, we do so by giving the second one at session 5 or 6. Whether we give two or three assignments is determined by the amount of time we have available after discussing goals. We never sacrifice goal discussion time to fit in all the assignments. In fact, on some occasions we have used only the final assignment because the goal work we were doing was particularly time-consuming and, in our opinion, more important.

The assignments that we use are designed to increase the participants' sense of competence, confirm their motivation for change, and increase their commitment to continuing their efforts after the group is completed. Assignments are given at the end of a session, so as not to distract from the work that needs to be accomplished at that particular meeting. We tell participants that for each assignment they must write a least one full page on a legal-sized pad of paper and bring it to the next group. If less than a page is turned in, we hand the paper back with a request for a complete page of work. We always completely review all expectations when we first give the assignment.

The first assignment is to write a page on "the small things that make a relationship work." We emphasize the small things because we believe that little changes translate into big changes and because we believe it is most helpful when people focus on small, doable tasks. We are essentially asking people to recall what they believe makes for a good relationship. This allows participants to bring to consciousness behavior that has worked in the past that they may have forgotten, as well as to consider new behaviors. The discussion of this question also creates an opportunity to learn from others in the group.

The fourth assignment is to have participants write about someone who has influenced them in a positive way. It often results in participants recalling useful information about how they themselves want to behave in relation to others. This information also relates directly to the goal work that participants are doing. The memories that are triggered by this assignment often increase participants' desire to work even harder at their goal efforts.

The final assignment is always given at the end of group seven. It asks participants to review what they learned in the group that was helpful and asks them to evaluate their commitment to their goal. Participants are asked to rate their commitment to continuing their goal efforts on a scale of 1 to 10, with 10 being highly committed and 1 being virtually no commitment. This prepares all participants for the discussion of these issues at the final group. This assignment also helps participants identify any adjustments or additions that they may want to make so that they can continue to be successful.

We return the last assignment to the participants 3 months after the final group meeting. We include a letter that compliments their work in the groups and also conveys a personal memory from us that reflects our appreciation of them as people. We mention that the last written assignment might still be of value to them and therefore we are returning it to them.

Working as a Team

There are many advantages to working as a team, as well as some disadvantages. Our preference for this arrangement was born out of our belief that this population would be difficult to work with and would present many in-session challenges that would be easier to deal with if two facilitators were working together. This has not proved to be a completely accurate assumption. The solution-focused approach we use creates an environment that makes change easier to produce, often in a conflict-free manner. We seldom face in-session challenges that we have not managed satisfactorily by ourselves with other populations. So why do we continue to work as a team and recommend that other facilitators do, too?

We work as a male-female team and consider this particularly helpful for a number of reasons. First, it tends to soften anger that might otherwise be directed at a single female facilitator. We do not assume that all the men we work with are angry with women, in particular, but we do recognize that some men will direct anger at a female facilitator and are much less likely to do so when a male-female team is used. In this case, working as a team saves energy that otherwise would be used to deal with misdirected anger and confrontation. A male-female team has the further advantage of providing a role model of a male and female "working together" and productively resolving differences. We pay attention to the little interactions of the team, always listening well to each other and respecting each other's desire to ask questions and pursue information from participants. We do not interrupt each other yet expect each other to allow space for the other's comments or questions. As a team, we openly disagree during sessions and discuss the disagreement, thus we model compromise and a willingness to "give in" and try an experiment. We do this with respect for our divergent views and our commitment to working together. We believe it is important to "walk the walk" of working toward solutions, trying something new and adjusting to each other's perceptions. Clearly, it is important that the disagreements of the team not be a significant focus of the group, since this would detract from the work of participants, but when they arise, we address them openly.

A major advantage of working with another person is that it takes pressure off both facilitators, allowing time for one facilitator to think of useful questions and compliments while the other is asking a question. This is particularly helpful when first using a solution-focused approach because it is easy to slip into problem talk or to begin mixing solution-focused questions with questions about problems, problem solving, or past emotional events. We believe this lack of focus is natural and that working with another facilitator makes it easier to stay committed to a solution-focused approach. Of course, all of this assumes that the facilitators are willing to hold each other accountable for staying on the solution-focused course.

Another advantage is related to the pace of interaction between the facilitators and participants. We find it helpful to keep participants fully engaged at all times, thinking and responding to questions and compliments. Given the brief nature of our approach, there is little time for interaction that is not purposeful. Participants quickly recognize that the pace will require them to be fully engaged in responding to questions and compliments. Some groups have referred to this as "being on the hot seat." We tend to see it as being fully engaged, being held accountable for responding. We are interested in being efficient with our work and find that efficiency is related to asking the most useful question at any given time. Working as a team makes it easier to produce useful questions and compliments at a pace that continually engages the group.

Another reason we prefer using a team comes from our experience with using one-way mirrors and phone consultation during individual and family sessions. We have noticed that it is often easier for an observer to produce useful responses. We suspect that this is because the observer has a unique point of view and can see the process from a broader, less engaged perspective. This is partly because the observer is not under pressure to provide an immediate response that is in balance with the therapy process. Within the group process, we view ourselves as "thoughtful observers" when our interviewing partner is engaged with the participant. We evaluate what is working and consider what might be more helpful, as if we were behind a one-way mirror. This allows us the most useful vantage point for being helpful.

When trouble does arise in a session in the form of a threat or a participant who becomes defensively focused, it is often very helpful to have the least involved facilitator take the lead in shifting the focus toward a resolution. In such situations, it is common for the anger or energy to be directed at one member of the team; generally, the other team member is able to ask questions that bring the focus back to the work at hand. The least affected facilitator can also elicit support from the group when the time is right to further defuse the situation. These types of situations are rare in our experience, but when they do occur, it is very helpful to be working as a team.

The team arrangement creates an excellent environment for training and professional development. We learn from each other, both by watching and by conversing after a group session. We support each other and compliment each other for our good work and hold each other accountable for not only "talking the talk" but also "walking the walk." Accountability for using solution-focused principles is easily accomplished by asking each other solution-focused questions after groups. These interactions reflect our commitment to our work.

The "How-To" of Being an Effective Team

Being an effective team requires an expanded commitment to solution-focused principles within the team relationship. For example, when we talk to each other about our work, we do so from the perspective of exploring and experimenting with ideas and approaches that may be more helpful. We compliment our efforts and remain conscious of what our partner is doing well. We compliment specific details and note what we felt was productive. We maintain a curious attitude that focuses on what we could have done differently.

In our work environment, time is an extremely valuable commodity. Because we are often limited to brief interactions with each other after a session, we must use this time efficiently to share specific thoughts that may improve our effectiveness. Following each session, we informally, as a team, self-evaluate our work performance in a brief verbal summary. In our evaluation of ourselves, we tend to be more self-critical, while in relation to each other, we focus on each other's strengths and what we noticed that the other person did well. This is not to say that we do not occasionally pat ourselves on our own backs, but we find it more useful to be critical of ourselves and not of each other. We are particularly aware of noting when our partner has done something in a session that was particularly effective. It is critical to mention such observations because doing so helps underline useful interviewing and builds commitment to the process itself.

When one member of the team feels frustrated by his or her performance, we focus on what we could have done that would have been more useful. This discussion is often twofold, the first focus being on possible different questions and or compliments, and the second being on how the observing facilitator could have been more helpful during the session.

Because being creative is part of what we believe is necessary in a constantly changing world, we want to foster creativity in each other. In working together, it is important to keep in mind that creative ideas can occur only if we are willing to suspend our notions of what can be done and how things should be done. This requires us as individuals and as a team to take pause and not react when a new idea surfaces. In some cases it requires rejecting the thought "That's the most ridiculous idea I've ever heard" and saying instead, "I wonder how that would work." Being committed to this basic shift not only increases the creative power of the team but also exponentially increases the fun factor.

When a team is most playful, it is potentially the most effective. Obviously, we are serious, diligent, and determined about our work, but we recognize that in part our effectiveness lies in our ability to get our participants and ourselves to play with ideas and behavior.

The following is a transcribed interaction that typifies how we discuss our work following a session. We believe that talking in this manner has multiple benefits.

Facilitator 1: Where do you think it would be most helpful to start?

Facilitator 2: I was most impressed by Rick. It seemed that the change he made was so profound. He was talking about taking his wife to dinner and making the reservations and his wife wasn't ready and he was getting very angry and he just started breathing and he said to himself, "What does it matter in the long run if we eat in this restaurant or not?" She was expecting him to be hostile and uptight. That surprised her a great deal. He was able to change all that inner emotion and uptightness and turn that around. I was just floored by his saying that he needed to see his wife in respect to the bigger picture and not just be concerned about himself and what he wants. He talked about how he used to look for all the little things that he could pick at that his wife would say, instead of really listening to her. Now he is listening to her in a more caring manner. Isn't that extraordinary?

F1:   I liked that he was forthright about his emotions, about how he's crying and that he is talking about how he is changing his ideas about how life works, in that he is noting that he wants to pay attention to other people's needs, not just his. He is applying this to his relationships at work, as well. He shared how he would go to work with the intention of making people miserable, because he felt miserable. He now realizes . . .

F2:   . . . he wants to do something different, for the first time.

F1:   I was also impressed by Anna in that she was clearly angry about having to develop a goal and then began to shift.

F2:   You know, I like what you did with her when she said she wanted to be calmer and you asked her where that calmness starts in her.

F1:   She said in her heart.

F2:   And you asked, "How do you make that happen?" That was really right on because she went on this search to find the way she makes that happen.

F1:   I liked that moment because it was a time when you don't have a clue about what she would create as a result of that question. It gave her the opportunity to create the details of what calmness in heart meant to her. I was impressed that she accepted that question, even though she is just beginning to build intention toward a goal.

F2:   Yes, pretty impressive for only her second group! I think that when people have children they want life to be different and better for them. I think we helped by bringing her caring about her children into the foreground.

F1:   Yes, the questions about "How would your son notice that calmness in you?" and "How would that make a difference to him?" were helpful to her. I believe that helped her draw on what she wanted when she was a kid. Those types of questions require a person to reflect on what they know a child wants to experience in relationship to their parent.

F2:   Yes, and then the question arises of "What do I have to do so that my children get what I wanted as a child?"

F1:   Yes, and "How committed do I have to be to be able to provide that kind of experience?"

F2:   I think that's where we worked well together with this woman.

F1:   Yes.

F2:   There was another question that you've asked in this area of "What would you like your son to say about his relationship with you when he's your age? What would you like your son to say about his experience with you?"

F1:   That question requires a huge amount of effort to answer. I'm always impressed that people allow us to ask these probing questions when it comes to their relationships with their children. It's the power of the group. Mo Yee and I were talking about how the group is this rare environment where people get to play with their ideas and thoughts and it's inviting, because you not only have the opportunity to be the main participant, but you also get to be a spectator of someone else's change process.

F2:   Yes, and that's part of our goal to create that environment. I was really rushed after the last group and started to think about Anna and her goal of being calm, and I thought, how would I work on calm right now? I'm learning from these people. Everything is interconnected; we're not separate from the group.

F1:   That's what I appreciated about Jerry and the dishes. He's almost like a storm, stirred up inside. He wants to do something to make it better, but on the other hand, he's so angry.

F2:   Yes, he's so angry with his wife and at this time feels staying with the family is what he has to do. I liked it when you asked him about that dilemma of how he will put effort into this relationship when he doesn't believe it will work.

F1:   I felt really confused about what to do because I wanted to ask him more about the times when he knew why he was with his wife and what used to work, but I was concerned about whether or not that would be productive, so I opted to lean toward questions that were more directly goal-focused. I was concerned about how much time.

F2:   That time pressure really drives us, and usually that is very helpful, but this was a time when you may have wanted to help him explore this issue of past exceptions. I thought about a scaling question related to how much he wants to be in this relationship or what is the level of confidence that this relationship is going to work.

F1:   I wanted to give him the opportunity to wonder about what had worked in the past.

F2:   When you explored with him how hard it is to be motivated to do something when you're no longer fully committed to a relationship, that helped him move forward into doing the dishes. Because prior to that he had made no commitment to do anything different, and after that work with him he decided to do the dishes, even if she did nothing all day after he had worked all day.

F1:   I think we set the stage for that by utilizing questions that asked him whether or not he was committed to putting in some effort, and then we pressed him to evaluate whether or not he was going to use his efforts in a way that would be helpful or that would be destructive.

F2:   Yes, you did that by stating that it depends how you do the dishes. You can do them sort of in her face or you can do them in another way. That helped him evaluate what his objective was, given that he also still had all this anger.

F1:   Yes, he had to decide whether or not his goal was to get back at his wife or to take some steps forward.

F2:   . . . and make things better. You know that helped him again focus on his children. I think we could have asked "What will your children notice that's different when you take that step forward?"

F1:   Yes, I think that's important. . . . . I struggled to find a manner of talking about how he was going to approach doing the dishes, and I really appreciated your being there, because your engagement with him allowed me to think about how to approach that issue.

F2:   Yes, and not dealing with the issue of his intention could have resulted in wasted effort. The other place I thought we worked well as a team was with the fellow who "bit his tongue" several times in his effort to decrease his negative remarks to his wife.

F1:   Yes, I got distracted by Anna's comments, and you brought it back to the details of what he needed to do to expand his goal effort. That needed to

happen, and you made it happen because you were able to keep that focus.

F2: It emphasizes how useful it can be to work as a team, particularly when there is so much to do and keep track of.

F1: I was so impressed with his effort in these first two groups.

F2: Yes, he's willing to do different things, and you can see a softer quality already in how he talks about his life and family.

F1: He's thinking and talking about his wife in a different way.

F2: He's said, "I was a biker and a tough guy, but now I want life to be different."

F1: And now he's asking if she wants to ride with him, and he's being patient with her to make that happen.

F2: And here we are at the end of the second group with lots of good things happening!

Working as a Team

Do be alert for what the team is doing well.

Do compliment each other.

Do compliment the work of group participants when talking about them to each other.

Do observe when someone does something especially well.

Do take the lead when your partner is being verbally assailed.

Do include each other in decisions.

Do talk as if you are a team.

Do model team work in front of the group.

4

Developing Useful Goals

Much of the work we do with group participants revolves around developing clearly defined goals. When goals are defined as a major focus of treatment, accountability for changing one's behavior can be achieved. The use of goals shifts the focus of attention to what can be done, as opposed to what cannot. It moves participants away from blaming others or themselves and holds them accountable for developing a better, different future.

Goals help participants construct present and future behavior that *they* are interested in. Goals also increase participants' awareness of choice because the range of possible goals is limited only by the participants' imaginations. Goals also offer participants an opportunity to play an active role in their own treatment. Within the collaborative process, they are invited to design goals that they believe will be helpful to them.

In our work, goals are defined as a mandatory part of group involvement. Participants are responsible for devising a goal that will benefit them and potentially benefit the people around them. They are also held accountable for reporting their efforts related to their goal in significant detail at each group session. We define the parameters of an acceptable goal and work with participants so that they have every reasonable opportunity to develop an acceptable goal.

Goals are used to create a context in which change is expected to occur. As participants begin to behave in a way that is consistent with their goal, we help them to see all the possible benefits of their goal behavior. Even the smallest change in behavior or thought is noticed and described as significant. It is our job to create an environment in which the goals our participants create and the resultant behavior are experienced as being of great benefit to them. Insoo Kim Berg, Steve de Shazer, and Gale Miller refer to this as "making the ordinary extraordinary." We often think of it as finding the little things that make a difference.

Much of what our participants do would not appear to be particularly difficult, nor are their goals particularly extraordinary, yet it is our task to notice how common behaviors have impressive benefits for them and the people around them. This context empowers participants to create new and useful descriptions of themselves. It is these new descriptions that we are interested in helping them discover and create.

Goals and Mandatory Participants

Mandatory participants are often defensive and worry that the therapy process will focus on their failures or shortcomings. They often conclude that the "authorities" have predetermined the problem and the solution. They also expect that the predetermined solutions will result in significant personal pain and humiliation for them. Thus, it should come as no surprise that when facilitators focus on problems, mandatory participants often deny that they have problems. This fact, tied with the common notion that people must admit to having problems in order to change, creates a difficult situation. The resultant struggle may lead facilitators to conclude that mandatory participants are difficult or impossible to work with, and mandatory participants are left with the feeling that treatment is painful and useless.

We contend that admitting to problems has no relation to changing behavior, and we further suggest that persistently pressuring participants to admit their problems, "to take responsibility" for their past behaviors, makes for a discouraging circumstance for both the participant and the facilitator. This is partly due to the fact that causation and blame involve complex, multifaceted descriptions that draw energy away from "getting on with change." At all levels of social and political interaction, people resist taking responsibility for their behavior, yet they can often agree that things could be better and as a result are willing to assume responsibility for making improvements when invited to do so. In many situations, the agreement to suspend judgment regarding blame allows people to move toward solutions. Truly taking responsibility for one's behavior can happen only in the present and future, since these are the behaviors that one is accountable for doing something about.

We find that participants are motivated to change when they are (1) invited to play an active role in determining the direction and focus of treatment, (2) respected as knowledgeable about their lives and what they need to accomplish to make them better, (3) in charge of determining their own goals within the defined parameters, and (4) held accountable for current and future behaviors as opposed to past behavior.

Using a structured goal-setting process offers the mandatory participant many choices. Therapy is immediately seen as more relevant and useful because the focus is on what the participant believes will be helpful and what he or she wants to achieve. These advantages result in a more efficient relationship, which means change can be accomplished in a shorter time.

Clearly, it is easier to develop a relationship with someone when you are helping him create a plan that is of interest to him, as opposed to trying to get him to admit to or focus on problems.

Participants have told us that they found it extremely helpful that we did not force them to review their problems. They have repetitively shared, "We knew we had problems when we came to you, and having to replay them would have only made things harder." We have noticed that many of our participants are comfortable sharing their old problems once they have begun to discover effective solutions. It is much easier for a mandatory participant to say, "I had a problem when I first came here" than to say, "I have a problem." We suspect that most people find it easier and more productive to focus on what they can accomplish, as opposed to focusing on their failures.

Goals allow participants to begin to explore possible solutions in a safe manner while allowing us to hold them accountable for doing something different in their lives. Accountability is expanded to creating a plan for change, creating change, and reporting on the impact that results from behavioral change. How many people can resist the opportunity to do something they really believe will be of value to them and of value to the people they care about?

Giving the Goal Task

Presenting the goal task to participants during the first group is relatively straightforward. We give the task of developing a goal and describe the parameters of a useful goal in the following manner: "We want you to create a goal for yourself that will be *useful* to you in improving your life." "The goal should be one that is *interpersonal* in nature, that is to say, that when you work on the goal, another person will be able to notice the changes you've made, and potentially they could be affected by the change in how you behave." "Another way to think about this is that if you brought us a videotape of yourself working on your goal, you would be able to point out the different things you were *doing* and maybe even note how these changes affected the other people on the tape." "The goal needs to be something *different*, a behavior that you have not generally done before." "Keep in mind that since you will be expected to report on your goal work every time we meet, it is important that your goal be a behavior you can do at least a few times a week." "It is important that everyone have an approved goal by the end of the third group; you cannot remain in the group after the third group unless you are working on an approved goal."

Thus, an acceptable goal is defined as *new, different* behavior that is helpful and that can be done with enough *regularity* that participants can *make reports* regarding their goal work at each group session. The goal is *interpersonal*, that is, it must have an impact on other people. There is no choice regarding developing a goal if one is to remain in the group.

Do's and Don'ts of Giving the Goal Task

Do get the group rules completely discussed and out of the way before the goal task is given.

Do be as clear as possible about the task.

Do cover the description of an acceptable goal.

Do be prepared for misunderstanding of the goal task regardless of how clear you are.

Do repeat the goal task.

Do use the notion of a videotape of the goal behavior.

Useful Questions That Help Clarify the Goal Task

What would we see if you were to do your goal right here today?

What might your wife notice that would be different when you are doing this goal?

How might she respond to your doing this goal?

Is this something different for you?

How do you think this will be helpful to you?

If this goal is helpful, how will you know?

Who do you think might notice that you are doing something different?

When will you do this?

When will be your first opportunity to do your goal?

On a scale of 1 to 10, if 10 is extremely confident and 1 is almost no confidence, how confident are you that you can do this goal?

Can you do this goal between now and the next group?

Creating Journeys: Developing Well-Formed Goals

Once we have explained the goal task, we ask whether someone has an idea for a possible goal. We find that some participants quickly grasp the goal task and begin exploring possibilities, whereas others find developing goals more difficult. It is particularly important to be patient and wait for someone to respond to the goal task. Filling any uncomfortable silences only displays a lack of confidence in the participants' abilities to begin the process. Inevitably, if you wait, the vacuum will be filled by a participant's ideas.

When the first participant responds to this task, we focus all our attention on helping him or her develop a goal that meets the criteria for an acceptable goal. To do this, we primarily ask questions interspersed with compliments whenever possible. We attempt to convey to the group members that we are willing to work hard to facilitate their success in developing a satisfactory goal. At the same time, we clearly convey that we do not have the answer or solution for them. We are willing to be lost with the participants, while taking an active role in helping them explore the possibilities for a workable goal.

The importance of allowing the participant to struggle with the process of creating a goal cannot be overemphasized. After many successful groups, we have asked our participants, "What could we have done that would have been more helpful to you?" The initial response is usually, "It was difficult to figure out what a good goal was." "Maybe you could have given some examples." This is quickly followed by, "No, I don't think examples would have helped." "I needed to find this goal myself." "I think examples might have distracted me from discovering the goal that worked for me." This type of response is so consistent that we have come to trust it and steadfastly refuse to give in to our urges to offer examples of goals to our participants.

The participants' search for a goal is critical to the overall success of the change process. The search builds commitment to the goal and may increase the goal's perceived utility. The very fact that participants are willing to look for a solution also implies that a solution is attainable. Looking for the "right" goal for them also implies that they need to discover for themselves what will be particularly useful.

The process of helping participants develop goals is similar to helping a person develop a plan for a trip. Once participants have established a general idea, we press them to describe as many details of the goal as possible, including what specifically they will do, when they will do it, who will be present, how they will get started, and how many times they might do a behavior before the next session. Such details are very useful because they create a description of change before it is enacted and help the participant evaluate whether the goal is useful and doable. In general, we want participants to feel as if they have already accomplished the goal in their thoughts prior to leaving the session.

The following transcript is an example of straightforward goal development. The participant has already developed a goal idea as a result of listening to other participants during the initial group. Participants often listen to other group members and find that a particular theme resonates for them. In this case, it not only resonates but also leads to an evaluation of previous behavior and a plan for change.

TOM: SESSION 2

Tom said very little at the first session and chose to listen to other participants as they explored potential goals. As Tom began to search for a goal throughout the following week, he, like many participants, did not immediately have a goal in mind, so he began to think of what might be useful for him to do. Tom was divorced, and he and his ex-wife, shared parenting responsibilities for and custody of their 11-year-old son. He began to reevaluate how he had been responding to his ex-wife and how his behavior might be affecting their son.

Facilitator 1: Tom, have you come up with any ideas for a goal since the last group?

Tom: Yeah, well I was thinking about what Bob was saying about his kids, and my son has been having some problems. He actually does well with me, but he is pretty disrespectful to his mom, and, uh, I think that's not such a good thing.

F1: So, what are you thinking that might be helpful, I mean, for you to do?

T: I don't really know. I've thought about talking to him about it, but I've always thought it was her problem and she should fix it.

F1: How is that working for your son?

T: That's just it. It's not working at all. I think it's getting worse, because she complains about it to me a lot when I pick him up.

Facilitator 2: What do you think you want to do that would be different, I mean, to make it better?

T: Well. . . . I think I need to talk to my son and tell him I'm not OK with his behavior, like with his mother.

F2: Wow, I'm impressed that you are willing to do that to help your son.

Up to this point the only therapeutic interventions have been questions that ask Tom to evaluate his thoughts and behavior. When Tom gives a specific detail of what he might do differently, the facilitating team gives a compliment.

T: I have to do something or it could get out of hand.

F1: When will you do this?

T: I can do it this week. He's with me most of the week, so I'll have time.

F2: What will you say to him that will make a difference?

T: I'm gonna have to think about that. . . .

F2: Sure, but what thoughts do you have right now?

T: I know I've just got to be real clear with him that I expect him to be respectful with his mother.

F2: Can you do that?

Once the participant has defined the details of goal-related behavior, the facilitating team asks Tom to make a commitment to do the behavior.

T: Yeah, I'm sure I can.

F1:   How will you know that it's working, I mean, that it is helping your son?

T: Well . . . I guess I'm going to have to ask his mom about that.

F1:   How confident are you that you can do that? Let's say 10 is you're completely sure and 1 is there is almost no chance.

T: Um . . . that's tough 'cause we don't really talk, and I don't do that well. . . . Maybe a 5.

F2:   Gee, I'm impressed. I thought you were going to say a 1 or a 2. You're halfway there already!

F1:   Is there any way you can see to move that number up to like a 5½ or 6?

T: I think if I just say I'm going to do this by next week that would help.

Note how the facilitator uses scaling questions to assist Tom to gauge and describe his confidence regarding accomplishing the goal.

F1:   So are you doing this by next week?

T: (laughs) Yeah, I'm going to do it by next week.

F1:   Is this a goal that you can work on for the next 8 to 10 weeks?

T: It's not going to be solved with one talk. I can see that I'm going to have to work on this for a while, every week.

F1:   OK, sounds good. We are going to be real interested in what happens with this goal.

F2:   Sounds great. Can't wait to hear about your efforts.

As is clear from this transcript, the facilitating team focuses on specifics while helping the participant evaluate whether the goal will be helpful and doable. Once this is established, efforts are directed toward building the participant's commitment to doing the goal. On the surface, this goal may appear small, but like most goals, it has considerable potential for expansion and unanticipated benefits. It is important to keep in mind that it is not the size or the complexity of a goal that counts. A small goal can be expanded both in scope and in the meaning the participant attributes to it once it is proved beneficial. Conversely, a complex goal can be narrowed to make it easier to approach and accomplish.

The following transcript of Tom's next group session illustrates how an initial goal is modified by the participant and the facilitating team. The original goal that focuses on Tom and his son leads to an interesting turn that pertains to Tom's relationship with his ex-wife.

TOM: SESSION 3

Facilitator 1: Tom, I'm real interested in what you've done with your goal.

Tom: Well, I picked up my son at my ex-wife's place, and we sat on the couch and I asked her what was going on with our son.

F1:   Um . . .

T: This just caught her by surprise, I mean completely, and I asked her to go to Bakersfield.

Facilitator 2: That's incredible. How did all this happen?

T: She thanked me for being so nice, and she spent the night for the first time in at least 5 years!

F1:   What do you think about your goal? Is it a good goal for you?

The facilitating team shows genuine interest in Tom's goal work, and even though it could be assumed that he is pleased by the results, the team asks him directly whether his goal is a good one. This is very important because it encourages Tom to make his own conscious evaluation and allows him the opportunity to confirm the value of his goal.

T: Yeah! The whole conversation wasn't about "This is your fault." It wasn't like that at all. I just asked her what she thought our son's problems were and what difficulties she was having and what we could do to remedy the problems with Jake. When I got done talking to him, he apologized to his mother, and she says he's doing better over the past 2 weeks. I'm not going to allow him to back talk to his mother.

F2:   Did it surprise you what happened?

T: Yeah! We didn't go into all that blame talk for the first time in 3 years.

F1:   That's quite a bit different. Are you pleased with how you handled your-self?

This question helps keep the focus on what Tom is doing.

T: Yeah, because I handled myself by saying, "What do you think *we* should do to correct this problem?"

F1:   What effect does all this have on Jake?

It is important to expand the meaning of the goal work. The facilitating team asks a question that invites Tom to attribute positive benefits to his new behavior. Tom accepts the invitation and projects the benefits into the future behavior of his son.

T: (pause) If he ever has a girlfriend, he would treat her better.

F2:   So you really want Jake to be successful in a relationship.

T: Yes, I want him to have success in whatever he does.

F1:   If she's in a bad mood some day, how will you handle that?

This question creates the opportunity for Tom to prepare for the inevitable ups and downs that occur in all relationships.

T: Take responsibility for part of the divorce, like I spent all my time working, and that was my problem, not hers.

F1:   Sounds like such a good goal for you.

T: Yeah, it seems to be working.

F2:   On a scale of 1 to 10, how confident are you that you can do well talking to your ex and your son?

T: I'm at a 10!

F1:   Good!
F2:   Great! It took a lot of guts to go over there and do this differently.

The change that Tom made was dramatic, and the response from his ex-wife was a surprise both to him and to us. In later sessions, Tom confirmed the benefits of his goal work by sharing how his relationship with his son was improved and that he and his ex-wife were able to be more effective in supporting each other's parenting efforts.

An important aspect of goal development is confirming that the goal *will* be helpful. Once the details are established, we often directly ask the participant if the goal will, in fact, be helpful. This helps the participant evaluate the goal, while at the same time inviting the participant to confirm that whatever he or she is going to do will in fact make a difference. If time permits, we elicit the specific ways in which the goal behavior will make a difference.

An important contribution of the facilitating team beyond eliciting details of the goal is to *encourage and compliment* any and all attempts to develop a goal. This is very important, even if the participant initially fails to meet the established criteria for a workable goal. Participants are not accustomed to thinking of what they want to accomplish for themselves in clearly defined terms. Because of this, it is important to remain patient and supportive regardless of their efforts. Initial attempts that result in poorly defined, unacceptable goals give the group and the participant an opportunity to explore the boundaries of a useful goal.

If a first attempt to develop a goal is not completely successful, we often state, "Well, you are beginning to sort out some of the possibilities for your goal, and we suspect that between now and the next group you may discover the specific behaviors that will make up this goal of yours." "We are very impressed with your efforts." "You obviously intend to have a goal that will benefit you." In this way, we display confidence that the individual will complete this task, and we also imply the participant's ownership of the goal.

Participant Who Has a Vague Goal

The following excerpt illustrates a common phenomenon at the initial goal-setting stage where the participant starts with a vague, ill-defined, broad goal. Instead of denouncing the goal or noting its inappropriateness, the facilitator must be patient and persistent in encouraging the participant's exploration. This is accomplished by asking evaluative questions and allowing time for the participant to come up with a useful goal. Participants often need more than one session to fully structure their goals. It is important for the facilitator to remain patient and focused.

THE CASE OF BOB

Facilitator 1: Is there anything you would like to talk about as far as a goal?

Bob: Um, actually, um, and um . . . I got a haircut; I shaved my beard off. I forgot your name . . . Jack, last time you quit drinking for over 5 years, and that's been one of my goals, also, which was about 1 year ago. [*Jack, another participant, had previously talked about quitting drinking.*] I quit for over a year and started back again. Tomorrow, I'm going to see the doctor and get peace and quiet, I'm just working on a lot of new things. I'm becoming a vegetarian, like I was, um.

Bob comes in with a vague desire to be different, but he presents no specific goal. It is important for the facilitating team to help him work toward developing a useful and focused goal.

Facilitator 2: Given that, you have, I'm assuming if you don't drink, you'll have time to do a few other things. Does that lead you to a goal, something you can keep focused on?

B: I just want to make myself stronger, because what happened to me is never going to happen again. I'm not going to get involved with what I got involved with ever again.

F2:   So, you seem to have some idea about what you need to do for things to be better for you.

The facilitator's language is directed toward doing something, even though Bob is still partially focused on not doing.

B: Just everything in general so that this will not happen again it's, it's . . . I will never be around another woman who does drugs and drinks anymore.

Bob continues with "not doing" talk, and facilitator 2 again invites Bob to talk about "doing" behaviors.

Facilitator 2: But, in terms of the specifics about yourself, when you think about this goal, can you talk about what you need to do at this point?

F1:   What do you want to work on in terms of a goal in this group? What is it that you want to work on?

B: Just being another person.

F1:   What would you be doing differently if you were this other person?

The facilitating team ignores Bob's blaming and generalities and persists in asking Bob for details of what he will do. Using the participant's language, such as "being another person," is often helpful.

B: Um, all I know is I won't be drinking, and that's going to give me a lot more time actually. I want to work. I want to get my body and mind to work together, um.

F2:   How would you know that is happening?

B: I'll know when I start feeling good about myself and I have a smile on my face.

F2:   Yeah, so that would be one of the signs of your accomplishing the goal.

F1:   So, what kinds of things would you do to put a smile on your face?

B: What makes me really happy is when I get really far out into the woods were nobody's at. I love to get out into the woods. I like to fish. I like to hunt.

F1:   Is that different for you?

B: Not really.

F1:   You already do the thing that makes you happy. But in terms of this group and the goal for this group, what do you think you can do to work on for the next 7 or 8 weeks that will help you be happier, different from what you already do?

B: Just be a better person. I'm so tired of stressing, I was stressing last night, but I normally don't drink coffee. See, I work at nights, and it was a quarter to one this morning, and I have to get up at a quarter to one again, but I drank coffee.

F2:   What would you do instead of the stressing stuff?

The facilitating team attempts to pursue exceptions to problems in hopes that this will help move Bob closer to a well-formed goal.

B: Um.

F2:   Have you done it before?

B: I never stressed, I never had any stress until this time. And I think I probably gained 5 years with all of the gray hair I got now.

Bob's statement about never being stressed creates an invitation to confront him with this point. After all, how likely is this to be true? However, our approach is not to argue such points and to approach Bob as the expert about his life.

F2:   So, how can you get back to the not-stress stuff?

B: Being around good people that actually do something with their lives instead of just doing . . .

F2:   What would be your first step in getting around these people?

B: Well, I'm going to move out of the county cause I know too many people here and get closer to Southern California to be closer to my daughter, which I haven't seen my oldest daughter and she's 21, and I haven't seen my second grandson yet and my other two daughters I haven't seen in a year.

F2:   Yeah, to reconnect with them.

B: I call them a lot. They know the situation that I've been in.

F2:   So, getting reconnected with them would be a good thing?

F1:   What I'm hearing is that you keep saying you don't want to let yourself
      be taken advantage of. What do you want instead?

B: I want to be in control.

F1:   So, were you ever in control before you were in this situation?

B: Um, pretty much because I did what I wanted. I wasn't involved with any-
      body, I had no stress. I tried to make life easy . . .

F1:   You had no stress at all?

*Here the facilitator cannot avoid at least a minimal challenge to
the stress issue. This is an indication for the team that we are
tiring or working too hard.*

B: I tried to make life easy, that's the way I liked it. Life is too short as it is.

F2:   Yeah, so do you want us to continue helping you develop this goal with
      you now, or do you prefer that we talk more next week?

B: I think I need time to just think about things, like I know I have to stress
      less and want to think about how I can do that.

F1:   Great, great!

B: I'm real comfortable with thinking about it by myself.

F2:   What we need to do is, we need to get down to it by the end of the next
      group. You need to get down to something specific that you are going to
      do.

B: I'll probably need some more help on it next week. I mean, I know what I
      want to do, I just can't say it real well yet.

F2:   So, we will talk to you again next week, and you'll have some more spe-
      cific ideas.

Bob clearly has difficulty focusing on a specific goal despite being
motivated to do something different in his life. In spite of this difficulty,
the facilitators persist in pursuing a specific, clearly defined goal. Bob needs
more time and probably assistance from the facilitating team. In this example, the team views all behaviors by the participant as attempts to cooperate. We do not judge a participant as resistant or uncooperative if he
or she finds it difficult to define a clear goal. Any initial difficulty is "normal"
and has little or no relationship to later success. We always work with the
belief that the participant wants to cooperate and is in fact cooperating. We
find that this approach translates into of a collaborative effort. The participant leaves this interaction with some confidence that he can discover a
goal and that it is his responsibility to do so. There is also a feeling that the
participant and the facilitating team are collaborating in the effort to create
a goal that fits for him. It is important to keep in mind that developing a
goal is a process that is often accomplished in stages. We often work until
there appears to be no movement and then "let go," preferring to take what
the participant offers while allowing the benefits of time to enhance the
percolation of ideas. It is similar to planting seeds, knowing that once they

are planted, one must pat the soil gently and firmly to hold them securely in place, water occasionally, and then patiently wait. In the next session, this participant actually develops a clear, well-defined goal that he actively works on both in and out of the group.

Simplifying Goals

As is apparent from the previous example, many participants begin with a complex, undefined goal and need considerable assistance in simplifying it. We find that participants benefit from thoughtful questions that help move the goal to a concrete, observable task. Simplifying a goal implies that the goal will not only be easy to define but also, ideally, easy to perform and remember. Goals are difficult for almost everyone to stay focused on, so keeping the goal simple in the beginning allows for early success and room to expand it later on in the process. For example, a common initial goal statement is "I want to communicate better." From our perspective, this statement has no meaning because it does not define what the participant will be doing. We ask questions that help participants begin to define more clearly what "communicating better" actually means to them. This not only helps them determine what they would do for their goal work but also helps them begin to evaluate whether "communicating better" is really a worthwhile goal to pursue.

The following transcript provides an example of how a facilitator can help a participant move from a complex goal to a simplified, workable goal.

THE CASE OF GARY

Gary: I think I need to work on communication, you know, communicating better.

Facilitator 1: What would we *see you doing* if you were communicating better?

The facilitating team wastes no time in pursuing observable goal behavior.

G: Well, I don't really know. I just think that communicating would be better, I mean my girlfriend and I don't really talk a lot any more.

Facilitator 2: Was there a time when you and your girlfriend were talking more and things were better?

G: We used to go for walks, but I've been coming home and watching TV. Just crashing in front of it, drinking a beer, and I don't really hear much after that.

F2:   When you went for walks, was that better?

G: Yeah, I had more energy and did more things.

F1:   I'm curious, what do you think was most helpful about what you did, I mean for you?

G: I don't know, but I know things were a lot better when we just did things

together, like the walking. I had forgotten about that! I think I need to
work on doing more things.

F2:   Doing more things?

G: Well, about 2 weeks ago I went for a walk by myself after work, I mean
before I went home, and I really felt relaxed when I got home. I think that
helped a lot cause she was stressed by the kids, and I was OK with it all,
and usually I would be all worked up and saying stupid things to her.

F1:   Wow. It was that helpful to walk after work?

G: Yeah, it made a big difference, me being calm. When we talk a lot about
problems, things get pretty messed up, so I'm not so sure about this communicating.

F1:   What about the walking helped?

G: I think I'm so intense about work, and I bring it right home, and I treat
her like she's one of my employees. That just isn't going to work. I mean,
I can see that even if I don't like what she's doing, that that won't work.

F2:   So what little thing will you start with to begin doing something different?
Something that we or someone else might see you do.

G: I think I'm going to exercise or walk before I come home from work. I
know that works, and I need to not treat her like an employee, that
would go a long way.

*Gary has become much more clear about what he will do, and
the facilitating team is interested in defining the possible
benefits in as much detail as possible.*

F1:   So what would your wife see you do that was different after you come
home from your walk?

G: I would just be calmer.

F2:   How would she know that?

G: I would take the time to just listen to her. I think sometimes that's all she
wants. I mean, I don't even have to really listen to her. I just need to sit
there and nod my head until she settles down.

F1:   Do you think you can actually do this?

G: Yeah, I'm sure I can.

F1:   Well, I'm really impressed by how you've thought this through, and I can
see how this will be helpful to you. When will be the first time you will
begin making these changes?

G: Tomorrow. I don't see why I can't begin right away.

F1:   How often do you think it makes sense to do this. I mean, to get the
maximum benefit?

G: I think I should shoot for every day, but I don't know if, you know, sometimes it might be impossible. I think most days I will do it.

F2:   So your goal is to do this walking or exercise most days after work and to
listen to your wife and nod your head until she seems to be more settled
down. Is that what you think will be the most helpful?

G: Yeah.

F2:   We will be very curious about how your wife responds to this. Can you keep track of how this affects her? Whatever you notice.

G: I think she's going to notice the difference.

F1:   So you're sure you're on the right track here.

G: Yeah!

Participants often feel a sense of accomplishment in developing a well-defined, doable goal. They know what they want to accomplish and how they are going to do it. They feel that the group process is doable as well and often are relieved to know they can be successful in meeting the requirements of the program. The experience of having a team asking questions designed to help clarify a plan of action to create change in participants' lives is both subtle and powerful.

Moving from a Big Goal to a Useful Goal

THE CASE OF BRIAN

Brian begins by describing a big goal that is too vague and broad to be helpful. The following excerpt illustrates the use of focusing or clarifying questions in helping participants to move from a big goal to develop a sense of what the parameters of an acceptable goal are.

Brian: I'm gonna try stress management 'cause I don't handle stress good. It doesn't work. I want to burn it, break it, or destroy it.

Facilitator 1: So how are you gonna do that?

B: Take a break instead of jumping forward. I think I'll try to just sit back and take a deep breath and cool off for a minute and reappraise my situation, day by day.

F1:   Have you done that already?

B: No.

F1:   You haven't ever done that?

B: Well, I said I had, but I haven't really.

F1:   So, did you have any ideas about what could set you off and then what you're going to do instead?

B: That is the hard part, is stress. Sometimes it slowly builds, and sometimes it's (snaps his fingers) right there in front of you. You have to, I'm gonna try, I won't say I'm gonna succeed. I'm gonna try to not be such a, what do you call it? Oh, an asshole. (Another participant laughs.)

Facilitator 2: How would you know that you're successful, Brian? What would tell you that?

B: How I felt. If the stress, if the anger didn't come out. If the belligerence wasn't there. If the, even if it's a lot, for 4 years now I've been hoping, but it's still been here (points to self) a lot of times. Like a volcano, wanting to explode.

F1:   So how will you know when you're being successful? What will be there instead?

B: My reaction, my attitude. I can change that. Then I'll know I'm successful.

F1:   OK, so what will, what will be, what will be there instead of the volcano?

B: I don't know. I'll have to experience that, and then I'll tell you.

F1:   OK, can you have some ideas between now and next time we meet of how you're going to implement this?

B: Yes, 'cause I live under a very stressful situation. I have a wife that's had six back surgeries. They're telling her she's gonna have to have another six, and it'll take her back, financial stress 'cause I just went back to work.

Brian mentioned a big goal of stress management, although he does not seem to have either a clear idea of the steps or past successes in dealing with his temper. While facilitator 1 attempts to use the "how would you know" questions to help Brian describe the envisioned behavioral changes, facilitator 2 steps in to help Brian evaluate the "size" of his goal.

F2:   It seems too big.

B: No, what's too big?

F2:   The goal.

B: No, why is it too big? Explain it. Are you saying you don't feel I can handle it?

F2:   No.

B: OK.

F2:   I think maybe I was saying that . . . because it's hard for me to see what you're gonna do that's going to get you from this place to where you want to go. I can't see the step yet.

B: You can't see the step?

F2:   No.

B: The step is to, rather than run away, a lot of times the stress happens you run away and hide and get away from it. You know, if there's a problem, there's only two things to do, you solve it or get rid of it. Most of the time I ignore it. So now I'm trying mainly to solve it, or to get rid of it, the problem that causes me the stress.

F1:   Has ignoring it helped?

B: No.

F1:   It doesn't help?

B: No, running away never does, does it?

F1:   Sometimes.

B: (laughs) Unless he's got a big enough gun, but no, it's not that kind.

F1:   Sometimes things change. Sometimes when you leave and then come back it's better.

B: I ran away five times. That's enough.

F1:   OK, so that doesn't work for you.

B: No.

F2:   I think what facilitator 1's trying to get at is he can't see a clear picture of what you're going to do that's different. Of what it is you're going to do specifically that will be different.

B: I'm specifically going to handle the situations that I'm involved in differently than I have been handling them.

F1:   Yeah, I hear that, but if I had a camera in your house?

B: I'd shoot you (laughs).

F1:   If we had a camera in your house, what would we see you doing now that would be different, that we wouldn't see a week before? What would we see different on that camera?

B: What I would try, try to have you see?

F1:   Yeah.

B: The, the lack of irritation and aggravation on my face almost constantly.

F1:   OK, so what would we see on your face?

B: Passiveness, I hope.

This is the first description Bob has created that begins to describe a "doing" versus a "not-doing" change in observable behavior. The team continues to help Bob create clear descriptions of change behavior that is different or new for him. This is a difficult but helpful exercise for Bob to do.

F1:   Passiveness?

B: More understanding, maybe.

F1:   So on this camera, what would we see on your face?

B: More understanding.

F1:   How would we see more understanding?

B: Because you would see verbal reactions even though they wouldn't be, wouldn't be, I don't swear, but still I can use words with more than one syllable to get my point across to aggravate those who are aggravating me.

F1:   So we would hear something different?

B: You would hear, I would be different. You would hear words coming out of my mouth different. I've already . . .

F1:   You've already what?

B: I've already started.

F1:   You have?

F2:   Great! Can you give us an example?

B: Oh, I started, what was it, last weekend, when a situation came up that normally I would have said something like, "I told you so." Now and my face would get as red as his T-shirt, "I told you." So I just said, "Well, you know, that's one thing about a mistake, you'll recognize it the second time a lot more than you do the first. Just try not to do it again." And she said, "huh?" (laughs). Because she expected me to really rebuke her. Because I had warned her of the situation, "Don't get involved, don't get in it. It's gonna be trouble."

F1:   So, how were you able to say something instead of "I told you so," which is what you really wanted to say?

B: Well, I'll tell you what I did. I went in the bathroom, took a deep breath, washed my face, and came out, and then I expressed myself. Rather than (smacks his hands together) shooting my mouth off like that.

F1:   OK, so that's what we'd see on the camera. We'd see you going into the bathroom, washing your face.

B: I just put cool water on my face because I knew I was getting ready to blow.

F1:   OK, so you put cold water on your face, and you took a deep breath. We'd see you taking a deep breath, and then we would hear you say?

B: I just, I said, "The thing about making a mistake is you'll recognize it real good the second time, but let's not try it again."

F2:   Well, how did you decide to say that, because that's amazing?

B: It just came out. It wasn't prethought or preplanned. I didn't have a script, I just, and it came out that way.

F2:   That's great.

F1:   Was it helpful?

B: Yeah, I felt better.

F1:   You felt better.

B: Yeah, because I didn't start arguing.

F1:   OK, that's exactly what we're looking for.

Brian started with a broad, vague goal of stress management that did not offer specific direction for how he was going to handle his negative feelings. By sharing with Brian that his initial goal was "too big," helping him look at the small steps, focusing on what he would be doing that was different, we helped him arrive at a much more specific and concrete description of "stress management." He moved from "Take a break instead of jumping forward. I think I'll try to just sit back and take a deep breath and cool off for a minute and reappraise my situation, day by day" to "I went in the bathroom, took a deep breath, washed my face, and came out, and then I expressed myself. Rather than (smacks his hands together) shooting my mouth off like that." The latter description offers a more helpful and specific behavioral guide to facilitate a change in Brian's reaction.

The process used here was subtle. Brian was able to arrive at a concrete description of "stress management" only after much probing and questioning. At one point, he got visibly upset in reaction to the facilitator's comment that the goal was too big, "No, why is it too big? Explain it. Are you saying you don't feel I can handle it?" Helping the participant to visualize a well-formed goal requires a lot of patience and consistency.

Do's and Don'ts When Developing Clear, Well-Formed Goals

Do persist in the pursuit of a clear, well-formed goal until the participant states he or she wants a break or the goal is developed to satisfaction.

Do pursue the details.

Don't get sidetracked by other issues.

Do use questions to help the participant think through ideas.

Don't suggest a goal or work harder than the participant.

Do restate a goal when it is well defined.

Do use a scaling question to help the participant state his or her level of commitment to the goal.

Do compliment all efforts made to develop a goal.

Do notice the participant's efforts to cooperate.

Do state your desire to help the participant develop a clear, useful goal.

Do ignore non-goal-related comments and redirect attention to the goal work.

Useful Questions in Facilitating the Development of a Well-Formed Goal

What do you think someone who knows you well might advise you to work on?

If you were to work on this goal, what would you actually be doing that someone would notice?

When things were going well for you, what sort of things did you do that were useful?

When your relationship was going really well, what did you do that you are not doing now?

If you were not doing this goal, what might you be doing instead?

What is the smallest thing that you could do that would help with that?

Have you done that before, and has it been helpful?

Is that something that you could really do?

On a scale of 1 to 10, how confident are you that you could actually do that?

On a scale of 1 to 10, how confident are you that this will be helpful?

What are the little things that you are going to do?

When will be the first time that you will do this?

How often will you do this between now and the next time we meet?

Who do you think might notice that you are doing this?

When Participants Present as "Stuck in the Muck" During Goal Development

Some individuals in every group find it very difficult to define a clear goal in their first, second, or even third attempts. These individuals often require more time, questions, and compliments to develop a goal. Some people state that their life is going so well that they can't think of anything they would want to change or work on. Others find the notion of setting a goal a completely foreign concept. Still others act as if the goal task will go away if they wait long enough. Traditional psychotherapy models tend to describe these people as resistant and sometimes use labels such as "anal retentive" or "personality disordered." We consider these descriptions disrespectful and believe they have a handicapping effect on the thinking of the facilitating team. We describe people as being stuck or unsure about what they want to do.

Our primary way of being helpful is to remain persistent regarding the formation of a well-defined goal. We also do our best to remember that everyone has a different style of discovering what is useful to them. It is important to remain aware that the experience of being in a group may in itself be new for some people.

Some participants find it difficult to adjust to the fact that we do not require them to have problems, and that we are only interested in their doing things that they believe will be helpful to them. They are accustomed to professionals exploring their problems and in many cases have become comfortable with this process. They are acclimated to a process that holds them accountable for problem talk. Such participants may feel that the rules of engagement with professionals have been unfairly changed when the "old answers" only lead to more questions related to what they are going to do. They are initially cautious of making commitments to do specific, observable, new behaviors. Because of this, we are mindful that they may need to adjust to a process that demands a focus on solution talk.

When people are particularly stuck and cannot seem to create a workable goal, we remain very persistent in asking questions that facilitate their search. We always frame our role as one of facilitating their efforts. We collaborate with participants in the search for options, but they are responsible for making the choices. If participants become frustrated with our questions, we encourage them to help us be more useful to them and ask them to advise us on how to do so. We act as partners with participants in a race against the clock because they must develop a goal within the agreed-upon time limits. In framing our role in this manner, we externalize the time limit and treat it as if it was a natural law rather than a limit we have imposed on the participant. It is in fact a limit imposed on both the participant and the facilitating team.

Developing a well-formed goal becomes an exciting challenge for the facilitating team and the participant in part because the challenge binds them together. When the resulting collaboration produces a workable goal, there tends to be sense of well-being that contributes to high levels of investment by the participant to make the goal work.

For some participants the difficulty in coming up with a goal is a reflection of their desire to use their time wisely; they do not want to develop a goal that will not have benefits. In this way, the most "resistant" participant may in fact be working to be the most cooperative. We will credit individuals by saying, "You are working so hard to find a good goal even when it seems impossible to find one, and we are very impressed by your insistence that the goal be useful to you."

In the following example, the facilitating team persists in helping the participant develop a new goal in spite of the fact that the participant indicates minimal motivation to do so.

Engaging the "I'm fine" participant

THE CASE OF DAN

In earlier sessions Dan had struggled to develop a goal, in part because he felt his life was in pretty good shape. He had noted, "I feel fine, and everything is OK." He finally was able to come up with the goal of displaying more patience while helping with his son's homework. He was able to define exactly what he would do that would indicate his patience, and he was able to effectively do these behaviors. This goal was clearly helpful to Dan and his son. He noticed that his son's school performance had improved, and their relationship was much closer. The school year ended prior to the fourth session, and he had not developed another goal to work on. In cases such as this, we require the participant to negotiate another goal; no one can be in the group unless he or she is working on a goal. Interestingly, Dan starts the process of developing a new goal in much the same way he had during the first group session by stating that his life was fine.

Facilitator 1: Now that I brought it up, what do you think you're going to work on?

Dan: Everything is fine.

F1:   That's what you said before, "Everything's fine, everything's fine," but still you came up with a goal, so . . .

Facilitator 2: Does this lead you to anything, maybe any half goal thing that, maybe, you could focus a little attention on?

D: Uh, not right now. I don't know. I haven't really thought about it.

F1:   But in order to be in the group, you have to have a goal you're working on.

F2:   Well, would it be helpful to you to kick this around a bit yourself, or would it be more helpful for us to talk about it, try to figure out something now? What do you think would be best for you?

The facilitating team quickly sets limits so that Dan knows he must have a goal to stay in the group. This is followed by offering a choice and asking him what would be most helpful to him. We find this a useful pattern of interaction.

D: I don't know.

F2:   You don't know.

D: We get along great. We do everything good. It's just the homework.

F1:   Yeah.

D: Something that I'm trying to avoid, but other than that . . .

F1:   I don't know what you're going to do, Dan. Do you want some other ideas, or um . . .

D: Sure. I'll tell you if I can do them or not.

F2:   It doesn't have to be a problem, it can just be something that is of benefit to you. It doesn't have to be a problem at all.

F1:   Something that makes your life better.

F2:   I don't know if it's a good idea for you to think about problems. It sounds like you don't have a lot of big problems right now. Things are going pretty well, so I don't think that's so helpful. So, I would maybe think about something that helps enhance your life. You know, brings some joy to your life or to your relationship.

D: My relationship is fine. It's really good. In fact, I can't think of a way to make it better.

F1:   Does anyone else have some ideas for Dan, so he can stay in the group?

This question invites the group to offer Dan support while again reinforcing the limits mentioned earlier.

Ppt 1:   OK. I got a question. The reason you had to take this class was why? Did you have an altercation with your kid? Your wife?

D: No, my ex-wife.

Ppt 1:   Your ex-wife.

D: I get along with her, too.

F2:   What do you think of doing what you did before? You went out, and the goal kind of came to you. I would suspect it would again?

D: Yeah, it probably will.

F1:   Yeah . . . yeah.

F2:   You were so good at that before. Boom, you found something that was useful. It wasn't a huge problem. It was just a little thing. You thought it made sense to work with your son. You did it. I suspect that will be the case again.

D: Yeah. It actually came to me when I was in my car.

F1:   Yeah, right.

F2:   So, I'm comfortable with that. On the other hand, are you comfortable with that way of approaching it, instead of trying to dig into all that to-day?

D: Yeah.

Dan clearly has difficulty coming up with a goal, even with probing, assistance, and limit setting by the facilitators and some other participants. The facilitating team had a choice of pushing Dan to come up with a goal or using his previous success with developing a goal. By reminding Dan of his previous success, the team was able to compliment him and express confidence in his ability to resolve this problem. Even though Dan did not come up with a goal in this session, he has made a commitment to come with one using his own method. He was allowed to move at his own pace and was reminded of his past success, and then he was able to develop a goal during the following session.

There is always an element of artful judgment in deciding whether to pull or let go. In our previous experience with Dan, we discovered that more pulling led to less goal development. He, in fact, told us that he needed space. In such situations we pursue an agreement that the participant will use his own manner of discovery to develop a goal. We clearly state respect for participants' methods and note our anticipation of their efforts and the results. We view this as their style of collaborating with the facilitating team. If we had become frustrated with Dan and attempted to force him to develop a goal in a prescribed manner, we surely would have been unsuccessful in helping him.

Do's of Engaging Clients in Goal Development

Do set clear parameters and expectations of goal development.

Do capitalize on previous successes.

Do allow space.

Participant Who Has a "Politically Correct" but Unhelpful Goal

Sometimes participants struggle with developing a goal because they believe that the solution must be accomplished by acting in a particular manner—a politically correct goal that makes good sense but has offered no success in the past. They repeatedly attempt a solution that brings them misery, yet they persist in defining it as a goal that will be helpful. When they are assisted in evaluating the goal, they often discover that what they thought was the perfect goal was actually part of the problem.

THE CASE OF SAM

Sam came up with the "classic" goal of spending more time with his wife, although what he really wanted to do was to get away from her because he felt she controlled him far too much. In situations such as this, it is very helpful for the facilitating team to assist the participant in evaluating the effects of potential goal activity. This helps Sam begin to identify the contradictions between what he says *should* be helpful and what he really believes *will* be helpful.

Session 2

Sam: My goal is spending time with the family. I have a stepdaughter. She's 5 years old, and I have a son who is 2 years, 5 months old, and I want to go out and play all the time, you know, and she tries to hold me down and keep me away from my friends. That just makes me want to stay out more, you know? She goes to work. She's been working. My work's seasonal, which will be starting in a couple weeks. But she just wants to hold me down all the time, and I just can't stand it. Like, whenever I go, she'll be following me around, driving the car, and she'll sit out and watch what I'm doing. Like if I'm at a buddy's house, she'll just sit out and wait in the car for me to come out and get in the car. Even though my car will be there, and she'll just stay there. I'll come home, and she'll want to smell, you know, certain parts, and you know, she has no trust, and it just makes it really hard.

Facilitator 1: Wow.

S: Like, I'll drive down to East LA to go visit my friends. Now I can hear my truck coming around the corner, you know, I know what my truck sounds like. So I hopped over in the backyard and looked over the fence, and I seen my truck right there where she could see my car. You know, it's really bad. The trust part. Even though I've done stuff to make her not trust me.

F1: So what are you thinking about as a goal?

S: Just spending more time with my family, you know.

F1: How are you gonna do that? It sounds like it's driving you crazy already.

S: No, but when she forces me, you know? Like I told her, "Let's go to Disneyland, let's go do this, let's go do that." "No, it's too far out. I don't want to go do it." But when it comes to Reno and to gamble she's all on it. But, just, I don't know. It's just all when she wants to, and I end up going snowmobiling, bike riding, fishing, four-wheeling, whatever I'm gonna do, camping. You know. (He laughs and gestures to indicate that he drives away without her.)

Ppt1: Sounds like you feel smothered.

S: Yeah, I'm only 25 years old, and I still, she wants to get married, and I don't know, man.

Ppt2:   If you already feel smothered, then why would you want to spend more time?

Ppt1:   Yeah.

F1:   That's a good question.

Facilitator 2: That's a very good question.

Ppt1:   I was married to one like that once. (Sam laughs.)

Both the facilitators and some other participants share their perception that what Sam wants to do is exactly the opposite of his goal of spending more time with his family.

S: Yeah, but I'm only gonna try it one time, you know? It's . . . I grew up without a father and all that, and I want my son. I know it's not worth it to go to court to, you know, keep him all to myself. But I want to be with her. I love my stepdaughter and all that, but . . .

F2:   You want to make it work.

S: Yes, I want to make it work, but I like just going out and leaving. I like going to have a good time fishing and all that but . . .

Ppt1:   Responsibility comes with marriage.

S: I know my responsibility. I've done everything I have to do—bills, food . . .

Ppt1:   But you can't go when you want. (Sam laughs.) That goes with the territory. I've been married five times, and I'll tell you it literally took a hammer to sink it into my brain.

S: She'll stand out there and literally jump on the hood of the car or whatever I'm gonna take off in, you know?

Sam seems overwhelmed by his life and problems, and most of his talk is in one manner or another focused on problems.

F1:   So, what are you gonna do for a goal?

S: I don't know.

F2:   You have to have a goal.

F1:   I'm curious about what it is you're gonna do.

S: Try and make her happy, stay home a little bit more.

F1:   But, like Mac says, it's tough to be there now.

S: Yeah, I want to be there, but when I want to go out and play, I want to go out and play.

Ppt1:   You've got troubles.

Ppt3:   I was thinking the same thing.

Ppt1:   Let's put it up front. It doesn't work.

S: I've been with her for 6 years, man, ever since I've graduated high school. I moved out of home, she moved in with me. And you know it's, if I never met her, I'd probably still be at home with my grandma.

F2:   Does anyone have a goal idea that might be helpful? Something that might be helpful for Sam?

S: I mean, I've tried to work it out, I've tried to work it out. I think I just need to try a lot harder.

F2:   I don't know. (Sam laughs.)

*At this point the facilitating team begins to openly challenge
Sam's suggested solution, and other participants also begin to
suggest Sam's solution is part of the problem.*

Ppt3:   No, 'cause trying harder will just make you more miserable.

Ppt1:   Yeah.

Ppt3:   I've been in your situation, and you really don't want to hear what I did. I
just gave it up. I said, "It's not worth it."

F2:   You've got to figure out a goal that's small enough that you can do that
might be helpful to you, might be helpful to her, too.

F1:   I think Mac's question is real important. Does this relationship matter to
you? Does it matter enough for you to do something different? Or do you
need to work on something other than your relationship?

S: Man, that's the only way, get in the house, you know how a dog has
some spots he just needs to go?

F1:   On a scale of 1 to 10, 10 is this relationship is totally important to you,
more than anything, 1 is that, you know, you really could care less. Where
are you?

*It is important to help Sam reevaluate the importance and
meaning of the family relationship to him as a way to
strengthen his motivation to develop a personally meaningful
goal.*

S: Ten. Because I grew up, and my father was never around, you know, and
my mom was alcoholic and shit like that, and it's just . . .

*At the time this was a shocking response to the team and helped
refocus their efforts to help Sam sort through the goal
development process.*

F1:   Wow!

F2:   Well, how are people to know you're at a 10?

S: I grew up in East LA all my life. My mom died when I was 9 years old. I
lost my dad when I was 18 and, like I said, I grew up on the streets of
East LA all my life.

F2:   So this is serious business for you.

S: I mean, my family, the way I was brought up was violence.

Ppt3:   You survived in East LA. You had to be violent.

S: I mean, I want to tell you where I came from. I came from a very serious
motorcycle club. I was never one to be brought up with a silver spoon. I
had to hustle for whatever I wanted.

F1:   That's right.

S: And, I mean, I'll tell you now, I've never been no angel since I've grown
up. So the only thing I love, and the only thing I got, my whole family is
dead except my uncle that lives up here. But I got my son, and I will give
him everything, and it don't matter what. If I'm with her or not, you
know? It's just, he's the only thing I got. If she don't want to make it

F1:   work like it should, then, you know, I'll pay for my son or I'll take him and live with him myself, you know? I grew up in a place where no one cared. I grew up around heroin and all that shit, you know what I'm saying?

F1:   So how, if we were to ask her how committed you are to this relationship, what would she say on a scale of 1 to 10?

S: Probably zero.

F1:   And you're at a 10?

S: Like I said, she wants everything her way, but it's hard, you know? I give her so much. But like this new car she's wanted, we're up here arguing, I says, "You don't want a new car." I sold back my truck for $19,000 before I moved up here, got a $5,000 paint job and all that shit. But I mean, it's just dust, rocks, all that, you know? You don't need no gold rims up here or nothing.

F2:   Yeah, so think a little here and try to find something little that might be useful to you. You have 2 weeks now to start to think a bit more. Because you care so much.

F1:   On the one hand, I'm hearing you say you really want a relationship because you never grew up with much family.

S: Oh, I grew up with no family. Except, from clubs to clubs to clubs, you know, that's my family.

F1:   Yeah, and so you really want this family business, but on the other hand, you're also saying this family business is driving you nuts.

S: Yeah, but if she don't want to go my way, you know, I got my motorcycle. I could go wherever I want, you know? It's just, but I'll never leave my son like my dad, you know, you know, left me. But my son's everything, you know, I don't know. It's just all I got to live for is my son. My son and my sister and her and her stepdaughter if she wants.

F1:   So how would other people notice that you're living for your son? That you'd do anything? How would other people notice that?

The team continues to bring the conversation back to what Sam actually does that reflects who he wants to be.

S: I don't care what other people notice. As long as I know what I'm giving to him and everything's fine with him, to tell you the truth.

Initially Sam thought that "spending more time with his family" would be the "ideal" goal. As he evaluates this possibility, it becomes evident that such a goal would probably drive him crazy. In fact, it may be that this goal will only lead to the "problem" rather then a "solution." It is a classic goal with a superficial appeal. After all, who could possibly argue with a man who wants to spend more time with his family? In this case, the facilitating team remained focused and patient with Sam to help him evaluate the relevance of his suggested goal. While doing so, the facilitators also reinforced and amplified his motivation to do something different for himself and his family. Sam clarified what he does not want to be and began to define who he wants to become. The result is that Sam's commitment to create a goal was strengthened as he began to recognize that there are people he cares about.

During the next session Sam is still without a goal, but he begins to share the details of his current relationship and as a result opens the door for realistic goal development. He continues to have great difficulty accepting responsibility for doing something, and yet the facilitating team continues to pursue the goal development as if this makes no difference.

Session 3

Sam: We've been getting along better since I got out of jail.

Facilitator 1: How's that?

S: I talk shit to her.

F1:   I don't know what you mean by that. What does "talk shit" mean?

S: When I get angry I just call her a bitch. She'd go cry, and I'd just leave. Then I come back in an hour and kiss her ass and she'd go, "Why did you do that to me?"

F1:   Is there something you want to do different there?

The facilitator assumes nothing and prompts Sam to evaluate whether he wants to change his behavior. This is helpful for three reasons. First, it helps Sam decide whether he wants to do something different. Second, by not assuming anything, we send him a clear message that it is his choice to do something or nothing. He is the center of change and takes ownership of the process. Third, if he does want to do something different, the question directs him to consider what this new and different behavior might be.

S: Yeah, I guess . . . watch the way I talk to her. Show her I love her more.

F1:   So instead of calling her a bitch, what would you do?

S: Probably blow up. You know just, if you don't let it out, I'm just going to build up. . . . You know just give her a glass jaw. I'd explode if I just sit there and give in.

Sam states he wants to do something different, but he quickly reverts to problem talk when pressed for details of what he might do.

Facilitator 2: So have you ever done anything . . . like talked shit for a while but then you went and did something else that kind of helped with that?

S: I just go tear up my trucks and dirt bikes.

F1:   Have you ever done that before you talked shit?

The facilitating team continues the search for possible exceptions, behavior that is not part of the problem or that modifies or leaves the territory of the problem. Notice that the facilitating team uses Sam's language, such as "talked shit" or "glass jaw."

S: Yeah, and I came back and talked shit to her.
F1:   Have you ever done that and worked it out and didn't talk shit?
S: No . . . no
F1:   You never have . . . not ever?
S: There's probably been a few times I didn't.
F1:   What did you do?
S: I go somewhere and eat it up.
F2:   What do you mean? How did you do that?
S: Go off somewhere by myself . . . take off for a couple days . . . my pager's going off all the time.
F2:   So that didn't work so well, or did it?
S: Just made things go worse.
F2:   So the talking shit stuff works the best.
F1:   But you'd like to do something different.
S: But I don't want to go out and live in the woods.
F2:   But you don't want to give her a glass jaw.
S: No.
F2:   I think you have a potential goal here.
Ppt4: He's trying to get it all together.
F1:   Yeah.
F2:   Impressive really.
S: I'm a lost man.

Even though Sam is stating that he is a lost man, the facilitators are acting more hopeful than ever. They compliment Sam and are definitive about the progress he is already making. Another participant is also chiming in with a strong positive statement.

F1:   I think you don't want to talk shit, and you don't want to give her a glass jaw, but how to get the pressure out?
S: But she's always . . . she talks shit to me.
F2:   Yes, well . . .
Ppt3: It's best to not talk back, but it's tough.
F2:   That would be a real challenge to figure out how you're going to deal with that. So how can you relieve the pressure without destroying your property and without destroying your relationship?
S: Get a pressure valve (makes the sound of air escaping while touching his forehead). I'd need a big one.
F1:   So this is a real challenge for you.

The notion of a challenge is again introduced to Sam. This offers him the opportunity to make a choice to do something different.

S: Yeah, it is.
F2:   I guess the question is, can you battle this huge thing that's like a monster?
S: Myself (laughs).

F1:   Yeah, that's what we're talking about.

F2:   So, what's a small thing you can do that will start on it?

F1:   Sounds like this has been hard for a long time.

S: All my life.

F2:   You've made big progress, all the way from this hitting stuff. . . . That was a critical challenge. . . . You've changed that, and now you are moving to the next one. What is the next step? How much less shit talk can you do and still do OK? What is your best guess?

S: What do you mean by that?

F2:   Is it possible for you to go a whole day without shit talk, or is that too much?

S: It's the way we always been, you know. Hit on each other, we're young, you know. Just playing around. All we're doing is horsing around.

F1:   If you weren't going to do shit talk, what would you do different?

S: Hop on my bike. She's always talked like, "Why don't you grow up?"

F1:   She's saying, "If you love me, why the shit talk?"

F2:   Where do you start in terms of this growing up?

S: When I'm 40.

F2:   When now? How old are you?

S: Twenty-five.

F2:   So, you've got some years to work on it. By the time you're 40, you'll be clear of this. So where do you want to start?

The team accepts Sam's description and accepts it as a goal Sam wants to accomplish even within his time frame.

F1:   You've already started with no more glass jaws. . . . It sounds like the next step is, you want to give up some of this shit talk.

S: Yeah, I guess I could start controlling myself, instead of hurting her feelings.

F1:   Yeah. How would you do that?

S: But, you know, I may be a big guy and stuff, but my feelings get hurt. She knows how to hurt me, make me happy, and make me sad.

F2:   So, is there something you need to say to her about that? What are you suggesting?

S: I guess we can't do this around the kids. They're getting older. We can only do this in the bedroom.

Sam spontaneously provides an interesting exception to the problem behavior that implies he has control over his actions.

F1:   You can limit yourself to doing this in the bedroom?

S: Oh, yeah.

F2:   So you do have some control over it.

F1:   You don't talk like this around the kids.

This statement allows Sam to clearly state that he can control his behavior.

S: No way.

F2:   So, you don't want your kids to experience any of this.

S: Not the way I grew up. Kids don't see that stuff. They don't need that.

F2:   It's not good for them.

S: My dad wiped my mom's ass, you know, my grandpa beat up my grand-mother.

F2:   So, what do you think of this as a goal, to lessen this pain for *your* children?

S: To learn to control this anger.

Sam brings up his childhood experience of witnessing abuse in his family of origin. The team is less interested in the history of the problem and the identified risk factors than in assisting him in using his bad childhood experience to reinforce his motivation to be a protective dad.

F2:   Is it OK to "shit talk"?

S: No, not really, I need to control my anger more.

F1:   You are starting to control it already.

F2:   If you can work on changing this "shit talk" and come back and talk about what you are doing different, then this would be a goal. If you can't talk about what you are doing different, then it's not a goal.

Notice that stopping the "shit talk" is not satisfactory as a goal. Sam must be able to define what he is doing differently and be able to talk about this difference.

S: Give it a few more years, and we will both be tired of it. . . . I need to control the way I talk to her.

Earlier in the conversation it was going to take 15 to 20 years to resolve, and now Sam is considering a few years.

F2:   Do you think this is an OK goal for you now?

S: To watch my anger toward her and to control my verbal abuse.

F2:   When you come in to group next week, you will be telling us what you are doing that is different about this and how this change affects you and her.

S: It should work. So, my goal is not to put her down with verbal abuse. That's going to be my goal!

In this surprising turn of events, Sam's long-utilized solution to his physical aggression is transformed into the problem, and he begins to explore whether or not he should give up "shit talk" and "grow up." He is clearly ambivalent but ends the session with a goal to stop this behavior. It could be argued that his commitment to change is poor—after all, he hopes to accomplish this goal in 15 years—yet the facilitating team is already complimenting him for how far he has come. In the following session, he dramatically states, "I've got to make these changes now, this week, because

I do care about my family." In a later session he shares how he held his wife while she cried after a painful loss. This was difficult and completely new for him. "I wanted to get out of there 'cause I hate that stuff, but I stayed because she needed that. In the past I wouldn't have even looked at her, it would have been her business to get over it." Throughout the final sessions he is able to clearly define what he is doing as he gives up "shit talk."

Suggesting Goals

On rare occasions we break the rule of not suggesting a goal to a participant. This occurs when a participant remains stuck and frustrated regardless of efforts to devise a possible goal. At such times we ask the participant if it might be helpful to request goal ideas from other people. We always offer "getting help" from others as a *choice* and respect the participant's decision. If he or she states it would be helpful, we ask, "Would it be most helpful to get some ideas from the group or from us or from everyone?" We always offer choice while at the same time asking the participant to make a commitment to what he or she believes will be most helpful.

Generally, participants state they would like ideas both from the facilitating team and from the group. If this is the case, we start by asking the group members to share any goal ideas they might have. When this is complete, we ask the participant whether the group's ideas were helpful. If the ideas were helpful and result in a goal idea, we help the participant define the details of the goal.

We compliment the group regardless of whether its suggestions lead to a goal idea. If the group's ideas are not seen as helpful, the participant may ask for other ideas from the treatment team. When this occurs, we ask the participant if it would be helpful for us to share some ideas. We also tell the participant that we have a history of coming up with poor goal ideas, but occasionally our suggestions have stimulated ideas for people. We then share any ideas we might have.

In 11 years of doing these groups, we have rarely come up with a good goal idea for a participant. Most of our ideas are instantly rejected, even when we thought that they were quite insightful. Our ideas have been like balloons that are popped as they travel across the room to the participant. The group suggestions often fare no better, with most being well received and then rejected. When ideas are not rejected, they are quickly modified. The process, however, can be useful because participants often devise a goal easily after the group and the facilitating team have failed to find a solution. We have come to view this process as the way some participants cooperate with the goal task. We attempt to address most goal development without using this process, however, because it can be time-consuming.

When participants get stuck, it is easy to attribute this to their lack of effort or, more generally, to "resistance." If we experience participants as "resistant," we work hard to notice and discover the their efforts. We also keep in mind that we may be out of step with the participant, moving too fast or demanding more than he or she can deliver at that particular time. We are very persistent in our efforts toward goal development. We find that participants appreciate that we do not give up on them.

> ### Do's and Don't When Participants Struggle with Developing a Useful Goal
>
> Do remain persistent and patient.
>
> Do offer choices as much as possible.
>
> Do ask participants what might help them discover a goal.
>
> Do look for the ways participants are cooperating.
>
> Don't define participants as resistant or uncooperative.

Participants Who Do Not Develop a Goal

In extremely rare circumstances a participant is unable to develop a goal by the end of the third session. When this occurs, we always offer the participant the opportunity to return to the next series of groups. This allows the participant to make another attempt at completing the requirements. We let the person know that we appreciate his or her efforts and that not everyone is ready to complete this group the first time they attempt it.

If the participant requests that we write a letter to the court regarding their efforts, we inform him that we will note his attendance and our willingness to have him come to the next series of groups. Even if the participant has presented in a most frustrating fashion, we always convey our willingness to work with him. In doing this, we have found that the few participants who have not been able to develop goals are later able to come back and successfully complete our program. We believe this is very important because research indicates that dropout rates for this population can be very high. We want to make change possible for participants who otherwise would have failed, and we believe this can happen only if we persist at extending our efforts while the courts hold participants responsible for completion.

One participant we worked with was unable to complete the goal development on three consecutive occasions. Because we treated him with great respect, he thanked us for kicking him out of the group on each of the three "failed" attempts. He was able to complete the group successfully on the fourth try. It was interesting to us that he seemed to use the group more effectively after each attempt. We now look at his "failure" as his unique way of working with us. This case also emphasizes the importance of the legal system holding people accountable for completing a program.

An alternative to having an individual leave the group if he or she has not developed a workable goal by the third session is to offer the participant an individual session between the third and fourth sessions. When this option is possible, we offer the participant the choice of doing this instead of leaving the group. We have found this to be a very effective option because it offers choice and conveys to the participant our willingness to go above and beyond the normal structure to help him be successful. This arrangement is also respectful of individuals who initially find it difficult to express themselves in a group situation.

Many participants initially find it difficult to cooperate in a traditional manner, yet with the persistence of the facilitating team and the recurrent opportunity to make important choices, they gradually move toward a collaborative process. Much of what the facilitating team does is directed at helping participants make the best choices for them given the circumstances. The group structure is designed to invite a cooperative effort. The team enhances the invitation by remaining respectful of participants' choices and by remaining persistently curious about how participants will resolve the dilemmas they face. Because of this, it is difficult for participants to resist the invitation to create a goal that is useful to them. There is nothing for them to fight against and significant opportunity for them to notice the potential benefits of working together.

5

Utilizing Goals in the Process of Change

By the end of the third session, all group participants must have a well-formed goal, which they will report on at each group. For some participants the goal behavior will remain relatively stable throughout the group process, whereas others will make many adjustments from one session to another. Our focus is to (1) encourage and compliment all efforts, (2) optimize the goal efforts by helping participants attach as much meaning as possible to their goal work, and (3) help participants evaluate and notice what is working.

In the first three sessions, it is easy to become narrowly focused on helping each participant develop a goal, and as a result it is possible to overlook the work of participants who have already done so. Therefore, it is very important to set aside time to attend to participants who have established goals and are already working on them. The benefits of doing so include the following: (1) It sets a pattern in which the group participants anticipate that they will be responsible for reporting on their goal activities at each session; (2) it reinforces the importance of working on the goal; (3) it allows for adjustments to be made in goals; and (4) it creates opportunities for further interventions, such as compliments and questions.

Sometimes participants will quickly identify a goal that is on target for them. They discover that the goal behavior clearly benefits them and results in day-to-day improvement in their life. These participants often report an almost religious devotion to their goal, months after they have completed the program. They state that the goal works for them, and they continue to focus on it. For them, the goal itself remains the critical factor, and they attach powerful meanings to the goal behavior.

Many other participants report that working on the goal and coming to group has transported them to a different place in their lives, a place of less intensity, or one that provides them with a broader view of what is good for them. Most of these participants note that working on a goal has shifted how they manage themselves in relationships and helped them evaluate what a good relationship is. Participants with this experience tend to view the goal as a vehicle for change rather then as a solution in and of itself. These participants tend to attach broader, more expansive meanings to their goal work.

We believe there are many ways in which people can be successful. Whether participants are expansive or narrow in the meanings they develop with regard to their goal work is not of great interest to us. We invite them to develop whatever meanings make sense to them, meanings that signify useful and important change.

When Participants Report Positive Results

When participants return and share that their goal efforts are helpful, it is important to use this as an opportunity to build on and encourage these efforts. We typically do this by becoming very curious and interested in what happened and collecting as many details as possible. We are curious in a manner similar to that of someone who is exploring something new and wants to examine all its possibilities and meanings. Great detail is re-quested so that the goal behavior is re-created in the group's presence. We also help participants evaluate the impact their behavior has had on others who may have directly or indirectly experienced the changes. This process of discovering the details and exploring the full impact of the goal behavior magnifies its importance and expands the meaning that is attributed to it. We often reflect on the courage that it takes to do something new and on participants' wisdom in picking a goal that is already showing itself to be beneficial. Direct and indirect compliments are critical to this process not only because they offer important feedback but also because they set a positive tone of expectation for the whole group.

In the following example the therapy team uses compliments and questions to help Peggy explore the meaning and impact of her goal effort.

THE CASE OF PEGGY

Peggy, a middle-aged woman, has developed a goal of remaining calm and lis-tening to her teenage daughter. If necessary, she "removes herself from the scene" until she can gain composure. Prior to this session, she has been very successful in her goal work. In this session she begins to share how her goal work is "spreading" to other parts of her life. The therapy team works to help her notice the significance of this and to explore what it means about her.

Facilitator 1: How about you, Peggy?
Peggy: I'm doing just fine. (laughter) No, well, let me see. My daughter was real good this week. The only thing that could have maybe exploded, I work at the hospital and, um, I seen these two "Bum Betty" women coming in with their hair all . . . well, anyway, they turn all the lights on and ask for the bell, you know. Her mother needs to get on the bedpan, so I ask

them to leave the room so I can put her on there. And I heard the daughter telling the other lady, "I wish that nigger wasn't taking care of my
mother."

F1:   Oh!

P: So instead of throwing that bedpan at her and telling her what I really
thought, I just waited until her mother finished, and I cleaned her up and
put her back in the bed. When I walked out the door, I told her, "Mrs. so-
and-so, I'm sorry that's the way that you feel, but I really enjoy taking
care of your mother." And I just walked off.

F1:   Wow.

P: I don't think I made any difference to her, but it made me feel better
'cause I really wanted to slug her.

F1:   Wow! What would you have done in the past?

*Notice how this question helps the participant evaluate and
validate the difference working on the goal is making for her.*

P: Cussed her out. I would have done something to her real nasty.

Ppt 1: Or threw something at her.

F1:   Oh, yeah, you would have thrown something?

P: Probably.

F1:   Ohhh . . .

P: Yeah, it just really hurt my feelings, you know.

F1:   Oh, of course.

P: But I got over it.

F1:   So how did it go from something hurting your feelings to just turning it
around?

*This question encourages the participant to reconstruct the
details of change.*

P: Because it probably wouldn't have made any difference to that lady one
way or the other. You know, if I'd cussed her out, I'd still been a nigger,
if I was nice to her, I was still one. So I just took the easiest way out for
me, which I still kept my job, 'cause if I'd have threw something at her,
shit, they would have said, "Get the hell out."

F1:   Do you think what you're doing with your daughter, the goal that you
have with your daughter . . .

P: Is working at work, too?

*These questions give Peggy the opportunity to see her efforts as
having multiple benefits. Her original goal was to keep calm and
not overreact to her daughter's behavior.*

F1:   Is it working at work?

P: Yeah, just trying to keep calm and not losing it. Like I said, when I start
yelling, I lose control. You know, if I'd have to start yelling at that lady, I
probably would have been . . . You know, made such a big scene. But it

all worked out. Like I said, I don't think it mattered to her, but it made me feel better.

F1:   Yeah, yeah, yeah . . . 'cause it's just another time that you're keeping your cool, even under very difficult conditions.

P: Oh, yeah, it was real hard.

F1:   Yeah, yeah.

P: That was real hard.

F1:   Right.

P: Yeah, I was proud of myself. I did it, 'cause I really wanted to tell her some things.

F2:   Yeah.

F1:   Um-huh. Good for you.

F2:   Yeah, that's big. That's really big. . . . That's the kind of thing where you could have . . . you could have done a lot of things and a lot of people would have said, "Right on." But you decided that you were going to handle it with some sense of how you wanted to deal with it.

The therapy team wants to gain as much as possible from Peggy's hard work. Instead of dropping this conversation, facilitator 2 expands the significance of Peggy's behavior by underlining her impressive decision making and emotional control.

P: And that lady didn't care. Like I said, she could care less one way or the other.

F2:   Right, right.

F1:   So, if that same situation, if you were to have handled that the best you could have and the worst you could have, how would you have rated that . . . how you handled that?

This question offers the participant the opportunity to again evaluate and confirm how well she is doing. Peggy compliments herself!

P: How I handled it this time?

F1:   Yeah.

P: Oh 10!

F1:   That's right!

F2:   All right, yeah! (claps)

When necessary, we help participants evaluate whether a goal is comprehensive enough to accomplish what they had hoped for. This is often helpful because it builds commitment to the goal as it is or permits expansion or adjustments of the goal task. This process is also respectful of participants' ability to evaluate their own efforts and emphasizes their choices regarding the goal work.

When participants find the goal helpful, they often make spontaneous adjustments to it as they begin to see their behavior and relationships from a different perspective. When this occurs, it is important for the therapy team to help participants notice these shifts and, if possible, incorporate these new understandings into the evolving goal work. To varying degrees, all goal work is organic in that the goal evolves from a basic structure and changes both in form and in the meanings attached to it from session to session. The following transcript clearly depicts the evolution of a goal.

THE CASE OF DANNY

Danny originally voiced his goal as "walking away if I notice the coming of fights." He also, in time, developed a secondary goal of starting a new business. With further exploration, he found himself evaluating his relationship and wanting to be in control of his life. In his words, "I want to stop allowing the relationship to control my life." The goal task was expanded and adjusted so that he was not just managing aggression but reevaluating his life goals.

Danny: Well, as you know, I've already started my goal and . . .
Facilitator 1: I don't remember, sorry.
D: My time out. Because, aggression to me . . . I've been hit in the face, and it's been really hard since I've been doing it, but I've been just walking away. Go see friends, go do something else. I hated it at first because I wanted to just really reach over and bite her damn head off. But (laughs), yeah, but I just, like the other day, she wanted to go at it, and I said, "Well, I guess you won't see me the rest of the day," and I left. Come back and everything there was no problem anymore.
F1:   So last week when you, when she wanted to get into it and you walked away . . .
D: I do that several times, sometimes.
F1:   And is that helpful?
D: Yeah, it's very helpful, very helpful. I'm getting used to it now, you know, where I can get away because I can see it coming. And a lot of times rather than using my defense, like "I'm out of here," I'm even getting to the point where it's like a secret. I just, "Well, I've got to go do the lawn. So as soon as I get that done, I'll be back to talk to you." Well, I might go out and do the shed and (laughs), you know. I'll do it 'til, I know the waiting period. Because I can still hear her as I'm walking out the door. She's in there arguing with herself, and I'm like, I don't want no part of it anymore. If it's gotta be that way and I've gotta sit there and do that and it's going to get violent, then I'm just gonna split. I'm just gonna take off on my own and the hell with her. Because if she can't make me happy, then I don't need her.

This is a good example of how a participant begins a goal of walking away when he sees a negative interaction beginning and modifies it to make it better. Danny now makes an excuse to leave rather than pointedly leaving and making an issue of his wife's behavior.

Facilitator 2: Do you notice anything with her now when you do this?

D: I do when I come back. It's like something I guess clicks in her head, "Well, maybe it wasn't that important because the subject doesn't even come up."

F2:   Oh, now, but I was curious about this part because you said that you were just doing this, you're doing it sooner. You're noticing something is coming.

D: Oh, yeah, I spot it sooner because I don't let my head get the violence in it, like it used to.

Danny has further modified his goal by anticipating problems and now leaves before trouble starts. Notice how his language implies that he is now in control of keeping the violence out of his head.

F2:   Yeah, OK, so . . .

D: Because that made me blind, and so I just went for what I knew. But now I sit back, and I watch all the time.

F2:   Watch, OK, so . . .

D: Oh, yeah, I watch for it to come . . .

F2:   OK, since you've started doing that, have you noticed something different about her, too?

D: Maybe it's not right.

F2:   Maybe what's not?

D: The relationship.

F2:   Oh.

D: But I'm still with it, but I don't know if it's gonna last.

F2:   Oh, OK, so you're not sure. You're evaluating that, too, whether or not its gonna work for you or not.

D: Right. If it doesn't work for me. I don't care whether it works for them. Its gotta work for me or it doesn't work.

F2:   OK, all right.

F1:   So, this business of leaving and noticing in advance when something's gonna come, and you're leaving sooner, is that giving you the opportunity to stand back more from the relationship?

D: It's like him (referring to another group participant), it's giving me a chance to wash my face. Because if I was to stay there a couple minutes longer, I'd be in it. Because that's the way I am. People come at me. I'm a very happy-go-lucky guy. I get along with almost everybody. But when ag-gression comes, I don't see any reason for, it's like if you're going to be aggressive with me, then I'm going to be aggressive with you. I don't care. And I'm trying to put a barrier there for that because when it's all over you just look at yourself and go, "Why did I even do that? That was stupid. I could have went and done something better that was more fun."

Danny is clearly beginning to evaluate his past behavior and question the choices he has made.

F2:   Are you beginning to figure out what that something is that would be more fun?

D: That's the thing, I've been doing a lot of work, I mean like my own business, and I really like that. People respect that I will do good work for them.

F1:   So, Danny, doing work, getting these jobs and starting work, how is that going to help?

The therapy team could easily construct ideas about how Danny's work might be helping, but instead they ask Danny to construct the ideas himself. This "not-knowing" attitude is more respectful of Danny and also gives him the opportunity to ascribe his own meaning to his behavior.

D: Well, it gets me off into other things, too. I'm not around as much and stuff like that. And then
                    I can make my own hours.

F1:   It's helpful when you're not around as much?

D: Hmmm, yeah, it's a different situation at home.

F2:   How so? Like how so for her? What do you notice?

D: The anger isn't as great because I'm not there as much. You know, it's like, the time spent that I'm gone, and by the time I get back, well, there's dinner or getting the kids ready for bed and stuff. And there are more things to preoccupy with. Because its like him (referring to another group participant) and his wife where she goes to school, also, so a lot of times she'll just run away with her books.

F2:   Does she notice that you're more of a happy camper then? Because of this?

D: Yeah, and it makes her mad.

F2:   Oh?

D: It pisses, I don't know why, but it pisses her off because she won't be happy, but she'll see that I am happy, so that pisses her off.

F2:   Confusing.

D: Or if I get around people that make me happy, like a relative or something. Like I was just talking to my aunt the other day on the phone. We used to, we were like this at one point in time (puts his fingers together). We were roommates, everything, and if she even calls me, I can see it in her face, "Ah, there's Gloria again." She can't stand my aunt because we get along so good. We're so much alike.

F1:   It sounds like you're really stepping back a little bit and evaluating this relationship, and taking this time out is helping you do that.

D: I'm not gonna screw myself up either.

F1 and F2: Yeah, yeah.

F2:   You're pretty focused. You look focused and you're clear, you know? In terms of what you need to do here and in terms of this thing that Facilitator 1 just said, too. What do you think that says about you now?

This type of question implies that the participant's efforts are affecting him personally. It invites him to draw powerful conclusions about the impact of his efforts.

D: It basically says that I'm gonna be my own person again. I'm not gonna be, let a relationship run my life.

Danny seems to be developing another more personal, as yet undefined, goal of "being my own person." This goal is interesting in that he is also beginning to develop a goal of owning his own business and is taking steps to make this a reality.

F2: OK, that's the big theme here, for you.
D: I've gotta be my own person or I'm not happy. If I'm not happy, then I don't need the situation.
F2: Yeah, OK.
D: No matter what the consequences are at the end, I'm gonna do what it takes to make me happy.
F2: It kinda keeps you safe, it sounds like, too.
D: It does.
F2: Yeah.
D: Safe is a good feeling.
F1: Sounds like you're really taking charge of your goal.
D: I am.
F1: Yeah.
F2: I would like, I think I want to hear examples when you come in next time.
D: OK.
F2: Do you think you're gonna be able to do that pretty clearly? The examples of like when you do this and how you're going about doing that? And anything else I think, you know, that helps you know that you are your own person now.
D: I haven't got to there yet.
F2: OK.
D: That's still questionable.
F2: OK.
D: I still get to sit back and watch a little, and, you know, when I make what I want to make of myself.
F2: OK, so you know you're on course.
D: Yeah.
F2: But you're not quite sure what the details are.
D: Well, I'm not sure quite what the details are or how it's gonna end up. I know it's gonna end up good for me, but I'm not sure it's gonna end up good for everybody else. But that I can't help.

Danny's goal work is on target, and he is able to identify the benefits. It is not clear how the goal will impact him personally, but it is clear that he is comfortable with his efforts. Sometimes participants feel a goal is not comprehensive enough. When this occurs, we express curiosity regarding what adjustments they think might be helpful. We then help them describe the details of how this additional goal behavior will be enacted. During this process, we also help them describe how these changes will be experienced by others. We always ask participants to evaluate how helpful the adjustments they are going to make will be by asking a direct question such as, "Do you think this will make a difference?" Or else we ask a scaling question such as, "On a scale of 1 to 10, how much difference will these adjustments make, 10 being a great deal of difference and 1 being virtually no difference?"

Once participants begin to focus on the positive results of their efforts, we begin to expand the meaning they might attribute to these changes. This is accomplished most efficiently by asking participants direct questions such as, "What do you suppose this means about you that you have been so calmly asking your children to do their chores?" or "What do you suppose your children would say these changes you have made mean about you?" or "Do you think this means you have become a more patient person?" or "What do you suppose your wife would say this means about you as a person?" All these questions invite participants to create or confirm a new description of themselves, thus confirming the importance of the changes and solidifying the change itself.

In the following case example the facilitation team uses the participant's life events, memories, and goal work to confirm her value, efforts, and human beauty. The process allows the participant to draw her own conclusions about her past, her future, and what she has learned.

THE CASE OF JOANNE

Joanne has described her goal as regularly taking some quiet time for herself so that she could be emotionally calmer when spending time with her family. Here Joanne begins by sharing an important event in her and her family's life, and the therapy team helps her evaluate what this event says about her, her relationship with her mother, and her relationship with her children. In this interaction Joanne is in the lead, yet the therapy team maintains focus to help her integrate these powerful memories into her goal work.

Joanne: And, um, when I brought my mom to my house to die, my kids were there 'cause that was their grandma, and they saw all the stages, and they were there with me, they were there with me the whole time. And that was very important to me that they did that. I'm not going to say that they allowed me to let my mom stay there 'cause . . . that's not the right word to say . . . it was something that they understood because that's what I needed to do for me and my mom.

Facilitator 2: And they were willing to be part of that whole circle between your mom and you and the kids.

Facilitator 1: What do you think it says about you that your mother wanted to die in your home?

J: I don't know. I asked myself a lot of times that question, she would say no one could take care of her the way I could 'cause I took care of her before she died. Before, when I lived in Southern California, I went down to take care of her and then I came back here, and so she just got worse, so she came up here. I kept telling her, "Mom, you've got to go back to Southern California to your doctors," and she said, "Sweetie, I don't want to go." Well, um, have you ever heard of the ugly duckling that grew up to be a beautiful swan? There was a little ugly duckling, and he was already hatched, and he couldn't find his mama, and nobody wanted him because he was an ugly little duckling. And so he would walk around, walk around, and walk around, and you're my mama, no you're ugly, we don't like you, we don't want nothing to do with you. So finally these two little kids found this little ducking and thought it was the greatest thing in the world. And they had a pond, and they put him out in the pond and the next morning they looked up, and it wasn't an ugly duckling after all, it was a beautiful swan, and my mother used to tell it to me.

F2:   What do you think she was saying to you?

J: I thought that maybe she thought that I was a good person and she loved me with all her heart.

F2:   So, I guess this is worth all the effort?

J: I wouldn't take back anything, and I don't regret anything I did.

F2:   It doesn't sound like you have any regrets about what you're doing now, you now focus on taking care of yourself and your kids. How are you doing with that, what is your confidence now on a scale of 1 to 10, 10 being completely confident and 1 being just kind of confident?

J: I wouldn't be anything less than a 10, a 10 or more.

F2:   Wow, you are superconfident then.

J: Yeah, I need that, I need that time by myself. I need that space so, that way things keep on going good.

Even though Joanne is clearly on target and confident, the therapy team wants additional details regarding the goal work.

F2:   Have you kind of figured out the balance now, the number of times, um, because some days you were taking the time and some days you weren't, what do you think now?

J: About 3 days a week, but if I know I'm getting like, you know, on edge or I'm tired of everything, then I'll take a break.

F2:   You'll watch yourself, yeah.

J: Well, after my daughter got in my face last time, I . . . you know, when she came up to me and asked if I took my time out, so but, um. [In a previous session Joanne shared that her daughter had confronted her about not doing her goal when she noticed her mother was more irritable. This was significant for Joanne because until that time she was only partially convinced that the goal was helpful.]

F1:   I just have one more question for you. What else do you recognize is different in your life?

This open-ended question invites Joanne to search for and create new meanings.

J: Well, I think I'm pretty, pretty inside.

F1:   How do you know that?

J: Just when I look at my life and what I've been through, I know it, and I have friends that are really truthful, 'cause your friend forgets that you did your stuff, and I have some true friends.

F2:   Well, you've got that reflection of your mother, too. You only have to think about what you see in your mother's eyes.

Do's and Don'ts When a Goal Is Helpful

Do help the participant notice all the benefits of the goal behavior.

Do compliment the efforts.

Do offer the participant the opportunity to draw conclusions about what the change means.

Do help the participant assess whether the goal is comprehensive and helpful.

Don't overlook small change.

Useful Questions When a Goal Is Helpful

Who noticed that you were doing this?

How do you think it affected them?

Do you think you can continue doing this?

What other benefits do you think will occur as you keep doing this?

How much more committed are you to this goal now that it's working?

Is there something you intend to add to the goal, or is it most helpful as it is?

When Participants Report No Change or That Goal Is Not Helpful

Attitudes That Promote Positive Change

Working with participants who do not notice benefits from their goal work presents an interesting, stimulating challenge. It is critical to keep in mind that a participant's response to his or her goal work is simply a response. There is no good or bad response, and the participant's response always has great potential to be useful. As inexperienced facilitators, we tended to feel more comfortable when participants came to us and said that things were much better, that "their cup was full." Yet there is a very old saying that reminds us that a cup is at its most useful state when it is empty. When participants report that something did not work, they are often much more open and available to creating new ideas. Keeping this in mind is very helpful because there is no reason to be discouraged by participants being stuck; in fact, the opposite is true.

From our point of view, all goal-related behavior is helpful, even when a participant states that a goal effort has failed to produce the desired results. At the very least, a goal that fails to produce the desired results always helps the participant discover what is not a solution. It encourages the participant and the facilitation team to look in another direction that will likely hold more promise. It is also important to keep in mind that if a goal does not solve a problem, it can still have unanticipated benefits and thus remain useful. In this case the question is whether the participant is able to notice how the goal is useful and whether the facilitator can help the participant to do so.

Another advantageous perspective is that whatever the participant states is not written in concrete; it can always be modified. This may seem obvious, yet we find that people commonly treat participants' descriptions and statements as if they are solid and inflexible. In our experience, these descriptions and statements are extremely flexible and constantly changing, and treating them as if they are solid objects creates a distinct disadvantage if change is the desired outcome. The alternative is to know that language is a creative medium, with few boundaries or limitations, and that transitions from one description to another can happen very quickly. Goals that were described as useless can be dramatically transformed to being very helpful within the span of minutes when language is used to focus attention in a search for the useful aspects of the participant's efforts.

Helping Participants Notice Change

One of the best ways to approach participants who say that a goal was not helpful is to ask them to state their goal. This helps them organize their thoughts and allows for the opportunity to focus on what they did, where they did it, and who may have been affected by their behavior. Reviewing details of the behavior in this way is important for the following reasons: (1) Many times people fail to notice secondary benefits or do not recall the positive results of their work until they review it; (2) sometimes people become distracted from the original goal benefit by refocusing, and (3) some participants attempt to accomplish too much in their first effort, causing them to miss small, important changes.

A number of years ago we were conducting a group in which a man stated that his goal—which was to do more activities with his mother— was not working for him. He had lived with his mother most of his life and hoped that doing more activities with her would improve their relationship. He discovered that doing the activities mildly strained the relationship rather than improving it.

At first it appeared that the goal was not helpful to him. As we explored the details of the goal, however, it became apparent that because his relationship with his mother was more tense, he was more motivated to work hard at college. He had not noticed this until the goal was reviewed. His working harder in college did not result in any recognition from his mother, but it did yield positive comments from a sibling and two instructors. The man did not recall these comments until he was asked if other people noticed any positive changes. In evaluating this, he decided that this secondary benefit of doing better in school and the praise of the sibling and instructors made it worth while to continue working on the goal.

The man continued to do much better in school. In time, his mother began to notice this change, and as a result she was more positive with him and expressed admiration for him for the first time in his life. He continued working on the goal of doing activities with his mother for 8 weeks, which resulted in his doing so well at college that he was offered an excellent employment opportunity. His acceptance of the new job led to his moving out of his mother's house, which he realized was an extremely important change for him.

The most important aspect of this case, from our perspective, is that this participant discovered that his goal was useful in creating the kinds of changes he felt were important, even though at first the results were a complete contradiction to his original expectations. Because of this and many similar experiences, we find it useful to help participants evaluate any and all possible secondary benefits of a goal. When participants are narrowly focused on one specific outcome, they commonly miss positive aspects that have resulted from their goal work. Participants will state, "I worked hard on my goal, but it was a bust." After we spend 10 minutes helping them search for unanticipated benefits, they will state, "You know, I think this goal is right on target."

Participants often fail to notice useful changes and benefits of their goal work. Some participants have developed a pattern of noticing negative events and have become increasingly problem-focused throughout their lives. Sometimes they anticipate that professionals are primarily interested in their problems. Redirecting these participants to describe their goal and helping them explore what they did related to the goal gives them a second opportunity to notice potential positive benefits. As these benefits are identified, compliments can be used to invite participants to develop a stronger commitment to the goal work. In the following example, benefits are identified and compliments are used to increase commitment.

MIKE

Facilitator 2: So, Mike, what's happening with your goal?

Mike: I don't know, it doesn't seem to be making much difference for me.

F2:   Umm, what were you going to work on?

M: Well, I thought getting things on a list and organizing my life would help, but she doesn't seem to notice much.

F2:   What did you do with that, did you develop the list and do things?

M: Yeah, I actually have the list in my head, three things. I pulled my bike out and cleaned it up to sell, I called about the removal of a fuel tank, and I worked on a slash pile.

Facilitator 1: Wow, I'm impressed. You are serious about accomplishing things!

M: I was hoping she would notice that I'm doing things.

F1:   How do you know she hasn't noticed?

M: I don't know, but she didn't say anything.

F1:   Did she act any different?

M: That's hard to say. She came out and brought me a drink when I was working on the slash pile, but I don't know what that's all about.

F2:   So you just don't know yet.

M: Yeah.

F2:   Did you notice that the goal was good for you in any way?

M: Not really.

F1:   Not at all?

M: It was good to get things done. I don't know if I would have gotten it done. . . . I felt more organized. I tend to have a million things going on, and that drives her nuts, and I like it and hate it at the same time.

F1:   It sounds like you did a great job of organizing the three things you worked on.

M: I think that is more what I need to do. Do like three things a week. Make it three things that I need to get rid of.

F2:   How would that help?

M: She's always complaining that I have too much going on and junk, and I hate to say it, but I have always lived that way, but it doesn't work very well. I mean for us. It worked good for me. It's going to sound stupid, but that's why I'm here, the man who couldn't let stuff go. It drives me crazy, too.

F2:   So what will you do? What will help?

M: I think it's not getting organized, it's also getting rid of things. I could sell a lot of things. I mean a lot of things, every weekend for a year and have more left over. I've got storage rentals that I could empty.

F1:   I'm amazed at how you are willing to make such a big change and how you are actually thinking of doing this different. What difference do you think it will make as you work on this?

M: I'm not sure that she will see it at first, but I know I would feel better. I know this drags me down.

F1:   And if you weren't dragged down, what would people notice?

M: Well . . . umm, it's not so much confidence, I think just calmer knowing that I don't need all that, that distraction.

F2:   If you woke up in the morning, and your wife noticed this difference, what would be the first clue to her that this was creating a change for you?

M: I think I wouldn't just be running out the door chasing after cars. You know like a dog. I had a dog like that. He would run after everything without a thought.

F1:   So what would you do?

M: (pause) . . . I would have a cup of coffee with her.

F2:   Taking some time with her?

M: Yeah.

F2:   Would that surprise her?

M: She wouldn't know what to think. She'd probably think I was sick or something.

F1:   Wow, this would be a change. Would it be helpful?

M: Yeah, I think so.

F1:   How would you do this?

M: I would just do it.

F2:   Like when and how?

M: Saturday morning, I mean she gets up late, so I would have to come back in and just . . . Well, I guess I could get her a cup of coffee, and we could just sit and talk.

F2:   Do you think that could work? I mean so you could do that?

M: Yeah.

F2:   So it sounds like you are going to change your goal so it will work better for you?

M: I think getting rid of stuff is big for me. Three things a week, and then slowing down with her and no chasing cars.

F2:   Well, I'm sure we can't wait to hear about the three things you get rid of and this coffee break.

The process of evaluating the details of the goal is very helpful for participants who are attempting to accomplish too much at one time. Participants who desire a lot of change in a short time often fail to recognize small changes and underestimate the significance a small change can have over time. Focusing on details amplifies the little changes and helps participants observe otherwise unnoticed benefits. We typically ask participants to tell us whether or not something was a little better, particularly if they note that something different occurred. It is also helpful to have participants evaluate the effect that their goal behavior will have over time. To do this we ask, "Do you think making these little changes will make a real difference if you keep doing them?" This type of question helps participants assess the impact of little changes, gives them the opportunity to predict further changes, and confirms that change is already occurring!

When participants are attempting primarily to change or influence the behavior of another person, it is more likely that they will report that their goal is not working. In these situations, it is often helpful to assist them in evaluating the potential for success in their attempt to change the other person. This helps participants give up or modify a goal that has poor chances of success and allows for the redirection of efforts to a goal that can make a difference. In this process participants often discover that they must focus their energy on a goal that is designed primarily to change *their* behavior so that they can cope better or live a more functional life.

When participants have made progress that they did not initially notice, we ask them whether they want to continue with the goal or if they want to modify or change it. Participants often will stay with the goal if they can see it as useful and they become better at noticing the little changes that signify progress. Once participants are able to identify benefits and make progress, it is relatively easy to help them expand upon the changes. Once changes are recognized, we help participants attribute meanings to them.

Evaluating and Changing Goals

Most participants either find their goal helpful or are able to modify it in ways that are satisfactory to them. On the rare occasions when participants have seen no benefit to the goal or even view it as making things worse, we help them evaluate whether changing goals makes sense. Before doing this we (1) ask detailed questions regarding their goal work, (2) help them search for unnoticed benefits, and (3) help them evaluate whether persisting in the goal work might bring results. We do not give opinions about persisting in the goal work even when we suspect that continuing with goal might be beneficial. We assume that the participants knows best.

Once it is determined that a new goal is in order, we begin by being positive and curious as to how the participants will go about discovering a more useful goal. Often we will ask, "Did doing this goal give you any clues regarding what might be a better goal?" or, more simply, "Since this isn't working, what do you think you need to do different?" These open-ended questions help participants begin to explore new possibilities and imply that they are accountable for creating a more useful goal. We also state,

"Everyone must have a goal that they are working on. If you are to remain in the group, you must have a well-defined goal before you leave group today." This statement creates anxiety for many participants, so we balance it with a supportive attitude and let them know directly that we will work hard to help them develop a goal. This is important not only because it supports participants but also because the whole group recognizes that we are being as fair as possible. The perception of fairness and a supportive attitude are so important that at times we will invite a participant to come in for an individual session to further work on developing a goal if he or she is unable to develop a goal by the deadline. We make this invitation in front of the group so that all participants can see our efforts to be helpful and fair.

The following case example shows how a participant moves from a goal that is producing unanticipated negative results to one that may offer more opportunities for positive change.

THE CASE OF ED

Ed originally felt that making an effort to "get to know my father better" would help him feel more confident. He did not know how his father would react to his efforts, since they had not talked in over 2 years. During the first two sessions Ed reported that his father had been hard to approach in part because he was drinking heavily. In spite of this, Ed made a number of phone contacts and had even briefly visited him. In the third session, he begins to consider changing goals.

Facilitator 1: Ed, you have been doing a good job of making contact with your dad. What have you noticed about this?

Ed: I don't really know. I'm pretty discouraged 'cause he doesn't seem to respond much. I don't know that he can.

F1: What have you done over the past week to work on your goal?

E: I went over to his trailer and, uh, on Sunday, and I thought maybe we could watch some football. I just dropped in because he wasn't answering the phone, and he was drunk at 10:30 A.M. I just didn't know what I could do. I guess it surprised me, but I don't know why.

Facilitator 2: You don't know why?

E: Well, yeah, I just thought he would be in better shape, but that doesn't make sense. I mean, he's an alcoholic, I know that.

F2: Is that helpful to know?

E: It's helpful not to forget.

F1: How so?

E: Well, I can't expect that he can really be there, you know. I started picking up things just to do something, and he got all pissed like I wasn't supposed to help him and he didn't need me around. I know he won't even remember that, so I don't know if it makes a difference.

F2:   Does it make a difference to you?

E: Yeah, yeah, I'm . . . I don't know that I can have a relationship with him. I don't know if he can have a relationship with me or even if he wants one.

F1:   How will you find out?

E: I think I am finding out.

F1:   Is that helpful?

E: God, I hate that question. Yes, it helps, but it kinda hurts.

F1 and F2: Yeah, yeah.

F2:   I'm just very impressed that you chose to do this work with your dad. I think that took a lot of courage, and I don't know that a lot of people would have been so diligent in their efforts. Would it help to keep pursuing your dad?

E: I just don't see how. I mean, I can. I probably will see him, but I wouldn't call that trying to make things better. I don't see things being better.

F1:   Has it been helpful to do this, I mean, pursue this relationship with your dad . . . I mean for you?

E: For me? Yeah, I know that this is an end in a way. I mean, I have to accept that it's not what I want it to be and then . . .

F1:   How would that help to accept this is the way it is?

E: I don't know, I think that's a million-dollar question, and I don't know.

F2:   But you know this is helpful in some way to have reached out to your dad.

E: Yeah, I know something I knew, but I know it in another way.

F2:   How do you think that will benefit you?

E: Well, I need to get on with my life. I've known that, but now I think I will do something about it.

F1:   So, where do you go from here with your goal?

E: I don't see how it would do any good for me to push it any further, not now.

F2:   So, does this lead you to another goal? You know you have to have a goal to remain in this group, so does doing this goal give you any ideas about another goal? Maybe something that helps answer this million-dollar question?

E: I don't know.

F2:   Do you want to think about it while we talk to some other people, or do you want us to ask you some questions, or what would be most helpful?

Ed has done a lot of work, and this question offers him the choice of taking a break or continuing a search for a new goal. Usually participants will choose to continue to work, but it is often more productive when they make the decision to do so.

E: I don't know, but I want to work it out now, so maybe you could ask some questions, but it was real hard for me to come here, and I . . . just want you to know that.

*Ed has answered that he doesn't know to the last few questions,
yet he shifts to an area that he knows will benefit him. It is as if
he does know but didn't know that he knew!*

F1:   Hard for you to come here, I don't understand.

E: I'm sure you saw me shaking the first group. I'm really scared to be in a group like this. I mean, it's really hard.

F1:   I didn't know.

F2:   I didn't see you shaking.

E: It felt like I was going to bounce off the chair.

Ppt1: I didn't notice.

Ppt2: I could tell you were nervous, but that's because I was nervous, too.

F1:   Well, I think you've done great talking and thinking and planning your goal.

F2:   Definitely. You are such a clear talker in front of all these people.

E: Believe me, I would not be here unless I had to.

F1:   If 10 was how nervous you where at group 1, and 1 is as relaxed as you can get, where are you now?

E: I'm at about a 6 or 7 right now, but that's still pretty high.

F2:   So you're more relaxed but not as relaxed as you'd like to be. Wow, how did you do that?

E: I think just coming and having to do it.

F1:   Is it better each time you come?

E: Yeah, I think so, but I don't know how far that will go.

F2:   That's right, you really don't know how far that will go.

F1:   So does this lead to a goal?

E: My goal in the group is just to come and do what I have to do. I know I don't get out enough. I avoid people. I hate to say this, but I just don't talk to people unless I have to. I know I should, but it's tough.

F1:   It's tough, but you've been doing it here.

E: Yeah.

F2:   So, is there a goal here about this talking with others? Do you think that would be helpful?

E: I know I get real negative if I don't talk to people. I start thinking that they aren't any good, like you can't trust any of them, so I think if I even said "hi" to them it would help.

F1:   So, could you do that and see whether or not it makes a difference?

E: Yeah, I think so. I would have to get out more to do it.

F1:   Can you do that between now and the next group and give us a report on it and what you discover?

E: Yeah.

We find that many people have similar worries regarding social contacts, and the group context is often very helpful to them. In these situations, we often assist participants in developing goals that are worked on in the group, such as contributing verbally, expressing an opinion, or asking a question in each group. This is negotiated as a goal only if a participant believes it will be helpful and is in addition to his or her out-of-group goal.

Participants Who Make Multiple Goal Changes

On occasion we have worked with participants who have readjusted or changed goals over three or four consecutive sessions. Some participants have dramatically altered their goals from session to session. We see this as beneficial if the following conditions are met: (1) The participant is able to clearly define the new goal behavior as a well-formed goal and (2) the participant is able to define how the new goal behavior will be more helpful to him or her and the people affected by it.

On one occasion we were working with a man who modified his goal on each of four consecutive sessions. During the first three of these groups, the theme of the goal related to pleasing his wife. His efforts were impressive but utter failures; in fact, his wife became increasingly verbally negative. On the fourth modification, he decided to do things that related to taking better care of himself. The result was a much improved relationship with his children, a moderate and gradual improvement in his relationship with his wife, and a significantly more relaxed feeling about himself and his life.

In this case the participant initially made changes in his goal that left its main theme unchanged as he continued to pursue different ways to change his wife. From our viewpoint, the participant had not really changed the goal in a meaningful way. We sometimes point this out directly to the participant by stating, "Maybe continuing to try to please your wife isn't going to work." More often we find it helpful to ask participants questions that assist them in evaluating the situation for themselves, such as, "This seems very similar to the goal that is not working. How is this different than your original goal?" or "What do you think will make this goal more helpful than your first goal?" This helps participants search for a difference that is meaningful to them. If they can not initially find or create that difference, we continue to ask questions that help them explore alternative ideas.

We find it very important to compliment participants efforts. With few exceptions we resist suggesting alternative goals even when we feel confident that we could do a better job of living their lives. Instead, we continue to ask questions that help them search for possibilities.

Participants Who Become Distracted by Problems

Sometimes a participant becomes distracted and actually loses focus on the goal. This most often occurs when participants have been stressed by various personal events. During these times, some participants will ventilate regarding the situation they are struggling with. On occasion, participants will become emotional, particularly if they have experienced a loss. During these times, we focus on listening well, by which we mean listening with little or no comment. We do not engage participants in "problem talk" and rarely reflect feelings. Nor do we interpret or ask questions that encourage participants to talk more about the problem. We respect that a person may find it useful to ventilate thoughts and feelings. We remain alert to how participants are coping with their current stressors. We compliment their ability to "get through" a tough situation and wait until they are ready to make a transition to their goal work.

JOHN

Facilitator 1: So, John, are you getting any closer to having a clear goal?

John: Well, I can't hardly get to these groups. For one thing, I have this 20-year back problem. I'm in terrible pain today. It's a spear in me, and I'm going to the chiropractor tomorrow. I've been working with this guy. If I can't resolve this I'm going to try to, um, the institute. I won't lose my job over it. I didn't do it on the job; I did it before. I was actually hired on this job, that's the reason I quit floor service jobs because I could no longer do the physical work, and of course they did X rays, but I've been on and off worked despite injured for about 20 years. This last week it hit me hard, and I went to the chiropractor last Monday, and he said I have to go to-morrow, and that's one of my goals is to get this pain taken care of now. He did, I saw him, start seeing him about the end of July, August, he got the spear out of my back. For 3 weeks I was doing really good, and I started working on my upper neck pain, and that's when the spears came back and I know it's curable. A lot of time, I learn to live with it. I know if I was a quad in a wheelchair, all I could move was my tongue. I want to live, you know.

F1: Yes, of course you do.

J: You know they just like fire people, and the downsizing all the time, I had to put in a claim for my earnings. The dentist has been great. He's given me more money than I give him; he sponsored my band so I gave him a check, he gives me the check, you know. I've got seven digits on the in-surance, but I can't put any more on the insurance without them wanting me to state whether it's an accident, illness, etcetera.

Facilitator 2: So, you've done incredibly well just to get here today.

J: I was injured on the job, and we had one piece of furniture to move from down stairs to upstairs, and it was a big entertainment center. It weighed about 400 or 500 pounds. We used the pulley, and I started pushing, and I go all the way straight up like this, and we're going up another step, and he slipped, and all that weight came right on me. I let out this big scream, and the guy we're moving for was about 400 pounds, and he walked over and put his arms up and he held it, my back was still sore.

F2: So, you want to do something so that you're not as irritable at home?

J: Yeah, I want to understand that behavior.

F2: What would they notice at home if you changed?

J: I could just shut them out and try to be easy on the kids.

F2:   Wow, how would you do that?

Do's and Don'ts When Participants Become Problem-Focused

Do listen without encouraging problem talk.

Do look for how participants are doing well.

Do compliment the participants' efforts.

Do look for transition opportunities to redirect the group to goal work.

Do, if necessary, ask participants directly about how much problem talk will be helpful.

Participants Who Have Not Worked on Their Goal

Occasionally participants state that they have not worked on their goals. It is helpful to accept this report and immediately begin pursuing exceptions to this statement. We begin exploring for exceptions by asking, "What was your goal?" This is a very useful question because it directs participants to review what they have stated they would do. It also helps trigger associations to possible exceptions to their statement that they have not done any goal work. Often by answering this question, participants will begin to recall examples of goal work that they have accomplished. We also ask, "Was there some little thing that you did that relates to the goal you set for yourself?" Many times participants have done something that they consider too small to mention. Our experience has been that these "small" events are great building blocks for significant change. The following case example is typical of how we find the small events that participants typically ignore as great opportunities for change.

JERRY

Facilitator 1: Well, Jerry, what have you done with your goal?

Jerry: It's been a really bad week, I haven't had much time to do anything. My truck broke down, and you know how it goes.

F1:   Was there something little that you remember about things related to your goal?

J: Not really, I mean this week was a mess.

Facilitator 2: What was your goal, I mean, the little things that you were going to do?

J: Something with my wife, like when we first met. I thought about that, and there were a lot of things we did like the flower thing.

F1:   Wow! You thought about some of the things that you did in the past when things were better?

J: Yeah, the flower thing made me think, but I couldn't do that because I didn't have any money, so I just picked her a plant.

F1:   You picked her a plant!

J: Yeah, a wildflower, roots and all. It was kind of dried out, but she really liked it.

F2:   Incredible! How do you know that she liked it?

J: She just smiled, and she still has it. I think she's going to dry it and keep it.

F1:   Amazing. Did you think it would mean so much to her?

J: No, not really, but things are a lot better, and I guess it is kind of a big thing.

F1:   Does this mean that you were right about your goal, that doing these little things from the past will make a difference?

J: Yeah, I can see that. I've been picking up things a little, too. She's working now, and it helps if I do more.

If, after exploring for unnoticed goal work, we find the participant has not done any, we reaffirm the importance of doing goal work and ask what the plan is related to his or her goal. We help the person create a specific plan by asking detail-enhancing questions. We also use a scaling question such as "On a scale of 1 to 10, 1 being working on this goal is meaningless and 10 being it's very important to you, what number would you give?" This helps the participant and us gain a sense of the level of commitment to the goal. Usually a participant will state a high number; if not, we pursue what can be done to increase the level of commitment.

Do's and Don'ts When Participants State They Have Not Worked on Their Goal

Do accept the statement.

Do look for exceptions.

Do ask participants to state their goal.

Do compliment any goal work.

Do help participants evaluate their commitment to the goal work.

Do help participants detail future goal work.

Summary

Helping participants use goals to create change in their lives is exciting. The excitement is often a result of being surprised by the creativity of people when they are in a situation that respects their abilities and holds them accountable for change. The process requires the facilitation team to be persistent and flexible. As can be seen from the case examples, questions and compliments play an important role in the process. It is important to remain conscious that the goal is a structure, which is used so that participants can create new meanings about themselves and the world around them. Ultimately it is less important what the goal is and more important that the participant creates new meanings as a result of the goal efforts. In this respect there are no right or wrong goals. There are only goals that are easier or harder for participants to attribute meaning to. As a result, it is critical that the facilitation team set a structure that optimizes choices for participants and respects the individual nature of each person.

Do's and Don'ts When Participants Report the Goal Was Not Helpful

Do ask what their goal is.

Do help them be specific about their goal behavior and the responses to it.

Do look for exceptions to "not helpful."

Do compliment, compliment, compliment.

Helpful Questions

Was part of the work on your goal was helpful?

Did you discover any clues about what would be more helpful?

What do you think you will need to do differently to be more successful?

Are there some adjustments that you would make?

6

Consolidating Change
The "Language of Success"

There is a temptation for some participants, especially court-mandated participants who do not voluntarily come for treatment, to view the final sessions as a celebration for having completed the group. Even though we respect this, we believe the ending sessions require a strong focus on accomplishments and constructions of future behavior. As a result of developing and accomplishing self-initiated, personally meaningful goals, participants usually have a positive outlook about themselves and their lives during the latter part of the group treatment process. The pertinent question, however, is whether they will be able to maintain or follow the paths they have started. A major challenge in the field of treatment of domestic violence offenders is the reduction of recurrence of violent behaviors after completion of treatment. Because of the brief duration of our treatment program, it is important that we help participants affirm and consolidate changes while further developing a road map for the future. In other words, from a therapeutic point of view, it is important to help increase participants' awareness of the positive changes so that they develop the "language of success" in place of the "language of failure."

We believe that several important therapeutic tasks need to be accomplished during the final sessions:

- Review goals, evaluate progress, and make future plans.
- Consolidate personally meaningful change descriptions and/or "new" identity.
- Develop connection between participants' actions and positive outcomes.
- Owning goal accomplishments.
- Acknowledge and compliment goal accomplishments.

Review Goals, Evaluate Progress, and Make Future Plans

Final sessions provide an opportunity to help participants evaluate how they have changed as a result of working on their goals. Often, participants have some idea that "things are getting better," although they may not have registered clearly what, where, and how they are better. Therapeutically, it is important for participants to develop a clear indicator of change so they will know where they are in terms of accomplishing their goal. Such a realization is important for participants to consolidate an image of "success." The personal meanings of change and progress are subjectively defined; scaling questions provide a simple tool for people to quantify and evaluate their situation and progress so they can establish a personally meaningful indicator of success for themselves. "Suppose when we first started the class, your problem was at a 1 and where you wanted to be is at a 10. Where would you say you are at today on a scale of 1 to 10?"

Besides evaluating progress, it is important to help participants assess how confident they are of maintaining their successes, for example, by asking, "On a scale of 1 to 10, with a 10 meaning you have every confidence that you will keep up with your progress and a 1 meaning you have no confidence at all to maintain the change, where would you put yourself between 1 and 10 today?" We want to help participants make a realistic appraisal of how confident they are about staying focused on the beneficial goal behaviors and what can be done to maintain those changes. Also, when participants speak aloud of their confidence, they reinforce the "language of confidence" and are more likely to create a confident image of themselves.

Our program also uses written assignments to assist participants in reviewing and consolidating positive changes and planning for the future. We routinely ask participants to "write down what you have learned from the group, and what you feel you need to do if you want these changes to continue."

Consolidate Personally Meaningful Change Descriptions and/or "New" Identity

The very nature of a "final group" primes participants to evaluate what they have accomplished and what their changes mean for them and their future. They are receptive to the notion that they are in some way changed by the process they have experienced. As the team explores what people in their social milieu are saying about the participant, a prevailing theme often emerges such as "the father who's there for his kids" or "the boss who listens" or "a man of patience." The development of such themes establishes that change has occurred and is now part of the individual's self and social context. The notion that a person actually becomes an "honest man" or a "caring mother" helps to solidify the change process; in many respects this process is the antithesis of diagnosing problems, since participants solidify descriptions that match the solutions that they themselves create.

To this end, we tend to help group participants in much the same manner as in previous sessions except that we focus more on connecting their goal work to the future while consolidating change descriptions into phrases that encapsulate the overall change that has occurred. Consolidating change descriptions often involves using the participants' own language in a manner that underlines their overall behavioral intention. This requires the facilitator to be alert for brief encompassing descriptors that may be useful. At times such descriptions include conflicts for participants, who may have to give up or modify previous ideas to accept their own suggested description. For example, one group participant noted that she would have to become a "soccer mom" to achieve meaningful change, but she did not want to lose her "right" to speak her mind and dress in the manner she preferred. Initially, when she suggested the soccer mom image, she implied that it was an unlikely future image for her. The interview team listened intently and helped her to explore the possibilities that might be available to her. When first asked to evaluate what her being a soccer mom would mean for her and her children, she saw that the description contained many of the benefits that she wanted for herself and her children, yet she perceived that her choice was to be either a soccer mom or "herself." The interview team remained curious and "not knowing," posing questions that helped her evaluate whether it was possible to be a soccer mom, while at the same time speaking her mind and dressing in the way she felt most comfortable. As a result, she was able to consolidate the two roles into an all-encompassing description that had the potential to work for her and her children. This example emphasizes the importance of taking participants' surface descriptions as meaningful territory for exploration and expansion. It also emphasizes the facilitator's responsibility to help participants explore areas of potential that they might otherwise overlook.

As a further effort to consolidate change, we also push a bit harder for participants to observe the broader impact that their efforts have had on their personal development and the development of others. Generally, participants are very receptive to this, since they have often already begun to recognize that their efforts have benefited them as well as the people they care about. When the social aspects of change are examined, participants begin to see their world from a wider perspective. They begin to notice the interconnectedness of people and behavior. For example, in most cases participants begin to reflect on the fact that doing something different and staying committed to a goal results in change, but not necessarily the change that they predicted. They notice that sometimes the people they care about respond favorably, and other times they do not. In retrospect, they often recognize that their goal behavior is most beneficial to themselves even when they originally designed the goal to affect the behavior of another person. For many participants this recognition serves as further motivation to stay the course. For some participants it represents a fundamental shift in how they view relationships. In either case it is helpful to explore how their goal-related efforts have affected the social dynamics of their lives.

Develop Conscious Connection Between Beneficial Efforts and Goal Accomplishment

Change is more likely to be sustained if people can develop a connection between what they have done and their goal accomplishment. Participants may use the "language of success" to describe their newly found identity as an "honest person" or "a responsible dad," or they may have confidence in their ability to make further progress. We believe, however, that for positive changes to be part of their lives, participants have to be consciously and clearly aware of the beneficial behaviors, efforts, and changes they have made that contribute to goal accomplishment. In this way, changes are no longer just random occurrences or a result of luck but can also be used in handling daily challenges.

"So, how did you do that, stay out of it instead of getting in the middle of it like you used to?"
"So, how did you figure out when it's time for you to take a breath and listen and when it's time for you to walk away?"
"How do you do that? How do you do that when somebody is irritable and you just let him or her be irritable without getting into it?"
"So how did you stop doing that?"

Another level of useful connection is between participants' behaviors and ascribed personal meaning. Joanna shared with the group the assignment in which she wrote a page about the most influential person in her life. She wrote about her mother, who had passed away 18 months earlier at Joanne's house. Joanne had cared for her mother during her last months, at her mother's request.

Facilitator 1: What do you think it says about you that your mother wanted to die in your home?
Joanne: I thought that maybe she thought that I was a good person, and she loved me with all her heart.
Facilitator 2: So, I guess this is worth all the effort?
J: I wouldn't take back anything, and I don't regret anything I did.

Other examples include questions such as "What difference would this mean to you, this stopping drinking thing?" or "What do you think makes you guys so committed?"

The tips for successful intervention include having participants clearly verbalize what they have done to contribute to positive changes, and searching for details. The elaboration of connection has to be powerful and strong enough so that participants clearly narrate, and therefore hear from their personal narration, about what they have done that was helpful. It may be tempting for facilitators to be the cheerleaders and "fill in the blank." However, it is much more important for participants to discover and construct helpful behaviors or meanings that are personally relevant in their lives.

Owning Goal Accomplishments

In our program, the participant is viewed as the center and the causal agent in constructing and accomplishing personally meaningful goals. We believe that maximum and long-lasting therapeutic gains are more likely to occur when participants own the treatment process and, ultimately, the successes. When a person owns the change, nobody can take it away. By asking "ownership questions," we create a context in which participants can consciously and clearly verbalize and elaborate their personal decision, and therefore their personal ownership of the changed behaviors. Ownership questions emphasize the participant as the center of change and the person who actively makes a decision or commitment to engage in the change process.

"When did you decide to do that?"
"How did you decide that stopping drinking would benefit you?"
"Did you always know you had this in you?"
"Where do you think it comes from for you, the commitment?"
"Where do you get that kind of strength?"

People are more likely to take ownership of positive change if they are explicitly aware of the choice they make. Such changes tend to be more sustainable because personal choice is involved in the process. Consequently, it is important to assist participants in making connections between their behavior or goal efforts and the choice that they make in the process. "Choice questions" ask participants to compare actions that they can potentially engage in and think about how or why they choose a certain action instead of others. In this way, participants have to mentally compare the choices that they made when answering the question.

"How are you discovering the more you give to people the more time you have for yourself?"
"How will you know whether to keep on hoping or to give up?"
"How has being aware of your anger made a difference for you and help you to start to listen to your girlfriend?"
"Is that what helped the most, do you think? Being aware of your anger, or was it something else that helped here?"

The Role of Compliments

Reviewing progress, consolidating change descriptions, making connections, and taking ownership represent a self-initiated internal feedback process in which participants use the "language of success" to describe their unique personal learning experiences. Compliments, on the other hand, represent an other-focused feedback process in which the facilitator, acting as the "community of other," provides external acknowledgment and appreciation of participants' goal accomplishment. We perceive both internal and external feedback as crucial in the process of consolidating change.

In our treatment program, compliments come in many forms, ranging from the use of simple linguistic cues such as "Wow," "That's incredible," "This is a great example," "That's a great story," "It's impressive," "Super," and "Great," to the use of questions that indicate surprise at the effort. In other instances, compliments are presented in the context of participants' goal efforts and involve more than the use of simple linguistic cues of positive affirmative or a surprise question. This type of compliment may not be associated with exclamation. We think this is a more powerful form because it helps connect the compliment to goal efforts and is less likely to be perceived as superficial, overly positive, routinized, or irrelevant to participants' context.

"Here there's this group, and you're the one who says you have a hard time being around people and you're really, really, shy, and now you can talk in groups and you talk more than anybody else."
"You know, I'm sitting here listening to you, and I got this image in my mind of this little stream, you know, moving through the forest, and pretty soon it gathers up momentum and speed, and now it turns into a river, and now you're just going downstream."

We perceive compliments as a powerful way to reinforce participants' goal efforts. They validate effort and instill hope. Giving authentic compliments is an art that can amplify positive experiences during final sessions.

Consolidating Changes

THE CASE OF JACK

In the following final session, we work with Jack, whose goal was to reconnect with his son. Jack begins talking about a secondary goal he developed to be supportive of his 10-year-old nephew, who was having adjustment problems. The time we take to talk to Jack is relatively extensive, given that there were seven other group participants in this final session. We chose to stay with Jack rather then redirect to other participants because he had a lot of energy and drive to share his goal work and, perhaps more important, to attribute current and future meanings to his behavior. This not only is important for Jack but also sets a powerful tone for all the other participants. This is particularly true because Jack has moved from being an extremely skeptical participant to a committed participant.

We begin by asking Jack to evaluate what his nephew has observed regarding the changes Jack has made.

Facilitator 1: What would your nephew say?

Jack: He would say I'm happier with myself. He would say I'm interesting and that I'm accomplishing things.

F1:   What would he say about your helping with his room and your helping him when he was scared?

J: He'd say that's great, he'd have me stay with him all the time, but he's got to handle that himself.

F1:   That's great. Let's hear about your other goal.

J: Well, it wasn't going very good last time, but then I decided to call my ex-wife's parents, and they said she had gone back to her boyfriend's place.

F1:   They had split apart?

J: Yeah, but they got back together. Her parents gave me the number, but the phone was disconnected. So I called her parents again and said, "I just called 'cause I was concerned and if they need anything and I have my own place, so just give me a call if you would." Well nothing happened for about a week, then out of the blue she called.

F1 and Facilitator 2: Wow!

J: She's back and her phone's hooked up and I didn't get to talk to my son 'cause he was busy, but we had a really good conversation, and she's going to bring him up to visit me on the 25th of this month.

F1:   Wow, that's incredible!

J: Yeah, that was really good; we had a really good conversation.

F2:   Your persistence is paying off.

J: It really seems to be. If nothing else, I haven't seen him, but I've built something to work off of.

F2:   It also tells everyone that you are serious about a relationship with your son.

J: Yeah, I was in a lengthy talk with her dad, and we talked about the Bible and stuff, which I read for the first time when I was in jail. I think he really appreciated that, and I let him know that I was going to put my son first and put what's happened in the past.

F1:   They have trusted you enough to make this connection. What do you think they see in you now that they didn't before?

J: I told them about these sessions and what my goal was. His advice was to put out the effort to see them. He said his daughter would keep him from me, but she is making an effort to make it work.

F2:   So what is it that they see in you now that they didn't before?

*The facilitator again pursues a clearer description of what people
see in Jack now. Jack is constructing the new Jack, and we want
the details.*

J: I think they see I care and that I'm really changing, not just talking about
        it. I had goals before these classes that I wanted to accomplish, but this
        helped and kind of put pressure on because it's weekly. I wanted to do it
        before, but there were no deadlines. That gave me motivation.

F1:   So you think that was helpful?

J: Yup, I'm sure I would have done something, but it would have been so
        random. When I couldn't get hold of her, I got a little depressed, and I
        didn't want to come to class and say, "It's not working," so I made a
        sideways movement. I went and started looking for a job that had health
        care benefits so that I had something to offer my son. That helped to
        keep me motivated to pursue the goal.

*It is common during final sessions for group participants to share
how they experienced the group and the pressures associated
with it.*

F2:   That's great. I'm impressed, not just with your success, but that you
        stayed so focused.

F1:   I know you want this relationship with your son, but what does this say
        about you that you persisted in spite of the fact it's been a difficult herky-
        jerky movement in that direction?

This serves as both a question and a compliment.

J: I always felt I could handle this. I've had bigger shortcomings than this
        that I've had to recover from. There's always some way to get through it.
        Sometimes you just close your eyes and hold on. You might not come out
        on the other side where you want, but you're going to come out on the
        other side. This showed me I wasn't putting enough effort in and maybe I
        was just closing my eyes through everything. You know, I do have some
        control of where I come out on the other side. I guess it showed me you
        get out what you put in.

*During final groups participants often reflect on the fact that
they have had previous problems. Sometimes they share details
or, as in Jack's case, simply share the fact that they have had
previous "shortcomings." This is not pursued by the facilitating
team. Instead, the focus is directed to expanding the solution-
based metaphor the participant is creating with the team.*

F2:   So it's not just holding on tight and closing your eyes. It's holding on tight
        and moving toward a direction in spite of the fact that the wind might be
        blowing you off course at times.

J: Everyone knows that you get blown back sometimes, and you have to
        move side to side, but it still helps me stay connected to my son.

F2:   Right, that's a real good point.

F1:   How confident are you that you will keep working on this goal?

The facilitating team routinely pursues the question of how committed participants are to continued work on the goal after the group is over. This allows participants to view the goal as solely related to them and what they want to do and what they find helpful separate from the group process. It continues the long line of questions that imply that participants are responsible for constructing what happens next in their lives.

J: I'm very confident, and I wasn't too excited about these sessions, but we're at the end, and I can see some things have actually happened since I've come here. It's kind of hard to admit. I'm in a different place now that I like a lot better.

F1:   So you're pretty high on that scale?

J: I want to say that I'm going to dedicate my life to this even when I'm working on other things. Because in the total picture I really am dedicated.

F2:   So, you're confident that you can keep the focus even though it won't always be the main focus. . . . It will always be in your field of vision.

J: Yeah

F1:   It's real clear to me, and I'm sure to other people, that you're real serious about wanting this relationship with your son.

J: Yeah, I think I need it, and as far as me seeing him, that will be a motivator. The more I see him, the more motivated I will be. It's a good conductor of what I should do with my time. It will keep me from straying and getting on the wrong side of things.

Jack is now fully creating a complex future that he believes will be helpful and productive.

F2:   Yeah, it's like a compass and the North Pole. It keeps you oriented to the direction you want to go.

J: The things that I used to not even think were wrong, I know are wrong. I now get down on myself and realize there are other things I should be doing!

Jack is not just concerned about doing the wrong thing; he now has an idea about the right things.

F2:   It sounds like you're holding yourself accountable for what you believe is the right direction.

J: Yeah, I'm taking on more responsibility.

F2:   I'm impressed that at times there is a pull to go in another direction, yet . . .

J: Oh, yeah, a lot of pull from a lot of different directions.

F2:   Do you think that in time the things that pull you away from your goal will be less difficult?

J: Yeah, I think it will be less and less as time goes on because if I move in this direction and stay on this path, it will become a lifestyle for me, and because of that friends that draw me in the wrong direction will fall away, and I'll be in this new routine.

F2:   Yes, it won't make it simpler, but it will be easier.

J: Yeah, it will be the path I'm on. I'll have temptation, but it will be easier.

F2:   It will be a well-worn path that you are familiar with.

J: And it's really improved the quality of my life.

F2:   How so?

J: Well, I'm contributing so much more to my relationship, whereas before I didn't want to get close to anybody. I would just go out and party and wall myself in a project.

F1:   And now?

J: I feel I'm accomplishing things rather then putting them off. I move from one good thing for me to another . . . instead of feeling bad about what I'm doing.

F1:   And that's different?

J: Yeah, it makes life better. . . . I don't worry.

Consolidating Changes

Encourage participants to

Review goals.

Use scaling questions to evaluate progress and confidence of staying focused on goals.

Make future plans.

Consolidate personally meaningful change descriptions.

Develop conscious and explicit connection between beneficial behaviors or efforts and goal accomplishment.

Develop conscious and explicit connection between beneficial behaviors or efforts and personal meaning.

Take ownership of accomplishments.

Verbally elaborate changes.

Ask for details.

Facilitators

Acknowledge and compliment positive changes.

Listen for change descriptions and help participants to elaborate, make connections, and take ownership.

7

Utilizing Group Process
The "Language of Sharing"

We use a group context in our treatment program. Unlike traditional group models that emphasize the transaction and interaction among group participants (i.e., the group process) as the primary venue of change (Yalom, 1995), we believe that people change more effectively when they focus on solutions. In other words, group process is rendered secondary to a person's active effort in search of solutions, which is essentially an individual exercise. On the other hand, we find it extremely valuable for group participants to observe one another and share their search for solutions. The existence of a "community of other" (Lax, 1996) whose members experience similar problems fundamentally alters the nature of treatment and embraces the curative factors of group treatment.

When people observe our work or read our transcripts, they are often struck by the fact that we appear to be doing individual therapy in front of a group. That is to say that both therapists are conducting therapy with one group participant while other group participants watch. From our point of view, we are conducting an interview that is being observed by the group and is affecting the whole group. Many participants feel a sense of relief just because they have found people in "the same boat." Group participants constantly evaluate how they will respond to questions we are asking and how the answers relate to their own lives. They also learn from each other's successes and failures. Thus, the group process is much richer than it might seem on the surface.

Since we believe that people change more effectively when they focus on solutions, we find it valuable when group participants hear and watch a search for solutions occurring directly in front of them. The interviewing team maintains a focus on solutions, future success, and what is working now. Gradually, the whole context of the group process becomes one of searching for or revealing solutions and heightened awareness of participant successes.

Goal Development Phase

Within the first session, participants realize that their role as observers is preparation for their role as interviewees. As a result of watching us interview other group participants, they realize that the questions they will hear from us will require complex constructions. This, in turn, stimulates numerous internal searches on their part to answer the questions that are being posed to another participant. This creates a degree of pressure to relate information and create possibilities. One result is that participants report that we made them think for themselves. If the process is viewed through time, it is apparent that the role of the facilitators changes from one of narrowly focused, supportive goal negotiators in early sessions to that of more broadly focused cocreators of meaning in later sessions. Early in the group process, within the first three sessions, the facilitators must help the group stay on task in developing workable goals. The participants are often anxious and sometimes poorly focused during these sessions. The facilitators must provide structure and direction and, when necessary, decrease problem talk and redirect the group to the work at hand. Problem-focused or distracting comments from the group are briefly and respectfully addressed, followed by a suggestion such as "Let's get back to the goal you were thinking about." The skills required of the facilitators during sessions 1 through 3 are similar to those of a director of a high school play, in that considerable energy is used to keep the cast on task.

Occasionally, group participants attempt to help one another. The facilitators must judge whether these attempts distract from the goal development process or instead are helpful. When this occurs, it is often useful to ask the group participant to whom the help is directed to evaluate the usefulness of the help. In doing so, the facilitators must always recognize and compliment the participant who is attempting to help. This underlines the importance of balancing the task of goal development with group participants attempts to play an active role in the group process. In general, we find it best to respectfully include the group when pressed to do so and then redirect to the goal development process.

An important exception to the relatively limited group interaction sometimes occurs later, in sessions 2 and 3. Once the facilitators have exhausted their efforts to help a participant establish a workable goal, it is sometimes helpful to request ideas from the rest of the group. This can be accomplished in many ways, but it is often most helpful to attain a clear statement from the struggling participant that help is requested and what type of help would be acceptable. In some respects, this process may seem a bit cumbersome, yet in the long run it pays dividends because it increases the level of collaboration and displays respect for the participant's desire for self-determination. Once agreed upon, the help of the group can be requested by asking the group an open question or by suggesting that the participants share any ideas they may have. Moving from one participant to another, sequentially around the circle, presses all of them to contribute and decreases the likelihood that one individual will dominate. Divergent views are also more likely to be produced in this manner, and, as a result, more choices are available for the group participant to consider. In spite of the fact that most suggestions are rejected, the process of including the group is often helpful because it can free up the "stuck" participant to develop his or her goal, if not immediately, then later. Group participants are respected for their efforts, participation, and willingness to help another person; they benefit from being part of a process in which being creative, contributing, and playing with ideas are more important then getting the right answer.

Goal Utilization Phase

Once the group moves from goal development to the goal utilization phase (approximately sessions 4–6), the role of the facilitators begins to shift toward inviting limited group feedback and interaction. The emphasis is on participants' reporting goal activity and responding to facilitators' questions, but the process becomes more open and inclusive of the group in general. During this phase, when group participants report goal progress, the facilitators may ask them to comment on the "good goal effort." Eliciting positive comments begins to expand the role of the group to that of supportive confidant. After the facilitators have elicited comments from the group on a number of occasions, participants often will begin to give spontaneous positive feedback to individuals who report goal-related success. If the group fails to initiate this pattern of relating, the facilitators can easily reinitiate it by asking participants what they think about the success of a another participant, or one facilitator can elicit comments from the other facilitator about the goal efforts. With very little effort the facilitators can help the group establish a complimentary pattern of sharing and recognizing successes.

It is helpful to conceive of this process in the simple phrase "You reap what you sow." Group participants freely build associations with whatever information they are exposed to and also tend to react in a reciprocal manner if invited to do so. The facilitators consistently notice and underline the successes of the group, drawing on the group's natural tendency to associate positive ideas and reciprocal compliments. The group begins to sow and recycle compliments and success stories.

Consolidating Phase

During the consolidating change phase of treatment, the group's role is still more restrained than in more traditional group process but somewhat expanded over previous sessions. The group is more spontaneous and positive in general and has established patterns of interaction that are primarily supportive, with little or no blaming talk. The facilitators ask questions that provide an opportunity for the group to notice and comment on the changes various participants have made. At times, the comments relate directly to the changes a particular group participant has made in his or her presentation, such as, "I've noticed that you are so much more calm. Have any of you noticed how much calmer he is compared to when we started these groups?" Whenever appropriate, the group can be asked to make observations that strengthen the awareness of positive outcomes and goal success or to confirm the benefit of the changes made. The facilitators can make a confirming statement and request further confirmation from the group, as in the following examples: "Bill, you have worked so hard to be more patient and a better listener. How do you think this has been helpful to Bill?" or "How do you think this will be helpful to Bill in the future?" or "How have you noticed this during the groups?" A second result is that during the final session, participants often comment on how helpful it was to listen to other participants' goal construction and goal development. They may say, "I feel like I had 10 goals because I felt like everyone's goal related to me."

Participants' Narration of Their Experiences of the Group Process: Language of Sharing

A goal-oriented, solution-focused approach to group treatment focuses on assisting individual participants to develop and accomplish their personal goals. Group facilitators do not explicitly utilize group interaction among participants as venues for positive changes. To better understand how participants view the group process, we conducted a content analysis of participants' responses to the assignment regarding what they have learned from the group. In addition, we included answers to one question from the follow-up phone interviews: "What things in the group have you found most helpful to you?" We received many comments from participants regarding the positive impact of group interaction and process in their learning and/or treatment experiences.

Curative Factors of Group Treatment

I Am Not Alone

One major curative factor of being able to listen and share is the feeling that "I am not the only one who has problems." The fact that "I'm not alone" or that "we all have problems" appeared to provide positive energy for change or at least made people felt better (less ashamed and more hopeful) about their situation:

- "I feel I learned the most from everyone around me. It touched me deeper because I am not alone, there are others like me, who seek to be all they can be by this training the domestic violence class offers."
- "I learned that I am no different than anyone else, we all put our pants on the same way. I don't have to hide in the back fort no more."
- "I found out I'm not the only one with problems and that we are similar to others."
- "Being in this class has made my life change a lot, meeting class-mates and hearing their problems, seeing that nobody's perfect, and everybody disagrees one time or another."
- "I realized that I am not the only one with problems."
- "I learned that we all have things, or problems to solve or work on. The old saying nobody's perfect certainly holds true."

We Have Different Perspectives and Ideas

Another identified benefit of sharing in a group context is the opportunity to be exposed to different perspectives and ideas that widen one's perspective, problem-solving abilities, or behavioral repertoires that are conducive to goal accomplishment:

- "I feel the class is helpful also by hearing how others cope and try to change things also, as I am able to try some of their ideas, too."
- "Listening to my other classmates talk about their goals and how or what they did to make it better, easier on them, all that gave me ideas. Everyone had their own little way to make these relationship goals better. Every little thing that helped in their relationships helped me in mine."
- "As I listened to others speak of their goals, and share their progress and growth, I examined within myself the same issues in my life. Each one touched on areas that I see I can still improve upon to make my life more peaceful and easier or smoother for the other people in my life."
- "I've found that I also have benefited, to varying degrees, from each participant of our group. Being exposed to others' situations has given understanding and insight I wouldn't have acquired alone."
- "I enjoyed this class because there were a lot of men in it, and just listening to them, their frustrations, expressing their feeling, because basically I thought they had a different outlook than women. Made me see them in a different light."

"Different" and the "Same"

Instead of being two opposing dimensions, "different" and "same" seem to complement each other in the change process. Comments from several participants vividly illustrate the juxtaposition of the theme "different" and "same."

- "I have learned that a lot of people have different kinds of problems in their relationships, and even though they are different kinds of problems, talking about them in a group, you hear a lot of things that relate to problems that you might not have had, and it helps you learn different ways to work things out in your relationship."
- "What I have learned over the past several weeks, during the sessions, is how we all had problems and such and the different ways everybody else used to work on their goals."

Positive Impact of Group Interaction on Participants

Many participants appreciated the opportunity to listen to one another's ideas and to share in a group environment. Such an opportunity appeared to have both broad and idiosyncratic impact that ranges from social benefits and affirmation to specific goal establishment efforts.

Social Benefits

Several members talked about the social benefits of sharing:

- "I really liked going to the class, not only to get away for my own time, but to see all my fellow classmates and hear the good things they had to share."
- "The fellowship with the class dudes was an interesting part due to talking and listening with others about their goals. This part of the class I will miss, because everyone has had a fun time, but serious about it."
- "I had bonded with the group and made some friends."

Affirmation

One identified social benefit is validation and support or positive social pressure from other members conducive to goal accomplishment or increased self-esteem.

- "I knew that I am a good person, but with this class, I now know that other people think that I am a good person, too!"
- "This class has helped me be a better person. Not only from what the counselors say but also the other students."

- "It may be that they know what I am trying to accomplish in controlling my anger, and that motivates me, not wanting to fail before them."

Specific Goal Accomplishment

Other members talked about how the opportunity to listen and share helped them to attain their personal goals or other accomplishments. As one member said, listening to others' experiences "sparks thought processes" that are helpful for individual members in their personal pursuits:

- "Going to class and listen to other people and their problem and it has also taught me not to think negative about everything that happens."
- "I believe that with the help of this class and my classmates and the instructors I have become more easygoing and friendly because of the shared personal stories."
- "This class has really helped me in many ways, being able to share my feelings, and what I've gone through these last 8 months has given me direction and problem-solving techniques. Sharing common concerns, interacting to solve problems has been educational in establishing goals and objectives in my life and in relationships."

The "Language of Help"

Helping each other is another mentioned positive attribute of group treatment. One participant referred to having "the help I will need from others." On the other hand, very few participants commented on the aspect of help, which is a contrast to the vast number of comments pertaining to sharing. It is obvious that the participants preferred the use of the "language of sharing" rather than the "language of help." This may say something about the mind-set of the group members, all of whom received treatment as a result of domestic violence. Such a language pattern probably reflects the more appreciated value of self-reliance and mutuality rather than the value of receiving help.

The message from our group participants is clear and unambiguous. They benefited both socially and therapeutically from the group process in significant ways. While maintaining an approach to working with each individual participant in a group context, we firmly believe that treatment for domestic violence offenders is more effective in a group context than in an individual therapy context.

Do's and Don'ts about Group Process

Do maintain a focus on an individual's goal effort.
Do invite helpful compliments and ideas from other participants.
Do encourage the language of sharing.
Don't let an individual's goal effort be sidetracked by small talk.
Don't permit blaming talk.

8

Useful Assumptions and Tools

Throughout this book we have provided numerous examples and descriptions of what we do. In this chapter we highlight tools that we have found helpful in working with domestic violence offenders. The description is not, nor can it be, inclusive, since there is always an element of creativity that continually generates new and valuable ways to approach life and its challenges. Our hope is to simplify the complex so that the reader can attain another perspective that will enhance the understanding of what works and what does not work. We have used the word "tools" to describe the solution-focused language structures that we use and also have expanded its meaning to include the assumptions that are critical in our work. In many respects these assumptions serve as the foundation for constructing useful questions and compliments. It is possible to be effective by using solution-focused language structure without exposure to the underlying assumptions, but we believe there are advantages to being familiar with them. One distinct advantage is that helpful questions and compliments are more easily discovered when the clinician is operating from particular assumptions.

Useful Assumptions

We routinely use five core assumptions in our work. These are not intended to be moralistic but rather are utilitarian and minimalist. They are not hierarchical, as one assumption may be more helpful at any given time. These five assumptions are as follows: (1) It is more helpful to not know than to know, (2) creating choice, (3) change is constant, (4) everything is connected, and (5) play invites change.

Not Knowing

Many mandated participants have experienced the feeling that other people know the answers better than they do, and they often have already rejected these predetermined solutions. These individuals come to our groups as if they were prepared to eat a most undesirable meal that they suspect we have cooked up for them. They are initially confused when we note, speaking metaphorically, that we have no idea what they want to eat or what might be most nutritious for them, while at the same time noting that we are confident that they will discover something useful to prepare.

They discover that we are interested in facilitating their cooking rather than cooking for them. In this respect, we believe that participants are capable of being the experts regarding their own lives. We find it very useful, if not necessary, for participants to discover their own goals. We define goals as being experimental. This allows participants to be the experts, while playing with possible solutions. We display confidence in the participants' ability to discover something that works for them while resisting the temptation to act as if we might know how to make things better for them. When we "know" the solution, we limit the possibilities and tend to decrease our drive to assist participants in exploring the possibilities. When we have an attitude of knowing, we also convey to participants that there is no reason to explore because the solution has already been determined.

We believe that the essence of change lies in the efforts of the participant to create and discover a solution. A solution can only be attained by the participant's search. In some cases, we have noticed that the solution is itself the search. If in our haste to help, we offer our solutions, we undermine the participant's opportunity for change. This is particularly ironic, since we have discovered that most participants quickly move to practical, concrete behavioral changes when they are given the opportunity to explore a range of options.

Our expectation is that participants will discover that they can create the changes that make a difference in their lives. The changes required are often not based on a dramatic new insight, a technique, or a profound emotional experience in the therapy room. Our participants discover that they are the authors of their lives and that they can and do write their own stories. The stories they create are made up of the little ordinary behaviors that they display and notice on a day-to-day basis.

It could be asked, "What is the facilitating team to know?" We know that participants are experts at discovering their own solutions, that when we are confident in their abilities, they arrive at solutions that fit them better and are more sustainable, that we can help them by asking questions that stimulate their personal search, and that we may help them see important changes and resources that they otherwise might fail to notice.

Somewhat tied to the position of not knowing is the notion of minimalism and economy of motion—or, as we have come to think of it, the economy of "notion." If the facilitating team were truly unknowing, it would seem only reasonable that it would naturally be curious and primarily ask questions, while the participant would primarily be creating solutions and/ or descriptions. This leads to minimal intrusion and intervention by the facilitating team and maximum invention by the participant. We find this type of relationship most useful because it optimizes the participant's involvement in creating and thus increases his or her ownership of solutions. By doing so, it increases the likelihood that the solution will be put into place and is, in fact, a solution. Metaphorically, this relationship is similar to teaching someone to ski. The first lesson the ski instructor must learn is not to help a skier up, once he or she has fallen. Doing so results in the novice skier learning how to use the instructor as an expert lifter and, of course, drains every ounce of energy from the instructor. The more useful approach in assisting fallen skiers is to ask a series of questions that helps them assume responsibility for getting up and assists them in discovering how to do so. It is helpful to ask questions such as "Should you have your skis pointing down the hill or across the hill?" "Where will your poles be most effective?" or "Should you dig the edges of the skis into the snow?" All these questions involve minimal effort for the instructor and maximum engagement of the novice.

The not-knowing posture is perhaps the most important notion that contributes to one's effectiveness. When the participant takes ownership of a solution, the potential for change is enormously increased. The type of solution is often inconsequential to the outcome. In many respects, the solutions appear to be randomly correlated to the problem. That is to say that they are correlated in some manner by the participant, but there appears to be no reason to believe that the prescribed solution is any more related than dozens of other possible solutions that could have been chosen. This leads us to believe that it is the seemingly random choosing of a particular solution and the participant's investment in describing it as a solution that make it useful. As with the fallen skier, it is not the getting up that counts; it's the fact that the person discovers his or her own "how" that matters most.

Creating Choice

Many of our participants feel that the people and events around them are controlling their lives. They are often described as controlling, while at the same time they are focused on how others control them. They fail to notice that they have numerous important choices. One of the more important aspects of working with participants is increasing their awareness of choice and encouraging them to view themselves as the experts regarding their lives. In the goal development process, we define the limits of an acceptable goal, but the specific goal is the invention of the participant. What is useful to one participant is sometimes not useful for another.

In a recent group, one participant decided to make his wife number one in his life, while another participant felt he needed to take care of himself and stop trying to please his wife. They both developed clear, specific ideas regarding what they would do to accomplish these goals, and both found their goals made a big difference in their lives. Such examples have convinced us that our participants are in the best position to discover what goals will be most useful to them in their unique life contexts.

Experience has taught us that participants construct goals most effectively when they are the inventors and designers of the goal. We tend to be most helpful when we act as curious onlookers who desire to know the details of how the goal will actually work in practice. Within the context of the details are numerous choices that can be made by the participants. We ask them which choices work best for them. For example, if someone buys flowers for his wife, we might ask, "How did you decide to stop at the flower vendor to buy those flowers?" or "How was buying flowers helpful?" These questions regarding simple details imply that the participant made an important decision purposefully. The question requires participants to consider their motivation and attribute meaning to their behavior. "What do you suppose stopping and buying the flowers means about you and what you have been learning?"

A facilitator who values creating choices makes a conscious effort to see alternatives in every sentence and interaction. Every opportunity to offer choice should be taken, including the first contact with a participant. For example, the facilitator might ask, "When is the best time for us to meet?" or "Would 9:00 be better than 10:00?" In the office, offering a choice of chairs and suggesting that the participant can move the chair to where he or she feels most comfortable is a simple way of emphasizing choice. Giving a participant an opportunity to select a drink—"tea or coffee?"—creates respectful exchanges that offer choice. When giving a direct assignment, we explain that participants have the opportunity to approach the task as they see fit. For example, "Write about someone, anyone who has had a positive influence on your life," or "Write about what you believe are the small things that make a relationship work." The manner in which these assignments are presented implies choice. In the first example, participants can pick anyone they choose; in the second example, they can approach the assignment from their own unique perspective.

Sometimes participants are initially confused or even irritated when we ask questions to which we do not know the answer. We suspect that they are in part bothered because we are not "playing our part" as the expert. In some cases, when participants feel we have betrayed our role, we find it helpful to share a metaphor that clarifies our expectation of our relationship with them. We do this by noting that we are not teachers and they are not in school. We explain that there is no single correct answer to the questions we ask and that it might be more helpful to approach the questions as if we were out on the playground playing with our ideas. This simple, straightforward explanation has been helpful in stimulating participants to relax and move into the "world of playful choices" and solution-building.

There is an extraordinarily important connection between not knowing and the notion of creating an environment of choice. Not knowing increases the participants' accountability for searching for their own solutions and as such implies that they have choices to make that the facilitating team cannot even contemplate. Not knowing requires that we suspend or release our assumptions. A common occurrence after we have completed a group is for a participant to wait for all the others to leave and then to tell us that at first he or she had assumed that most of the other group members would not make any progress. Such participants share their initial belief that many of the others were unchangeable and their surprise at how much everyone had changed and how dramatically their impressions of them had changed. We reflect on how wonderful it can be to be wrong. It is the element of not diagnosing, of suspending assumptions, that creates the vacuum in which group participants can create new constructions of who they are and who they want to become.

Do's and Don'ts of Creating Choice

Do assume that participants have the capacity to create an effective answer.

Do take a not-knowing position.

Do leave space for participants to respond. If you don't respond, it's their turn.

Do say, "I don't know."

Do say, "What do you think?"

Do be patient and persistent.

Do ask yourself if and how it is helpful when negative assumptions are created.

Do stop yourself when you take the role of the expert.

Don't give advice. If it's your idea, it's not their idea.

Change Is Constant

We find the concept that change is constant to be a powerful one, yet at times it can be difficult to maintain an awareness of it while working with domestic violence offenders. This difficulty is probably the result of the tendency to view people and problems as static or stable. From a descriptive standpoint, this is practical because it decreases the overall complexity of the issues that are presented. Simple problem descriptions are more easily tolerated than complex problem descriptions; as such, it is more convenient to categorize or describe people and problems using simple summaries rather than complex descriptions. There also has been a strong historical bias toward categorizing and describing activities as part of scientific research. Such an approach, however, tends to ignore complexities and to imply that individuals are, in fact, their prescribed descriptions. When people are categorized as "batterers," "victims," "depressives," and "manic depressives," it is easy to lose awareness of the fact that they are complex and constantly changing. When people do "change," the change is often negated by saying, "Well, they must not have really been that bad," "I guess they were misdiagnosed," "It's a flight into health," or "It's only temporary."

Yet, when change is the goal, we find it is more effective to become sensitive to any and all changes that are occurring that can be used. Effective facilitators know that all changes can be attributed to other changes or suggested changes. In our work we remain hyperalert for small changes that can be built or expanded upon.

Fostering Change

Do notice any small changes that are helpful.

Do ask questions that create a search for change that is already occurring.

Do ask questions that help the participant expand the change behavior.

Do expand the meaning of changes.

Everything Is Connected

In the biological sciences, for some time there has been an acute awareness that small changes in the environment result in other, related changes. As a result, small changes in an ecosystem are monitored because they are viewed as indicative of potentially bigger changes. No individual organism lives in a vacuum.

We find this way of thinking helpful because small and sustained changes have the potential for far-reaching impact. Small changes can be used in an individual participant's search for goals, as well as in the group process. As discussed previously, assisting participants in noticing the impact of a small change and of sustaining a change can lead to a profound shifting of behavior for everyone involved.

Within the group process, it is not necessarily discouraging when participants initially are negative or defensive. If only one participant begins to consider the potential for change, we are confident that this movement can be expanded upon. The process is similar to the impact of water on concrete. Once it has worked its way into a crack, it will relentlessly expand the crack. Even if the environment turns cold, the water turns to ice and becomes even more effective at expanding the crack. If the group presents as harsh and cold, the consistent positive and complimentary nature of the team becomes even more powerful as participants experience the contrast between compliment and negativity. Knowing that even a small shift will result in significant change because of the group's interconnectedness gives the facilitating team an important edge.

Early in the group process it is important to evaluate a participant's ability to cooperate in developing a goal. If the participant can develop a goal, this process begins a flow toward other participants' making similar efforts. If a participant struggles with goal development, it is important that the process of attempting to develop the goal encourages others to further explore possible goals. This is accomplished by communicating great respect for all efforts at goal development, even those that appear to be attempts to resist this task. This approach is guided by the assumption that all interactions in the group are interconnected. Other participants see this respectful process and are affected by watching the interaction. This tends to push the flow of the group toward cooperative exploring interactions.

The concept of interconnectedness frees the facilitating team to pursue changes that are easiest to initiate with the participants who are most likely to change, knowing that doing so will pull others into the stream of change. As more participants are pulled in, the current becomes stronger and more compelling. When the current becomes strong enough, the group pushes itself forward, increasingly interested in the changes that participants report and curious about how the changes are affecting their lives.

Everything Is Connected

Do elucidate the interconnectedness by asking questions that invite an awareness of it.

Do be patient. Any small change can lead to more change.

Do focus on participants who get the ball rolling and gradually expand on their efforts.

Play Invites Change

It may seem a bit irreverent to include the notion of play in a book that introduces an approach to treating a problem so utterly serious as domestic violence, yet we contend that play, as we define it, is an important element in the change process. Much of what children learn occurs through play. Every interaction has the potential to invite new learning, and children are receptive as a result of their playful attitude. Many of our participants initially approach the group as if it will be work. They spend a great deal of energy defending themselves from a potential attack and assume that we are going to attempt to control them, impose our ideas upon them, or make them do things that will require using more energy than they want to expend. Since many mandated participants view the "therapy world" from this perspective, we have come to respect the fact that the initial sessions will have a serious tone. In fact, we pace the participant's expectation that the group process will be serious by talking about "the rules and expectations of the group." We talk about how we expect participants to work hard, contribute in group, and complete all assignments. Early on this explanation helps participants feel comfortable because they understand the relationship with the facilitating team, yet for the team the goal is to shift the relationship into one in which everyone not only works but also begins to play. The transition to an environment that encourages and compliments a playful interchange of ideas helps participants to suspend their preconceptions about what is possible or potentially beneficial.

In our context, play occurs when participants allow themselves to stand back and entertain new possibilities of doing, thinking, and feeling. They begin to consider the "what ifs," the potential of what they can become. We expand the process by helping them play with the details of what this new piece of life will look like. Once a playful environment is established, participants' views of their lives change from high-intensity defensiveness to a broader, more open position. This in and of itself represents a significant change in positioning for many of the individuals with whom we work. This shift is similar to the experience young musicians have when making the transition from playing music alone to playing with others. Even if they play the same melodies as before, playing with other musicians changes the experience, the music, and their perspective. Our process is similar to jazz, in that we invite participants to improvise new life changes through, or over, a preset structure of goals. We allow plenty of room to play, while insisting that the participant stay focused on what will make a difference.

To begin playing, it is necessary to enter the world of "supposes," a world where almost anything is possible. Carl Whitaker, the famous family therapist, was an expert at entering this world. Sitting on the floor, wearing a three-piece suit while playing with a small child, he asked a woman what she thought it would be like to go on a date with her son-in-law. Although the woman was taken aback by such a thought, Whitaker persisted in pursuing details of where they might go and whether they would dance! The word "suppose" invites participants to enter the world of play. Participants initially anticipate that we will "impose"; instead, we "suppose," and in so doing begin providing the opportunity to create new stories.

It could be suggested that play could be taken too far and lead to a lack of focus, no structure, chaos, and a failure to address the critical issues. Participants might, for example, misinterpret the notion of play as an opportunity to avoid addressing serious issues. We agree with this notion and consider it critical that facilitators structure the process so that playful idea construction occurs within the context of developing useful goals and real-life changes. Strong, clear expectations regarding goal construction and goal utilization must be used to help balance the concept of play. In many respects, the play that we are talking about here is actually focused, purposeful play.

Fostering Playfulness

Do think about your work as the most wonderful opportunity to seriously play.

Do use words that encourage play, such as "suppose," "what if," and "what will that look like when you do it?"

Do wonder about the possibilities in your own life.

Do take the opportunity to create, doing activities you normally would not do.

Do make a point of playing.

Do ask yourself, "What would I be doing if I were being more playful right now?"

Do play with words.

Do notice how work is or might be play.

Do consider outlandish ideas that might be practically applied.

Do create a view of the world as offering endless creative opportunities.

Do know play is free and valuable.

Useful Therapeutic Dialogues

Often, the core assumptions discussed here serve as the foundation for us to construct solution-focused therapeutic dialogues with participants. The focus of such dialogues is on creating searches, eliciting and expanding descriptions related to goal efforts, rather than trying to understand the problem. Also, we use therapeutic responses to facilitate a process that provides feedback to participants regarding their goal efforts. We believe that people need useful feedback in the process of change. In our work, we favor certain types of therapeutic dialogues that lend themselves to constructing useful descriptions and providing helpful feedback. The facilitator provides direct feedback via listening responses, affirming responses, restating responses, and expanding responses. We also use a great number of what we call "evaluative questions" that help participants provide self-feedback by reevaluating different dimensions of their doing, thinking, and feeling.

Helpful Therapeutic Responses

I'm Listening

The importance of listening can never be overestimated in our work. When we listen attentively to what participants have to say, we convey the implicit message that we expect them to have something important to share. It is also their time to work. In addition, listening has been identified as an important component of building relationships. Being listened to by an attentive person is one of the identified curative factors of therapy. In our program, facilitators convey their intention to listen through the usual linguistic cues, including "Oh, yeah, yeah," "Hmm-mm," "Wow," "Okay," and "Right." Such cues not only convey the message "I'm listening" but also provide feedback to the participants that "I'm interested in what you are saying" and "what you are saying is important." These messages encourage participants to elaborate and continue their thinking process. Sometimes, facilitators may paraphrase the participant's statement or give a brief comment as a way to convey that they are attending to and understanding the conversation.

Affirming Responses

Affirming responses provide validation and affirmation of a participant's behaviors, feelings, and thinking. This type of feedback instills hope in participants, and encourages them to further pursue their goals. In our treatment program, compliments come in many forms, ranging from simple linguistic cues to questions that indicate surprise at the participant's effort:

"Wow," "That's incredible," "This is a great example," "That's a great story," "It's impressive," "Super," and "Great," "You did? Really?"

In other instances, compliments are presented in the context of a participant's goal effort and involve more than the simple linguistic cues of positive affirmation or a surprise question. We think this is a more powerful form of compliment because it assists participants in making a connection between the compliment and their goal efforts. Compliments given in this form are less likely to be perceived as superficial, overly positive, routinized, or irrelevant to participants' context.

"Here, there's this group, and you're the one saying you have a hard time being around people, and you're really, really, shy,

and now you can talk in groups, and you talk more than
anybody else."

Restating Responses

Restating responses simply paraphrase participants' words as accurately as possible in a manner that allows participants to feel that they are understood. Restating responses represent the facilitator's effort to share with participants what has been said as understood by the facilitator. They function as a mirror or sounding board that provides feedback to participants, further clarifying and reinforcing the described behavior, meaning, or feeling. This approach is particularly helpful when the participant wants to be heard and is not ready to explore solutions, as well as when the participant has accomplished something and is receptive to hearing someone restate his or her achievement. This form of recognition can be a powerful reinforcement for the participant's efforts. It also is helpful when the facilitating team is unable to create a useful question or is completely at a loss as to what responses would be most helpful. At these times, restating is almost always a safe, useful response. The rule is: If unsure, restate the participant's thoughts.

Expanding Responses

Besides listening, showing understanding of, affirming, and restating what participants have said, we also use what participants have said and expand their words to produce new meanings and new possibilities in their goal efforts. An expanding response is usually preceded by a restating response. Expanding responses are similar to reformulation techniques that have been discussed in the literature (e.g., Aronsson & Cederborg, 1996; Troemel-Ploetz, 1977).

"I hear you said your dad taught you something very useful in
this situation and now you're trying to pass on the useful
things."

Evaluative Questions: Creating Searches and Providing Feedback

There is no other language form that we work harder to develop than asking good questions. We videotaped and transcribed all group sessions for purposes of conducting process research of our program between October 1996 and January 2002. One session was randomly selected from each of the 14 groups. We conducted detailed content analyses of the therapeutic dialogues of these 14 sessions with the assistance of the software QSR NUD*IST Vivo (Nvivo). Findings indicated that facilitators initiated 51% of all dialogues, and 46% of those dialogues with participants are in the form of questions. We are always alert for questions that will trigger useful responses from our participants because we believe change occurs when participants begin to search for and create solutions. In this respect, a participant's response determines if a question was useful or not. Does the question help the participant begin or expand a search for a description of a solution? To some degree, responses are individualized, yet we find that certain types of questions seem to be more helpful than others and that some questions are almost always unproductive.

We follow certain guidelines in deciding what type of question we might ask. For example, we seldom, if ever, ask participants *why* they behaved the way they did. In our experience, asking a "why" question leads participants to search for explanations for their behavior. This is almost always unproductive because it forces participants to justify their behavior and directs energy away from efforts to move toward solutions. In many cases, the participant will actually create a well-formed reason for why change is impossible! If you have doubts about the negative impact of asking "why" questions, consider the response when someone asks a child why he or she misbehaved. When faced with this type of question, children will often search for what others believe is the right answer, and inevitably the "right" answer is not only unfavorable but also demoralizing for the child. In many cases, the child will form excuses or explanations in response to a "why" question, and these responses are seldom helpful. It is almost always more helpful to ask what the child could have done differently or what can be done now to make things better. We assume that participants are doing the best they can at the time and that trying to discover why they behaved as they did is unproductive or sometimes impossible.

What we have found most helpful is a group of questions that we call "evaluative questions." These differ from facilitator-initiated therapeutic responses because, instead of directly providing feedback to participants, they initiate a self-feedback process within the participant. Evaluative questions represent questions that ask participants to self-evaluate their situations in terms of their doing, thinking, and feeling. The facilitator abstains from making any interpretation of participants' situation or suggesting any ideas; he or she just asks good questions that help participants evaluate different aspects of their unique life situations. Evaluative questions operate from the stance of curiosity and convey the message that we believe that participants have the answers and we do not have the answer.

Exploring Questions

We commonly ask exploring questions at the very beginning of the treatment process. These are simple questions aimed at getting participants to explore and play with different ideas for developing useful goals.

"What are you thinking?" "Any of those possibilities?"

Planning Questions

Planning questions help participants to evaluate what action or behavior needs to be taken for positive change to happen. These questions focus on planning for future action and anticipating what needs to be done.

"Is there something you'll need to do to make sure that you stay focused?" "So how are you going to do this goal, then?"

More sophisticated planning questions assist participants in focusing on doing something different from what they have done before. It is also important to help participants evaluate whether what they are doing now as a goal is different from past behaviors. We believe that positive changes are usually associated with new and different behaviors. Repetitive past behaviors are more likely to maintain the problem rather than solve it (Nardone & Watzlawick, 1993).

"So what would you do different to try to get along better with your dad?" "How has being aware of your anger made a difference for you, not to lose your mind and not to say things that wouldn't be helpful?"

Indicator Questions

A solution-focused approach emphasizes establishing a clear indicator of change early on in the treatment process so that clients will clearly know when they have accomplished their goals and when they can stop receiving treatment. All too often participants know when they have problems, but not when the solution has arrived. Constructing a clear indicator of change is an integral part of the solution-building process.

"How would you know that you have accomplished your goal?" "Yeah, but say 2 months from now, you're going to bed at night, and you can't go to sleep, and you ask yourself whether you are still focused on your goal or not. And you ask yourself, 'Am I doing okay? Am I doing what I want to do?' How would you know?"

Exception Questions

In the process of developing useful goals, it is helpful to ask questions that lead participants to consider alternatives to their current behavior or questions that ask them to search for times when things were better. These are called exception questions because they ask participants to look for an exception to the problem (de Shazer, 1985). This type of question is often a "when" question, such as "When was the last time you and your wife felt things were going well?" Once an exception to the problem is discovered, detailed questions can help the participant expand on it. As implied, these questions ask for the details.

"What did you and your wife do when things were better that you are not doing now" "When did you do that?" "How did you do it?" "How often did you do it?"

Scaling Questions

We have found that scaling questions are a particularly useful form of evaluative question. They allow participants to affix a numerical value to their evaluation. They are also helpful to the facilitating team because they give a unique view into participants' vantage points that cannot be objectively defined, such as their motivation, confidence, commitment, and progress in the change process. As a team, we have often been surprised by the numbers participants have indicated when we have asked scaling questions. As a result, we have been able to build on participants' evaluations that otherwise would not have been noticed.

Initially, scaling questions can seem a bit awkward, but in time and with practice they become second nature. They begin with an explanation of the scale and then note the behavior that is being evaluated. For example, "On a scale of 1 to 10, 1 being that it doesn't matter that you get a job and 10 being it is the most important thing for you to accomplish, where are you at on that scale?" An interesting aspect of using numbers is that even though numbers have an implied value, the value in any given interaction is always to some degree negotiable. One person's "2" may be another person's "5," and a "5" may mean a person is halfway there, as opposed to not really committed. It is the conversation that occurs after the scaling question is asked that determines and creates the meanings of the numbers.

Effect Questions

Effect questions assist participants in evaluating what they expect to see happen as a result of their behavior or goal efforts. These questions help participants to clearly think about the impact of their behavior or goal efforts and what they want to accomplish by their actions.

"What are you hoping will happen when you are friendlier to people?" "Do you have any thoughts of what you're hoping will happen if you do this?"

One specific type of effect question is the "relationship question" (Berg, 1994). Because all behaviors occur in a social context or have social implications, we find it very useful to help participants evaluate the social connections that will support desired changes. To this end, social context questions are used to help expand the solution talk into the area of relationships. They ask for the details of the solution as it relates to others.

*"Who else knew that you were doing it?" "What do you think
will happen when you spend more time with your family, be
more of a family man?"*

Helpfulness Questions

Helpfulness questions assist participants in evaluating and delineating how
their behavior will be helpful in accomplishing their self-initiated goals. We
have found this type of question extremely useful.

*"Was it helpful that you were aware that you were angry?" "So
how will that be helpful to you if he [participant's son] finishes
his homework, if he does his homework?"*

Feasibility Questions

Besides evaluating whether certain behavior or change is helpful, it is important to assist participants in evaluating the feasibility of their behavior
or goal effort. Small, sustainable, and realistic goals or behaviors are more
likely to be useful for participants than big, dramatic changes because the
latter may set people up for failure. Also, a realistic appraisal of the situation
increases the chance of success.

*"Where it's easy and where maybe it's not so easy?" "Are you
feeling it's reasonable to do it?" "Have you ever done that in
the past?" "How likely are you to be able to do that between
now and the next session?"*

Connection Questions

Change is more likely to be sustained if people can make an explicit cognitive connection between what they have done and the desired outcome.
In this case, change is no longer just a result of luck or randomness. Participants will have more control in accomplishing their goal if they consciously develop a connection between useful behaviors and goal attainment.

*"So, how did you do that, stay out of it instead of getting in the
middle of it like you used to?" "So, how did you figure out
when it's time for you to say you know this is the rule and when
it's time for you to walk away?"*

Meaning Questions

When a participant makes a change that is defined as significant, it is useful
to help him or her describe the experience as having a deeper or notable
meaning. For example, if a participant cries with his wife for the first time

in his life, an evaluative question such as "What does this crying mean about you as a person?" gives him the opportunity to attribute important meaning to this event. In most cases, people will apply positive connotations to their behavior when the opportunity is given, such as "It means I really do care" or "It means I'm a sensitive person." This allows them to construct who they are and who they want to be.

Often, beginning with an evaluative question allows one question to be built on another, for example, "Do you think it would be helpful if other people knew that you are such a caring person?" "How do you think it would be helpful?" "What can you do to help people notice this?" "What do you suppose will happen when you do this again?" Notice that the first of these questions is much different from asking, "Do you think that it would be helpful if other people knew that you cared so much?" The first question focuses on the person's self, whereas the other limits itself more to the person's behavior. We generally believe it is best, when possible, to shift the focus to conclusions about the self. In doing so, the conclusion is not concentrated on a set of behaviors but is more generalized as to who the person "is" or wants to be. This allows for questions such as "As a caring person, what do you think would be helpful to do next in relation to your wife?" In this case the conclusion about being a caring person is already drawn, and it is now a matter of identifying what a caring person would do next. This question also has the benefit of strongly implying that there will be a continuance of the caring behavior.

Evaluative questions that focus on conclusions about the "self" can be formed in various ways.

"What does this say about you?" "What does this say about who you are?" "What does this mean about you?" "What does this mean about you as a person?" "What would your father say this means about you?" "If _____ saw you do this, what would they say this means about you?" "What do you suppose _____ would say this means about who you are?"

Ownership Questions

We believe that maximum and long-lasting therapeutic gains are more likely to occur when participants own the process of treatment and, ultimately, the successes. When a person owns the change, nobody can take it away. By asking ownership questions, we create a context in which participants can consciously and clearly verbalize and elaborate their personal decisions and, therefore, personal ownership of the changed behaviors. Ownership questions emphasize the participant as the center of change and the person who actively makes a decision or commitment to engage in the change process.

Jack was sharing with the group his new commitments to spend quality time with his children. "When did you decide to do that?" "Where do you think it comes from for you, the commitment?"

Much of what is said and how it is said is subtle and easily missed. Yet there is nothing more critical than having an awareness of language and its implications. It is important to keep in mind that the greatest value of any question is its ability to provide a structure that allows for creative, playful thinking and collaboration. Some questions quickly discourage such a process, whereas others offer a wide variety of opportunities for dynamic conversation. We strongly believe that words are our tools and that our effectiveness is determined by using words in such a way that they elicit useful responses. We try to provide questions that elicit a clear and detailed goal description, such as "What will you do?" "What will others see you do?" "What will the benefits be?" or "Where will this happen? Notice the use of the word "will"—a small word that carries the implication that the behavior is sure to occur in the future.

When a participant reports success in doing a goal-related behavior, we typically use language that solidifies the change, for example, "How did you overcome this fear?" or "Where do you suppose you learned to be such a caring father?" These questions use words that define the behavior as already accomplished. "You really went out of your way to work with your son. What do you think that means about you?" All these questions require participants to draw conclusions about themselves, ones that will likely build their own sense of accomplishment and confidence. We find it is much more effective to offer participants the opportunity to draw conclusions about themselves than it is to offer our own "insights" about the changes they are making. We find it is the participants' perceptions that count, not ours.

Do's and Don'ts of Therapeutic Dialogues

Do use language that implies the participant wants to change.

Do use language that implies that participants are capable.

Do use language that implies change has occurred or is occurring.

Do use language that implies the changes are meaningful.

Do use language that encourages participants to explore possibilities for change.

Do use language that suggests that participants can be creative and playful about life.

Do use language that conveys recognition of participants' evolution of their personal stories.

Do limit energy expended in unproductive areas such as negative, blaming, self-defeating descriptions.

Don't ask "why" questions.

When Doing Less Is Best: Vortexes and Black Holes

It is often helpful for the team to remember that most behavior and language can be used in some manner to help the participant move toward useful change. There are, however, circumstances that we call vortexes or black holes, which seem to suck the energy from the change process. Theoretical physics describes black holes as having such a powerful pull that they actually suck nearly all the surrounding energy into them; not even light can escape. The critical element for the facilitating team is to recognize when energy is being pulled away from building solutions so that it can be redirected. If this is not done, the efficiency of the facilitating team and the participants' efforts are diminished. In understanding this concept it is often helpful to think of personal interactions that have repeatedly been ineffectual.

For example, a participant was experiencing marital problems at the time of the group. He began to see that all the energy he was using to solve the marital problem was actually maintaining the problem. His energy was creating an enormous vortex that only served to exhaust him and his wife. He concluded that he would be far better off doing nothing, at least until he could think of something different. (It is interesting to note that doing nothing was, in fact, a manner of doing something different.) Realizing that if he did not allow his energy to drain into the vortex, he would have energy to do other things, he began to search for something he could do differently when an argument surfaced between him and his wife. His search produced the idea that he would ask his wife to play cribbage whenever it appeared an argument was on the horizon. Instead of allowing himself to use his energy to argue, he would focus on the cribbage play. The outcome was more positive than he had anticipated, as energy was freed up to enjoy life in a more meaningful and self-directed manner.

Recognizing a Black Hole

In the physical world, black holes are elusive, but in the world of language they are relatively easy to identify. The characteristics often include at least one of the following elements: (1) repetition of ideas that amplify or maintain problem talk; (2) one individual working much harder than another with no apparent benefit, particularly if this is one or both of the facilitating team members; (3) Evidence of attempts at problem-solving suggestions rather than solution-focused exploration; or (4) decreased energy of the involved individuals.

When any one of these characteristics occurs, it is often helpful to consider doing something different. Specifically, it is often most helpful to stop whatever you are doing and either stop sending energy into the vortex or do the opposite of what you are currently doing. Usually doing the opposite involves redirecting energy to other activities that have been neglected.

9

Working with Special Populations

Individuals Who Are Court-Ordered to Receive Treatment

Individuals who have been ordered by the court to receive treatment are generally considered challenging and difficult. The therapeutic literature and research focus primarily on voluntary clients, and there is little information on effective treatment of mandated clients. This is partly due to the fact that mandated clients are not viewed as good candidates for treatment because they typically deny that they have problems and often are defensive and suspicious of those providing service. Furthermore, mandated clients primarily view the therapist as an extension of the judicial system and anticipate that the facilitator will judge, blame, control, and possibly humiliate them. They expect that the therapist will take the role of the expert, and that they will have to assume a subservient, conciliatory role in order to meet the requirements of a treatment program. As a result, some mandated clients present as angry and hostile, in some cases harboring anger and resentment toward the person or persons they consider responsible for putting them in this humiliating situation. They feel that they have been judged, found guilty, robbed of their dignity, and now are being punished.

Traditional treatment approaches for domestic violence offenders have focused on the importance of convincing participants that they have problems and need help. Some treatment programs use confrontation in an attempt to get mandated participants to see the error of their ways. Most programs propose implicitly that participants must be held accountable for their past behavior and that such accountability is the first step to accepting responsibility and moving toward an improved future. Such approaches attempt to meet mandated participants "head-on," challenging their basic beliefs and assumptions. This requires considerable effort and confrontation and risks creating significant resistance. Under these conditions it easy for the facilitator to slip into unhelpful response patterns and negativity.

From our perspective, confrontation is very time-consuming, puts the facilitator in the role of judge, sets the participant up to be resistant, and

149

turns the participant-facilitator relationship into an adversarial one. In addition, being accountable and taking responsibility for past behavior does not help the participant ascertain what to do differently and can be done just to appease or placate the facilitator or the court.

How to Engage the Court-Mandated Individual: A Solution-Focused Approach

Solution-focused therapy invites participants to be the experts regarding their lives. A solution-focused approach assumes that individuals have the skills and ability to make the changes they want, as well as the ability to create a better future for themselves. According to DeJong and Berg (2002), respect for human dignity through acceptance and a nonjudgmental attitude is the foundation for the development of trust in the client-practitioner relationship. Working within participants' frames of reference and accepting their perceptions communicates a willingness to listen and understand. DeJong and Berg (2002) indicate that client resistance and challenging or confronting the client's perceptions play no part in the solution-focused approach. De Shazer (1985) has suggested that therapists think of resistance as a form of cooperation, that it represents clients' unique way of perceiving and being, and that it is more useful for the facilitator to view clients as competent, while searching for ways to cooperate with them. Solution-focused treatment enhances clients' competence by searching for strengths, building on them, and encouraging clients' participation and self-determination.

Working Collaboratively

Part of the task of the solution-focused facilitator is to demonstrate that he or she is not interested in controlling or dominating mandated group participants and is willing to work collaboratively with them. The challenge is to change the power differential so that participants recognize and experience themselves as having power and choice, and view the facilitator as a person who does not know the answers but who can help them discover possible solutions. In the solution-focused approach, the hierarchy of power is much less pronounced than in traditional approaches, since group participants are invited to be experts in their own lives, and the facilitator becomes the expert in asking good questions. DeJong and Berg (1999) suggested that co-constructing a basis for cooperation is the sole productive way in which to engage mandated participants. One way to encourage group participants' cooperation is to treat them with dignity and respect, help them see their own strengths, allow them to make choices where choice is an option, and let them know what is and what is not negotiable.

In this model, when an angry participant states, "I don't belong here, and I don't want to do the group," we respond in a calm, friendly manner:

"OK, so what do you want to do?" Participants are typically surprised by this approach. They expect us to tell them that they are court-ordered to receive treatment and that they have no choice. Instead, we look to them for the answer, thereby indicating that they indeed have choices. Letting group participants discover what works and what does not work for them is respectful and helps them understand that they must produce their own answers.

We do not try to convince group participants that they shouldn't be abusive or shouldn't drink. We indicate that we believe they are capable of figuring this out for themselves. We do not teach or lecture. By not assuming the role of expert, we are implying that participants have the skills, tools, and information they need to change whatever they want to change. Our philosophy is to cooperate in helping them reach their goals. By not confronting group participants, we give an unexpected and compelling message to those who anticipate that they will be judged harshly for their past behaviors. The message is that we are not going to try to control them. Participants feel valued when we carefully listen to them, and consequently they are more interested in listening to us as well.

A typical example of how this process is enacted is evidenced in our work with Eric, a potential group participant who, upon initial assessment, decided he was not going to attend the group, refusing to sign the required forms. Instead of confronting him and informing him that he had no choice, we asked what he was going to do instead. Eric decided to go back to the court and tell the judge he was not going to do the program.

A month later, Eric returned and requested to enroll in the program. We did not ask him what happened with the judge or try to reexamine his previous decision making. We treated him as though this was the first time we had seen him. Eric worked diligently on his goals during the group, and upon completion of the program he rated himself at a 10 (on a scale of 1 to 10) in terms of his commitment to continue working on his goals. It is doubtful that Eric would have responded as well if we had confronted him and insisted that he had no choice regarding his participation in the program or argued about his desire to talk to the judge. Instead, we did not interfere with his decision-making process, respecting that it would be helpful to him. As a result, Eric was able to allow himself to cooperate. In his final group assignment he wrote:

> I have learned that a lot of people have different kinds of problems
> in their relationship and even though they are different kinds of
> problems, talking about them in a group, you hear a lot of things
> that relate to problems that you might have had, and it helps you
> learn different ways to work things out in your relationship. I think
> it is good to have goals in a relationship. That way you can work
> on problems and if your goals do not work out you can think of
> new ones. In my goal, communicating with my daughter has

helped my relationship with her and her mother, and that makes me happy. And I think it makes all of us happier. I feel confident that I will continue working on my goals, because it makes me feel good and I think it makes my daughter feel good and her mother proud.

It is notable that this was written by a man who, when initially referred, insisted that he was not going to attend the program. We believe that by not confronting Eric, we made it possible for him to come on his own terms.

Focusing on Participant Goals as a Way to Engage the Mandated Participant

Goals are an excellent vehicle for eliciting commitment and developing initiative for change. When used effectively, goals offer multiple choices, imply that change is possible, and permit change to be generated in manageable stages. Goals also create the opportunity to talk about change in a manner that stimulates participants to view themselves and their lives from a unique perspective, one in which they determine where they want to go and how they will get there. People who set their own goals, in their own terms, are more likely to work on them and maintain investment in them.

The group participants' responses direct the session. Because we listen carefully to each group participant and ask questions directly related to the participant's responses, each person feels heard and is assured that his or her thoughts, experiences, and opinions matter.

Utilizing Referral Source as the Leverage Point for Constructing Useful Goals

Many mandated participants express confusion about why they are being referred. Facilitators frequently hear, "I don't know why I'm here, they just told me to come," or "I really don't have any problems, but I was told I had to be here, in order to get my children back," or "The court said I had to come, but I really didn't do anything wrong." In our groups we often hear, "I really don't have anything to work on, because everything's going fine in my life" or "It's not really my problem, she's the one with the anger."

Insoo Kim Berg (1990) has suggested questions that can be used effectively with mandated clients to facilitate cooperation and elicit engagement. Questions such as "Whose idea was it that you come here?" "What are they expecting as a result of your coming here?" "What do they think will be different?" "What do you need to do to get them to leave you alone?" "What will you be doing that will tell them you don't need to come here anymore?"

These questions are very effective in soliciting cooperation from the mandated participant. By exploring the answers to these questions, the facilitator helps participants to discover for themselves what they need to do differently. The questions imply that the participant has the answer, that the solutions to their dilemmas lie within them, and that they are capable of achieving their solutions.

Utilizing Strength-Based Questions as a Way to Elicit Cooperation

Strength-based questions point out that group participants are competent in some areas of their lives and that solutions can be found in these areas of competency (DeJong & Berg, 1999). The answers to these questions give participants hope about their future, helping them to recognize that they are competent and capable of addressing issues and problems. When they recognize that the questions are sincere, and that we are genuinely interested in their strengths, they become more engaged in the program. Examples of strength-based questions asked during the assessment phase of the domestic violence groups are "What have you done that you are proud of?" "What have you accomplished that took a lot of hard work?" "What do people compliment you on?" "What are some of your recent successes?" "Have you ever stopped a habit that was hard to stop?"

Use of Group Rules as a Way to Enhance Participation

Group rules are an excellent tool for engaging the mandated participant. The rules specify what participants must do to be part of the group: They must attend, they must be on time, they must participate, and they must engage in behavior change. The arrangement is similar to being on a sports team: You may not like the rules, but in order to be on the team, you have to play by them. In this respect the use of rules allows the facilitators to be somewhat removed from the role of control agent. By clearly specifying what is not negotiable, we also set the stage for what is negotiable (i.e., the goals), which are primarily the creation of the participant.

Do's and Don'ts When Working with Mandated Participants

Do elicit strengths and accomplishments.

Do affirm and reinforce any changes and strengths that are noticed.

Do help participants define what they want and how it will benefit them.

Do help participants redefine their perceptions of themselves through utilization of their strengths and accomplishments.

Do help participants deal with the choices they do have.

Do accept that the choices may be limited.

Do respect that some participants want to experience consequences.

Don't confront.

Don't demand conformity.

Don't extract confessions.

Don't be the expert.

Individuals Who Have Substance Abuse Problems

Substance abuse is a significant factor in the domestic violence population. Between October 1996 and January 2002, 61.4% of our program participants presented with behaviors consistent with substance abuse and substance dependence disorders. This is not to imply that substance abuse causes domestic violence, yet for many individuals it does play a role in the events that bring them to us for treatment. Such observations have led some professionals to conclude that domestic violence treatment programs should include a substance abuse treatment component.

The fact that there is considerable controversy regarding both the etiology and the treatment of alcoholism and drug abuse or dependency presents a challenge to a facilitator attempting to choose the right treatment. After all, numerous approaches are available, including behavioral, biopsychosocial, cognitive, disease, physiological, psychoanalytic, psychosocial, and Alcohol Anonymous, to name a few. It is not easy to integrate many of these approaches, since some seem to conflict with one another.

During the early development of our treatment approach to domestic violence, we ignored the substance abuse issue with the exception of requiring group participants to be sober and clean when attending their groups. We did not allow participants to have a goal of abstinence because it did not require them to actively do anything other than stop a behavior. It required *not* doing. In many respects this narrow and limited approach was useful because it shifted the focus away from the substance abuse issue and helped individuals get on with something new and different in their lives. In many cases participants began doing something other than drinking or using. Group participants often found that their new behaviors and evolving lifestyles did not leave room for alcohol and drugs.

Gradually we began to notice that some individuals would share the importance of stopping drinking or stopping drug use. They talked to us as if this was significant in spite of the fact that we did not consider it an acceptable goal. As a result, we began to listen intently to their stories of how they were dealing with or addressing their substance abuse or alcohol problem. We now believe that how we listen and respond to this issue is important to the success of these individuals. Eventually we developed an approach that held participants accountable for goal development separate from the problem of substance abuse, while remaining respectful and curious about what they were doing to decrease or stop substance use. We were intent upon not becoming problem-focused in this area; instead, we listened to solution talk and directed participants back to solutions when they drifted into problem-focused substance abuse stories.

Our emphasis remains on cocreating stories about what is working, combined with helping participants evaluate what they need to do to continue to be successful. It is significant and advantageous that almost every group contains at least one participant who has already come to the conclusion that his or her alcohol or substance use issues need to be addressed. Often such individuals surface during the intake or goal development phase and typically share the importance of stopping drinking or drug use. At times they connect their alcohol or drug use to domestic violence, and at other times they simply note how destructive it has been to them. They often have already taken action to change their behavior and in most instances have discovered benefits to these changes. When given the opportunity, they readily describe what is working for them and create new benefits and avenues for change when invited to do so. As a result, they stimulate other group participants to actively evaluate this important issue. Helping participants focus on their own plans for change in this area is consistent with our experience that the vast majority of individuals with substance abuse issues change as a result of their own efforts, usually without outside intervention.

The following example illustrates how the team respects participants' effort to address their substance abuse issues while holding them accountable for goal development.

Larry: I've been thinking about this goal thing, and I think I need to not drink. . . . I know that since I've stopped that things are better because drinking, well, it gets me in trouble.

Facilitator 1: Larry, stopping drinking is not considered an acceptable goal because the goal has to be something that you do, rather than not do. So you will need a different or additional goal for this group. I'm curious how stopping drinking has made a difference for you.

We want to immediately let Larry know that he must work on a goal in which he actually does something new while also letting him know we are interested in how stopping drinking will be helpful.

L: Well, my wife, she isn't always complaining about me going to the bar, and I'm around more now.

Facilitator 2: How does that make a difference to you?

L: We don't argue as much, and it's calmer if we do. She still drinks some, which kind of bugs me, but things are calmer.

F2: How important is that to you, that it's calmer, let's say, 1 is it doesn't really matter and 10 is it's real important?

L: It's important, like a 9 or maybe a 10.

F1: What tells you it's a 9 or 10?

L: I've got responsibilities now, and I'm getting too old for this stuff. . . . I see my friends, and I see my dad, and I'm not going to end up like that.

F2: What will tell you that you are doing life different from your dad?

L: (pause) My dad was in the hospital last week, and he's going to die because he won't stop drinking, and I told him that, but I know he's going to keep doing it. I'm not doing that to my kids. I'm doing it different. I decided that I can't stop him, but I can do something about me.

F1: Wow, you are really serious about having a different life for you and your family.

L: Yeah, I guess I am.

F2: So, stopping drinking and doing something different is extremely important to you?

This statement both respects Larry's stopping drinking and reaffirms doing something different.

L: Yeah, it is.

F1: What would your mom tell you about this?

This question is a "shot in the dark" in that Larry has not said much about his mother and his response is not predictable, yet it allows Larry to assess how his social network is responding to the changes he is making. It also allows the facilitation team to know more about Larry's social context and possible resources. If Larry shares that his mother is an alcoholic who doesn't care about what he does or who he becomes, the team can only be more impressed by his intention to live his life differently. When the team responds to Larry from this point of reference, there are no bad answers. All responses can be helpful.

L: She's already noticing a difference, and she's proud of me.

F1: That's great that she believes in you and supports you!

L: Yeah, it helps, but I'm the one who has to do it every day.

F2: What do you need to keep on doing to be successful?

This question not only helps Larry assess what to keep doing but also defines him as already successful.

L: You know, when I get out of work I drive past the bar, and I see all those trucks, I know all those guys, and that's tough, but I just think about my dad, and I keep on driving. That's the most important thing.

Larry could have said that he needed to continue to see his alcohol and drug counselor or that he needed to stay focused on being humble by working cleaning floors at the church every Friday night. The important aspect of the interaction is that Larry

*is defining what will work for him; he is defining his own
solution or treatment plan.*

F1:   So driving past and thinking about your dad is huge for you?
L: Yeah, because I'm the kind of guy that can make up my mind to do some-
        thing and stick with it. I just needed to be clear about this.
F2:   Is there anything that would make it more clear to you?
L: (pause) Losing my kids, but I'm not going to do that, that isn't necessary,
        and I'm not going to do that to them.
F2:   You're really intent about this change you've made, not only for yourself
        but also for your children.
L: Yeah.
F1:   Does talking about this give you any ideas about what you might want to
        do for your group goal?

*Even though we could have expanded on the details of what
Larry could do in this area, we decide to shift to helping him
define his goal for the group; we know from experience that
Larry's goal work will no doubt dovetail with his effort to remain
free of substances. In later groups we will help Larry assess how
he is doing regarding staying away from alcohol and the specifics
of how and what he is doing differently. This allows Larry to
reaffirm his work in this area.*

"Waking Up"

A second common presentation of substance or alcohol use occurs toward
the end of the group process. In such cases participants have noticed that
alcohol impedes their goal efforts, or sometimes participants will share that
they are evaluating whether it is a problem for them. Often they will note
that another participant's comments have stimulated them to consider how
their own alcohol or substance use is affecting their life. We refer to this as
"waking up." These individuals present wonderful opportunities to help all
participants evaluate what works and what does not work, to develop commitments to change and to begin doing something different.

Jim: You know, I haven't said anything about this, but I stopped drinking and
        using because I knew it made things worse. Actually I stopped using
        about 4 months ago when I went to jail, and then the last month I
        haven't been drinking, and then last week my friends were kind of teasing
        me about it when we were at the lake. They were seeing if I would drink,
        my wife even offered me a drink. My friends were wondering if I was go-
        ing to get real crazy because I am a wild man when I drink.
Ppt1:   Well, you know, I can't do none of that.
J: Yeah, I thought a lot about what you said when these classes first started,
        and that got me thinking a little. . . . But I had one beer, and then I just
        hung out with my kid down by the water.

Facilitator 1: Did that work for you?

J: Yeah, I guess it did. I didn't get all crazy and act like a wild man, and I'm changing a lot, you know, and growing up. You wouldn't believe how different this is for me.

Facilitator 2: You're a young man who cares about more important things.

J: Yeah, more grown up and wanting my kid to have a good life.

F1:   What did your wife think about all this?

J: I think she was real nervous at the lake, but she was happy when we got home that night. I'm just not sure about the drinking.

F2:   What would your daughter tell you about the drinking if she could really tell you what she thought?

Jim's daughter is 9 months old.

J: She would tell me to get rid of it altogether, I'm sure of that.

F1:   How important is that advice to you?

J: Pretty darn important. She means everything to me.

F2:   How will you know that you're on the right track?

J: I know I'm on the right track. I know I'm not interested in being a wild man; it isn't worth it to me anymore. I think if I drank over two beers I would be in trouble, and I don't know if I should drink at all.

F1:   I guess that's where your daughter comes in.

J: Yeah.

When working on substance abuse issues, we find it most helpful to work in small time segments. Jim is clearly struggling with the question of whether he can drink in a controlled manner, or is that too risky? His own projective description of his daughter's advice is to stop drinking, although he knows himself as a person who drinks and is just beginning to consider an alternative identity. He has made significant commitments to himself, his daughter, and his family and is further evaluating what more he needs to do. We leave him with questions while being careful not to push him into a corner. After all, it must be his choice, and we are greatly impressed by how far he has come already.

Treatment Story and/or Solution Story

Individuals who are actively addressing substance abuse problems are unique in how they approach resolving this issue. Such individuals can be seen as belonging to two distinct groups, those who view their problem as requiring "treatment" and those who view the problem as one that they can address by making adjustments in their own behavior.

In working with individuals who have identified substance abuse as a problem that they can address, it is important to begin by exploring their "solution stories," that is, how they began to recognize that they need to do something different and how and what they have done that has made a difference to them. We have discovered that people are unique in their solutions, with some people finding success with highly structured, complex solutions and others with simple, straightforward rules of thumb. We respect participants' solution constructions by showing genuine interest in how they make their solutions work.

We have concluded that it is particularly important in the arena of substance abuse to help individuals evaluate what they need to do against the backdrop of their social milieu. For example, it is not uncommon for people who have had recurrent alcohol problems to say that they need to stop drinking, yet they often fail to recognize in what way it is important to them. The initial reasons for "stopping drinking" are often related to the problem context: "I always get in trouble when I drink," or "She's going to leave me if I drink." It is beneficial to help participants discover how it is important to them in the broader context, specifically the nonproblem context. To some degree we view change as solidified in the future context and the problem as solidified in the past context. This recognition leads us to pursue the future benefits of stopping or decreasing substance use. Thus we ask questions that facilitate searches for what these changes would consist of and who the benefactors of this new life might be. In many cases the benefactors are the group participants' children, spouses, employers, and themselves. We find that focusing on what a participant's child notices or would notice as a result of the parent's stopping or decreasing substance usage provides powerful motivation for change. This often leads participants to reflect on the damage they have caused themselves and others. When this occurs, we accept that temporarily reflecting on the past is part of the transition to future change. When the opportunity arises, we redirect to the future story that they are creating for themselves.

Participants Who Create an Alcohol and Drug Treatment Story

As noted earlier, some participants view themselves, the problem, and the solution from a specific preconceived framework. Often this self-imposed framework requires participants to receive some type of treatment. The fact that participants not only view their problems from a distinct perspective but also view the solutions from what might appear to be an equally distinct point of view is extremely important. For example, group participants may view drinking as a problem that possesses and controls them, and they may have attempted multiple solutions that require extraordinary effort. At times such participants remain committed to what appear to be nonsolutions with extraordinary persistence due in part to preconceived notions regarding what should work. They may even have been told by people they respect that they require specific treatment with which they must comply. When they do not succeed, they may blame themselves for not trying hard enough and may be sensitive to a similar message from others. This can lead to a pattern of trying harder in ways that are not effective.

When this type of situation presents itself, we find it most helpful to not directly challenge the participant's description of the problem or attempts at resolution. Doing so generally provokes the participant to defend with vehemence the problem description and the attempted solutions. It is often more productive to gradually assist the participant in evaluating and re-creating a "solution story." This requires vigilance on the part of the facilitation team so as to notice opportunities that permit the participant's evaluation of what is and is not working. As this evaluation process proceeds, the opportunity to help the participant determine possible modifications to the "solution story" becomes available.

When the participant's preconceived framework includes the requirement that he or she be treated, the "solution story" is more aptly described as the "treatment story" or a "solution/treatment story." Typically, participants who are focused on a predetermined "treatment story" such as "rehab" or AA meetings have not evaluated in what way this treatment is or will be helpful to them. Assisting participants in making such an evaluation has distinct advantages, including increasing commitment to a "treatment story that works," as well as the potential of modifying a treatment story that is not optimal or even disadvantageous. It is extraordinary how often participants are unable to identify how a particular preconceived treatment will be helpful and yet how capable they can be in identifying what has been and will be helpful to them in the future once they are given the opportunity.

It is often this opportunity to evaluate that allows participants to pursue a solution or begin to construct a treatment story that offers a specific plan for change. It is also clear to us that participants become more invested and assume more responsibility when they design their own treatment. It is critical that the preconceived ideas of the facilitator not interfere with this process.

In our experience, facilitators often have strong biases regarding alcohol and drug treatment. We find it most helpful to keep our biases out of any exploration so that participants are free to design solutions that make sense to them. For example, if a participant states that he or she needs to go to a support group two times every day, we never imply that doing so is excessive or wrong; rather, we ask how doing so will be helpful. We always assume that the participant will describe how this works or will be able to begin exploring a useful modification.

The hallmark of all change processes is assisting participants in seeing that they are the creators of solutions rather then being "possessed" by a problem. A solution-focused approach, particularly in the area of alcohol and drug use, does not challenge the participants' descriptions of the problem. Doing so only encourages participants to defend their behavior.

Do's and Don'ts When Working with Participants Who Have Problems with Drugs and Alcohol

Do listen for alcohol and drug successes.

Do encourage details of successful treatment stories.

Do encourage details of solution stories.

Do listen respectfully to alcohol- and drug-related misery and redirect to solutions when the opportunity arises.

Do respect all treatment and solution options.

Do create a playful dialogue regarding alcohol and drug issues.

Don't impose preconceived notions about alcohol and drug treatment.

Individuals Who Are Angry or Aggressive

Most participants start the program with the intention of completing the group so that they can comply with a court order and "get the authorities off my back." Our job is to help them be successful in reaching their immediate goal and to hold them accountable for expanding their goals in a manner that is consistent with making important and valued changes in their lives.

We seldom deal with overtly aggressive participants and have experienced no physical violence in our groups, yet many of the participants we see are angry, and occasionally they are verbally aggressive and hostile. When verbally aggressive behaviors do occur, they typically happen during the assessment phase or during the first few group sessions. After the first few sessions there is seldom any angry or aggressive behaviors, probably because most group participants begin to view the facilitators as respectful of them, not interested in controlling them, and very interested in having them benefit from their experience in the program. Participants also become focused on how they can stay in the group by developing and working on a goal of their choice. Using time to argue or to be aggressive becomes an expensive proposition because it decreases the amount of time available to plan and do something useful. Planning to do something useful and talking about what is working are requirements for staying in the group. In later sessions participants typically are so busy working on their goals and improving the quality of their relationships that there is no room or desire for a negative process, and defiance is often replaced by cooperation.

When anger or aggressive behavior does occur, we find it most helpful to view it as the best attempt the participant can make at the time to resolve the immediate issue he or she is facing. This is not to say that aggressive behavior is acceptable or effective in resolving problems. It is, instead, a recognition that facilitators are more effective in creating change when they maintain the assumption that people are doing their best at any given time. When the facilitators entertain other assumptions, such as "this person is sick, mean, sadistic, untreatable, or oppressive," they are less likely to recognize or even notice the potential for meaningful change. It is understandable, for instance, that group participants may be angry, hurt, and fearful. From their point of reference, their rights have been taken away, and they are being controlled, judged, and misunderstood by the "system." They have to pay large court expenses and may have spent time in jail. Some may have lost their jobs and families. Many participants feel the district attorney, the police, and the courts have mistreated them, and they may expect the group facilitators to treat them in a similar manner. In addition, most participants have never participated in a group and do not know what to expect. Facing the unknown can be a powerful trigger for anxiety.

With anger comes risk not only for the facilitators but also for the participants themselves, as well as other participants. Because of this, it is important to consider how to hold participants accountable for change while decreasing the risk of aggression.

There are a number of important aspects to addressing potentially aggressive individuals. These include (1) creating a safe and predictable environment, (2) monitoring the facilitator's emotional responses, and (3) defusing angry reactions.

Creating a Safe and Predictable Environment

It is especially important to create a safe and predictable environment for everyone involved in the process because doing so decreases confusion and increases the likelihood of successful outcomes. A safe environment also increases the confidence of the facilitators and thus often decreases the anxiety of the participants. The facilitators should be confident that they have the support necessary to accomplish their job. As a general rule, all safety considerations should be addressed prior to a challenging situation arising, thus allowing the full attention of the facilitators to be focused on the participants and on immediate issues rather than on safety-related issues.

From a structural standpoint this means that facilitators should have a safe physical environment, including emergency support, if necessary. The environment should be reasonably comfortable yet free of unnecessary objects that might be thrown or used to hit. It is often helpful to survey an interview room while considering the following questions: "What objects create or decrease risk of injury?" "If a participant got out of control, what would I do, and how would I do it?" "Who would help, and how would they know I needed help?" Consider asking these questions with a colleague or friend present in the room. This can be particularly helpful because it generates more ideas and options. As a general rule the facilitators and other participants should have access to leave if necessary and should consider their placement in the room with regard to their personal safety. They also should be clear about who is available to help and how help will be attained. Considering the time of day appointments are set and the availability of other staff can be useful. In our clinic setting, when voices are raised, a staff person outside the room begins to monitor the situation and is ready to respond. When the volume or content reaches a level of concern, that person will call or knock on the door to allow for "a break in the action." This gives space for the cooling of emotion and helps the participant pause to regain composure. Basic agreements about how and when support will be provided are an important part of establishing a safe working environment.

Few experiences are more frustrating to participants than being told one thing by one person and another thing by someone else. Thus, it is critical that the intake and group process be organized, systematic, sensible, and predictable. This is particularly important during the intake and assessment process, when participant anxiety and tension generally are high. One of the best approaches is to have one person address all information requests and complete the intake process. In our experience, this significantly decreases miscommunication.

Prior to or during the assessment, every opportunity is used to explain as thoroughly as possible to participants what the group will be like, what will be expected of them, and what they can expect from us. Setting clear, reasonable expectations and offering as many choices as possible helps participants feel more comfortable and less controlled. We suspect our focus on solutions rather than problems also contributes to participants feeling more at ease. We convey that we are interested in participants and what they want to accomplish and are not interested in controlling them. We elicit information on what they like about themselves and what others like about them. We explain that although the goal process may involve hard work, we will do whatever we can to help them complete the group successfully. We encourage them to ask any questions they may have about the group process.

At intake and later at the first group session, the rules of the program are reviewed as a way of setting clear parameters for what will and will not be tolerated in the group. The second rule clearly states, "Violence of any sort in unacceptable. Any use of violence will result in termination from the program." We let participants know from the beginning what is negotiable and what is not. Violence within or outside of the group is not acceptable or negotiable.

Monitoring the Facilitators' Emotional Responses

Even though creating a safe, predictable environment with reasonable expectations decreases the potential for aggression, some participants still present with anger, and it is critical that the facilitators be capable of responding in a useful manner. To be effective, the facilitators must be calm and clear about their roles. Clarity about the facilitators' role often contributes to a calm presence, and calmness contributes to a sense of clarity, both of which are helpful during stressful situations. The clarity is not about what the participant needs to do but about the facilitators' role. The facilitators must be clear that they do not need to fix, correct, confront, control, or educate. Once limits are set and expectations are agreed upon, the role of the facilitators is to help the participant explore what works *with* the participant. This may include helping some participants evaluate whether their anger is working for them, is working against them, or is distracting them from accomplishing what they really want to do.

It is important to keep in mind that addressing anger is not, in our opinion, the same as "treating domestic violence." When necessary, addressing anger directly with participants is done to help them more effectively use the program. In many respects anger is a barrier that for some participants interferes with their ability to work with others. Some participants, by virtue of their behavior, insist that this barrier be addressed before they move on to more important goals. When this is the case, we want to effectively help them remove the barrier.

Defusing Angry Reactions

When participants become angry, it is helpful to ask, "Would it be helpful to attend to this directly, indirectly, or ignore the response?" Because an angry statement can draw attention, it is easy for the facilitators to assume that a direct, balanced response—one that meets force with an equal amount of force—is required to immediately address the issue. In our experience this is often the least helpful response. It is often most helpful to react with considerably less intensity and in a very respectful manner. Doing so allows the participant to experience a lack of resistance as if he or she were punching the air. This creates a circumstance that increases the likelihood that the participant will evaluate the behavior. When participants experience this response from the facilitators, they usually quickly either become calm and refocus on other issues or increase the intensity of their reaction. When they increase or maintain the same level of intensity, it is often helpful to continue to remain calm, with minimal reaction. This again challenges participants to do something different as they attempt to react against no reaction. When this occurs in the group setting, the group will often react by encouraging the participant to move on to a more productive position. Group participants do this either with direct verbal suggestion or by ignoring the anger and moving on to other issues. During this process it is particularly important not to ask the individual to calm down or to argue with him or her; the participant often experiences this type of response as disrespectful. In most circumstances participants are able to calm themselves and develop a plan for the immediate future.

It is sometimes difficult to determine when a participant is ready to "get back to work," and as a result it is necessary to either ask him or her directly or to suggest that there is important work to do. In the group setting, we do this by asking questions such as "Would this be a good time to think about what you are going to do for your goal?" or "What is your goal?" or "What work have you done related to your goal?" At times it is helpful to shift the focus to another group participant by asking similar questions of that person.

One of the more difficult situations occurs when a participant directs anger at one of the facilitators, for example, as a result of a misunderstanding in which a participant feels offended. When this occurs, we find it most helpful for the least-focused-on facilitator to take the lead in defusing the situation, usually by asking questions that help us better understand the participant's point of view, then shifting to helping the person determine what would help him or her feel more comfortable. At the beginning of this process, the facilitator whom the anger was directed at remains mostly silent. In our experience it is often best for this person to do nothing until the situation is less emotionally charged.

It is often helpful to slow the pace of the interaction so that there is more time for everyone to think clearly about what is being said. When the hostile group member asks a question, we take our time responding, slowing the pace and assuring the participant that we want to be very thoughtful in responding. As angry participants regain a sense of control, they are often apologetic and seek some manner of saving face. During these times we find it best to be highly respectful to them and to offer them every reasonable opportunity to regain their composure and position in the group. In our limited experience with this type of situation, we find that participants often apologize to the group and the facilitators for any discomfort they may have created. They often realize that they misunderstood and overreacted. We find it helpful to listen to their new understanding regarding our relationship with them and then to refocus on what they are going to do that will make a difference for them in the future.

The following case example describes an individual who remained angry well into the group process and initially struggled to use the group in a negative way. The transcript provides insight into how such a challenging situation can be addressed from a calm nonexpert position.

Tim presented at the assessment interview with hostility, verbal abusiveness, frequent swearing, and yelling. He was angry with the judge and the district attorney. He insisted that he did not do what the courts said he did, and stated he only acted in self-defense. The loud, aggressive language did not stop during the entire interview, and completing the assessment interview and obtaining the necessary information was challenging.

The facilitator did not contradict Tim, ask questions regarding the offense, or try to determine whether he was telling the truth. The facilitator remained calm, spoke quietly, and asked questions relevant to the assessment interview. When Tim yelled that he was not going to take part in the group, the facilitator responded by calmly asking him what he was going to do instead. The facilitator did not confront, get defensive, or attempt to convince Tim that he had no choice, instead leaving it up to him to determine what he would do. When treated in this manner, Tim paused, took some time to respond, and decided that he would do the group after all. Although he did not decrease his verbal aggressiveness, he grudgingly completed all the required paperwork necessary to be admitted to the group.

At the first group session, Tim did not speak, and he turned his head away from the group for most of the session. During the second session, Tim faced the group, appeared to be listening, and even offered a few comments. He did not yet have a goal. By the end of the third session, Tim still did not have a goal, and the facilitators spent extra time after the group calmly setting limits and helping him figure out what he was going to work on. After considerable time ventilating, Tim was able to come up with a goal to improve his relationships at work. He would attempt to do this by experimenting with complimenting his coworkers.

During the following group Tim begins to recount his goal-related efforts, and the facilitators help him stay focused on his efforts.

Facilitator 1: So, Tim, what did you say your goal was?

Tim: My goal was to compliment my coworkers. I ended up screwing up, screwing me in the end, and you know what, I said it to him just like that—I said, "You're a fucking jerk. I complimented you, and the way you repaid me is I had to work twice as hard." So we talked about it, and I said, "You know, I can be nice to you, or I can be real rough with you—I prefer to be nice, but if you truly want me to be, I can be real rough. It's your choice!" So all last week they did it, and this week they had all their stuff done, and I'm like, "You know what? It's really nice coming in today. Thank you, guys.

F1:   This week they had all their stuff done?

It would have been very easy to get caught up in Tim's language and talk about his anger and verbal aggressiveness. Instead, the facilitators stay focused on whether his goal is helpful.

T: Yeah.

F1:   It sounds like you kind of complimented them for that?

T: I told them off first! I said, "You know—I complimented you and got slapped in the face. It's hard to do your work in the middle of my job." They thought about it, and I said, "Would you like me to do it to you?"

Facilitator 2: How did you figure this out? It sounds like things have changed?

The facilitators are continuing to focus on what is better,
bypassing the hostility.

T: No, they're still the same. They still think I'm a jerk, and that's fine with
       me.
F1:   So, this complimenting—did it help? It sounds like it made things worse.

The facilitators remain focused on Tim's goal while attempting to
help him determine whether working on this goal is helpful.

T: It did at first, and then I gave them smaller compliments, like "God, you
       really worked hard today smoking that cigarette" (said sarcastically). "Like
       you really worked hard today." And when I notice the difference, I say,
       "Wow! It's really nice, thank you very much."
F1:   Does that help?

Again the facilitators ignore the sarcasm and continue to focus
on whether this is a good goal for him.

T: Yeah.
F1:   It does?
F2:   How so? Do you think it helps them or it helps you? What do you think?

The facilitators help Tim develop clarity about how his
complimenting is helpful. They are genuinely curious about his
perceptions.

T: They do their job, so I don't have to do their job for them.
F1:   So, how did you figure out that you needed to make a smaller compli-
       ment?

This is a subtle compliment of Tim's inventiveness.

T: A couple of them are morons that don't understand. I don't think they
       had enough compliments when they were younger.
F1:   So, how did you figure out that instead of doing those big compliments,
       that you needed to tone it down to something smaller that they were do-
       ing?
T: Because I got slapped in the face when I gave them a compliment.
F1:   Yeah, but I might have stopped complimenting altogether.

The facilitator is again complimenting Tim for doing something
that appears hard to do and for recognizing that he needed to
adjust his behavior.

T: No, no, no. It's not O.K. I have enough crap on my crap list—you want
       my crap list? You know, I get here an hour before everybody else, and I
       start, and I set up. You wanna come in for me and start? That's fine—
       come here and tear down and clean up?

F2:   Since you've been doing these smaller compliments, have things been go-
      ing better at work?

*Like a dog with a bone, the facilitators stick to the goal and
bypass the hostility.*

T: Clint was fired or laid off today.
F2:   You sound like you're pretty tough with people there, and yet you still do
      the compliments.

*This compliment recognizes Tim's tough presentation and yet
credits his efforts.*

T: You know, as long as they get their job done, I can be fine. But I don't
      like carrying other people's weight, if something doesn't get done, the
      boss comes to me (makes a lewd gesture). It's my responsibility, it's my
      kitchen from 11:00 A.M. to 5:00 P.M.
F2:   Absolutely! So you're accountable.

*The facilitator agrees with Tim, and again compliments him by
noticing that he holds himself responsible for getting the work
done.*

T: Yeah.
F2:   And you hold them accountable.

*Another compliment for Tim, implying that a good supervisor
holds his staff accountable for their work.*

T: Uh-huh—they're responsible for their work, and they weren't getting it
      done, and now they're getting it done.
F2:   Were you doing this complimenting anyplace else? With your daughter—
      you have a daughter, right? Are you doing it with her or primarily at your
      work?

*The facilitators are looking for ways that Tim may have extended
his goal to other relationships in his life. Tim notes that he has
been complimenting his daughter, which provides the facilitators
with further opportunity to reflect on how responsible his 12-
year-old daughter is and that Tim must have been doing
something right as a parent.*

F1:   So, this complimenting business, do you think it's a pretty good goal for
      you?
T: Yeah, it's a good goal.

F2:   Is there something you would rather work on at this point?

T: You know, my personal life's going good, I'm working hard with my daughter, and my relationship is going great, work is going a hell of a lot better.

F2:   So, this goal is doable?

There are multiple opportunities to focus on Tim's hostility, anger, and verbal aggressiveness. However, the facilitators stay focused on his goal, bypassing all the invitations to be sidetracked and finding opportunities to compliment him, in spite of his anger, and pointing out that his life is getting better. This transcript also demonstrates how helpful it is to have two facilitators working as a team with aggressive group participants; such participants can be especially challenging, and working together helps both facilitators stay on track.

By the sixth session, Tim reports that his staff is working as a team. He has even received compliments himself, which he discovers are uncomfortable for him to accept. He comments that it is easier for him to give compliments than to receive them. At the final group, the facilitators ask Tim how helpful his goal is to him, and he notes that it is about a 7 on a scale of 1 to 10. When asked how helpful he thought it would be when he started, he responds that he would have rated it at about a 1.

It is easy to be intimidated and distracted by aggressive group participants, especially if they are angry with the facilitators. It is easy to feel on the spot, with the rest of the group watching to see how we will handle the situation. It is always a challenge to stay calm and focused when these situations arise.

We suspect our focus on solutions contributes to participants feeling more at ease, and therefore less angry. If one of the facilitators needs to miss a session, we recommend that it not happen during the first three sessions, because if aggressiveness is going to occur, it usually happens during that period. Our outcome studies indicate that participants who have initially presented as hostile or defensive, even those diagnosed with antisocial personality disorders, benefit from the program as much as those who were cooperative from the beginning. Some of the most appreciative participants are those who at intake were skeptical, defensive, and angry.

By setting up clear, reasonable rules, with consequences if the rules are violated, by remaining calm and not reinforcing aggressive behavior, and by focusing on participant goals rather than goals the facilitator thinks the participant should focus on, we are able to eliminate most opportunities for acting-out behavior. By the time participants start working on their goals, and their lives start to improve, usually by session 3 or 4, we see little, if any, negative or contentious behavior. Instead, we see cooperation and support, with participants enthusiastically complimenting each other on their progress with their goals.

Do's and Don'ts When Working with Angry or Aggressive Individuals

Do remain calm and listen respectfully.

Do offer choices when possible.

Do work together as a team with the cofacilitator.

Don't reinforce aggression.

Don't judge.

Don't engage in power struggles.

Individuals with Psychiatric Diagnoses

Ours is the only agency in our county that works with court-mandated domestic violence offenders. As such, we deal with a wide variety of individuals. As part of our agency procedure, we complete a mental status exam and provide a *Diagnostic and Statistical Manual of Mental Disorders* (4th ed.) (*DSM-IV*) diagnosis for all new intakes. Many of the people referred have Axis I and II diagnoses. Among the participants who enrolled in our program between October 1996 and January 2002, 18.8% had Axis I diagnoses, including major depression, schizoaffective disorder, post traumatic stress disorder (PTSD), attention-deficit hyperactivity disorder (ADHD), adjustment disorder, intermittent explosive disorder, and impulse control disorder; 25.5% of the participants had histories consistent with personality disorders such as antisocial, narcissistic, obsessive-compulsive, and dependent personality disorders.

In our application of a solution-focused approach, we do not find it helpful to focus on psychiatric diagnosis or mental illness in the assessment or treatment process. Traditional diagnostic approaches tend to focus on problem categories and on a person's limits and deficits. Labeling can inadvertently sustain a problem reality if the facilitator begins to make assumptions based on a diagnosis rather than the broader reality that reflects who the person is and what the individual is capable of. It is helpful to be aware that a person who has been labeled as having an antisocial personality is not antisocial in all areas of his or her life. A depressed person is not always depressed and almost always experiences times when the depression is less severe. A person with an impulse control disorder often experiences times when he or she manages to control inappropriate impulses. Individuals diagnosed with schizophrenia are unique in presentation and symptom description. Many individuals with this diagnosis are fully functional, whereas others are virtually incapacitated. Our role remains the same regardless of the degree of disability, and that is to help individuals effectively use their resources to accomplish their goals. Diagnosis provides, at best, an extremely limited perspective of an individual's ability to change, cope with, or manage his or her life.

We are concerned about the negative effect of labeling, in that focusing on a diagnosis limits the facilitator's ability to see the potential of the whole person. Furthermore, a label of mental illness can limit the participants' ability to notice their own strengths and resources, particularly when individuals begin to view themselves as the diagnosis. In such situations, individuals often state what they can and cannot do based on their diagnosis.

In our experience most people do not seek out a psychiatric diagnosis; they seek out assistance to treat a feeling, behavior, or experience that interferes with the way they want to live. We recognize the value of helping individuals respond to symptoms that interfere with their ability to function. When possible, individuals can play an active role in deciding how to respond to symptoms, including seeking a psychiatric evaluation and taking psychiatric medications. When individuals state that they have psychiatric symptoms, we ask them how they deal with them, what they have found that works for them, and how important it is for them to continue to do what works. It is not uncommon for participants to share different strategies that they use to their benefit, including in some cases taking medication. This type of interaction usually does not occur in the group process and is much more likely to occur after a group session, when a participant waits to talk to the facilitators in private or during a phone call between sessions. Often participants are seeking recognition or reassurance regarding what they are doing. This points to the importance of complimenting individuals for their efforts and their persistence in taking care of themselves. Complimenting individuals who are typically socially isolated and unsure during social interactions can be powerful, leading them to become more confident and involved in the group process.

Contrary to public opinion, individuals with mental illness diagnoses are no more likely to engage in domestic violence than the public at large. Our recidivism rates do not indicate that participants with mental disorders are more likely to reoffend than are those without mental disorders. Outcome research has shown that a diagnosis of mental illness does not predict or limit a person's ability to develop and attain useful goals. Research conducted at the Brief Family Therapy Center demonstrates as well that a successful outcome is not related to diagnosis (DeJong & Berg, 2002).

Making Adjustments

Given that we view diagnosis and labeling as counterproductive, the question remains, "What, if anything, do we do differently to address individuals who present with psychiatric symptoms during the group process?" The answer to this question is as complex as the individuals with whom we work, and yet often as simple as staying the course: complex in that we must be utterly respectful of an individual's unique perceptions, yet simple in that we hold all individuals, regardless of their unique features, accountable for meeting the expectations of the group. This requires that the facilitators put aside all assumptions about the individual's limitations and maintain an unwavering expectation that the individual has the capacity to do what it takes to be successful. Adjustments come out of respect for the surface presentation of the participant.

Participants who might be described as mentally ill sometimes challenge the facilitator's capacity to maintain a respectful response. For example, a number of years ago, Insoo Kim Berg saw a woman at our clinic who said her deceased uncle, who made unreasonable verbal demands on her, tormented her. The woman had seen numerous psychiatrists and had taken many medications, with little or no benefit. Insoo respectfully talked with her about her current relationship with the uncle, including asking if she, Insoo, could talk with him. This request was declined, but the woman did agree that she could give the uncle a message from Insoo. This allowed Insoo the opportunity to collaboratively develop an intervention with this individual. Insoo Kim Berg's communication was totally consistent with this woman's view of the world and was respectful of her desire to work toward the changes she sought. Such individuals challenge facilitators to respect an individual's unique presentation while at the same time expecting participants to build on day-to-day activities of change.

During the group process our approach is much the same: accept the unique presentation, focus on the expectations of the group, and avoid areas that typically distract from goal formation and goal work. In some instances it is necessary to adjust the pace and type of question. For example, some individuals require a slower pace or concrete, less complex questions. The slower pace may include the actual speed at which the facilitator speaks, as well as the speed of overall flow of the questions asked. As an adjunct to slowing the pace, it is sometimes helpful to ask the participant to reiterate his or her understanding of what has been said or agreed upon. This offers insight regarding the individual's capacity to use the process effectively and allows for meaningful adjustments.

Individuals who have difficulty organizing their thoughts or focusing attention often find it very helpful to work on a goal that is less complex and more well defined. Such goals are often easier to remember and to do on a regular basis. They permit the participant who is otherwise poorly organized to be successful in a meaningful way. Smaller, limited goals also make it easier for the facilitators to redirect the participant back to the goal if he or she becomes distracted by other thoughts. Concrete goals are often easy for participants to expand upon as the group progresses. This allows the facilitators to pace the expansion of the goal to match the participant's ability to handle complexity. For individuals with significant thought disorganization, it is often helpful to limit goal efforts to basic tasks and to help participants expand only the recognition of the benefits and meaning of their successes related to the goal. Most individuals who struggle to organize their thoughts readily recognize the value of working on less complex goals. We find it helpful to ask questions that allow them to evaluate the benefit of doing something "smaller" rather then "bigger."

It is important to remain aware of the value of compliments and attention, particularly with individuals who present with symptoms of disorganized thinking and/or a flat emotional response. Often these individuals fade into the background of a group, in part because they lack the social skills of other group participants. Thinking deficits often translate into social deficits or contribute to a pattern of withdrawal. Attending to individuals, including them, and respecting their ideas and efforts not only challenges the person in question but also challenges the group to recognize and respect the achievements of all participants.

Dramatic Presentation

On rare occasions participants present in a dramatic fashion that demands the attention of the whole group and facilitators. Individuals who present in this way often have been given a diagnosis in the broad category of personality disorder. The application of our approach to such situations requires the facilitators to remain calm, nonreactive, persistent, and able to set clear limits and exude a caring presence. It is also important that the facilitators remain sensitive to the immediate drama, while keeping in mind that the goal is to get back to the basic tasks of the group.

When individuals present with drama, they are essentially saying that they require special attention. In the most extreme situations, participants are implying that their needs at the moment are more important than those of the group and facilitators combined. It is foolish to argue this issue and much more helpful to accept that the participant requires attention. Our goal is to give the attention in a caring, receptive manner that deflates the drama and promotes a collaborative and cooperative response from the participant.

In doing this, it is often important to determine what will help deescalate the situation. In many circumstances it is possible to ask questions that allow the individual to ventilate or to share his or her perception. This can provide clues to what other responses might be helpful. The facilitators must listen closely and convey to such participants that they are understood. It is important that the facilitators allow them to share information but not get bogged down in a prolonged conversation regarding why they experience or behave the way they do. It is important to make the shift to "What can we do now?" as soon as possible. The facilitators must help these individual explore what they need while gradually bringing the focus back to basic group tasks. In some situations it is helpful to simply ask participants what would be helpful to them or to offer some concrete choices about how to proceed.

In our experience, effectively addressing individuals with "dramatic presentations" does not require new or specialized skills, but it does require facilitators to apply skills under challenge and stress. Sam was a group participant whose behavior was bizarre and intimidating. He had a *DSM-IV* diagnosis of organic brain disorder and antisocial personality disorder. Sam would sit and stare at a group participant or one of the facilitators for 5 minutes or more without saying anything. We chose not to respond to or comment on the behavior, and Sam would eventually shift his attention. During the third session, Sam initiated a hostile interaction with one of the facilitators. He expressed angry feelings about the group and questioned the competence of the facilitator in an aggressive and indignant manner. His behavior was quite unnerving, and, given his past unusual behavior, the whole group became tense. The facilitator at whom his attention was directed became quiet, and the cofacilitator started to ask Sam questions to help shift his attention and begin to better understand what Sam was reacting to. The pacing of the questions was slowed, and Sam was given an opportunity to state some of his concerns. Sam shared concerns and made some aggressive statements that were intended to engage the facilitator upon whom his anger was focused. No attempt was made to engage Sam regarding these statements or other statements that seemed charged with emotion. Attention was gradually shifted to the question of what Sam wanted to do. Did he want to continue the group? If so, was he willing to develop and work on a goal? Throughout this process, Sam regained a sense of control, refocused, and was able to appropriately continue with the group process.

Subsequent to that session, Sam apologized to the facilitators and to the group for any discomfort he might have created. He attempted to put the group at ease by saying that he would not hurt anyone. He told us that he was very involved in martial arts, and that the behavior we had thought was staring was a martial arts technique that he used for focusing on his opponent. He revealed that he had received some serious head injuries, in fact, had a metal plate in his head, but continued with martial arts in spite of that. The staring behavior did not return for the remainder of the sessions. The process allowed Sam to evaluate and modify his behavior in a way that permitted him to use the group effectively.

In the next session, Sam appeared very nicely dressed, clean shaven, and sporting a new haircut. He had been extremely isolated in his life and had very few social contacts. He noted how he had avoided relationships with other people and generally did not trust them. He felt this was not particularly helpful or good for him. Sam decided that he should challenge himself to make his life better; as a result, he developed a goal of learning how to relax in anxiety-provoking situations and to help out other people.

He not only worked on this goal between groups but also made a point of engaging in relaxed, reassuring conversation while he was in the group. He often provided wonderful, detailed examples of how he had worked on his goal by engaging with and helping people.

Another participant, Stephen, had a long history of mental health care dating back almost 30 years. He had various diagnoses, including schizoaffective disorder, major depression with psychosis, and generalized anxiety disorder, and had several hospitalizations, which included treatment with antipsychotic medication. In spite of this history, he was able to maintain a long and mostly successful work history. His goals during the group were to use language other than swearing when he became upset, to change his focus by engaging in an art project, or, if these did not work, to visit his mother's home.

Stephen was able to engage with other group participants in a helpful manner and was very committed to his goals and the importance of maintaining stability in his life, which included staying in mental health treatment. In his final written assignment, Stephen stated that the group had been a very good learning experience for him and mentioned that he thought the group was all about a religious proverb, which was "God helps those who will help themselves." He further wrote that he was proud of being a small part of a greater effort to put an end to domestic violence.

We have noticed that when we have a group participant who demonstrates unusual thinking, the rest of the group includes and supports that person. We have not witnessed any ostracizing or rejecting attitudes. Participants seem to want each other to be successful in completing the group.

Do's and Don'ts When Working with Individuals Who Have Psychiatric Diagnoses

Do recognize that each individual is unique.

Do look for the group participants' competencies and strengths.

Do be curious about what changes will occur.

Do work as a team.

Do slow the pace when necessary.

Do hold all participants accountable for goal work.

Do compliment and notice changes and involvement.

Do consider building on small, concrete goals.

Do help participants focus on the concrete details of the goal.

Don't label group participants or talk about them as if they were a diagnosis.

Don't attend to inappropriate behavior.

Don't give up or assume that participants cannot make meaningful change.

Individuals from Diverse Ethnoracial Backgrounds

One of the most important clinical challenges in working with participants of diverse backgrounds is engaging them in a meaningful process of treatment. For many cultures, disclosing problems of domestic violence to an "outside" helping professional can be perceived as disgracing the family name or losing face, especially for cultures that value male superiority, collectivism, and obligation. Other potential factors that prevent participants of diverse backgrounds from seeking help include, but are not limited to, feelings of being different, unfamiliarity with the service system, lack of confidence in and trust of the service system, fear of being misunderstood, cultural barriers such as diverse methods of seeking help and solving personal problems, and language barriers. As such, it is of utmost importance to successfully join with the participant to prevent early dropout and establish a helpful therapeutic relationship.

Engaging Participants of Diverse Backgrounds

Joining with Participants' Dilemmas of Seeking Help

Because of a strong fear of shaming the family name and losing face for some minority participants, issues of confidentiality should be communicated clearly and unambiguously early on in the group. In addition, it is important to explicitly recognize their dilemmas in receiving treatment and normalize the emotion of shame or guilt (Sue & Sue, 1990). Opening the door for domestic violence offenders to talk about their dilemmas serves to validate their feeling of ambivalence and educate the facilitators about the participants' culturally embedded perception of their problems and solutions. On the other hand, this model does not view drilling on problems or negative feelings as helpful in the process of change. It is more helpful to redirect therapeutic dialogues to reaffirm and strengthen whatever motivating factors are present in participants.

Strengthening Motivation

To reaffirm and strengthen participants' motivation, it is important to assist them in developing personally relevant goals that are viable and meaningful in their cultural context. Externally imposed goals are likely to be sabotaged with active or passive resistance. Participants will be more invested in change when they actively participate in the treatment process, determine the goal of treatment, and take charge of the change process.

Joining with Participants' Culturally Embedded Mode of Communication

Because people from different sociocultural backgrounds will have developed diverse "comfort zones" regarding modes of social interaction and communication, the facilitators should observe and respect characteristics of both verbal and nonverbal communication styles in their participants. For instance, some participants of diverse backgrounds may be more reserved and inhibited about emotions. They should be given time and space to open up at their own pace and in a way with which they are comfortable. Lack of direct eye contact should not be misinterpreted as a symptom of avoidance or anxiety; it may be a sign of respect (Chung, 1992). Being silent or reserved does not necessarily mean resistance or unwillingness to seek help; it may be just a matter of needing more time to open up.

Imparting Structure of Treatment

Many participants of diverse backgrounds may have no prior experience with treatment. To lessen their anxiety regarding seeking professional help, it is important for the facilitators to clearly explain to them the structure of the group treatment program. The facilitators should take the initiative to find out whether participants of diverse backgrounds may have any questions that have not been covered.

Pairing Participants of Diverse Backgrounds in the Treatment Program

It is common for participants of diverse backgrounds to feel isolated and different from other group participants, which is detrimental to meaningful participation in the treatment process. Having more than one such participant in a group serves to lessen feelings of isolation and increase the participants' feelings of connection to the group.

Asking for Feedback to Clarify Communication

Because of cultural and/or language differences or barriers, one person may understand, use, or interpret specific sentences differently from another person. For instance, "yes" may be a linguistic indicator of affirmation of what has just been said by another person. It can also mean "I hear you" without an affirmative intent. In case of doubt, it is important to clarify meanings of ongoing communication by cross-checking or asking questions such as "Is that what you mean?" or "Do you have any questions about what we have just discussed?"

Use of Interpreters

Because of the presence of language barriers for some participants of diverse backgrounds or participants with hearing impairments, interpreting services may be necessary. The presence of an interpreter creates a "triangular relationship" among the facilitator, the participant, and the interpreter, with implications for communication patterns and boundary issues. A facilitator using interpretive services has to attend to several guidelines to ensure effective communication, as well as to set up clear boundaries:

- Use professional interpreters for reasons of confidentiality and up-keeping standard of services.
- Briefly meet with the interpreter before the group to clarify his or her roles and responsibilities, explain your expectations, and answer any questions.
- Request the interpreter to use the first-person form in the process of interpretation to ensure direct communication between the facilitator and the participant.
- Be aware of technical issues that facilitate the process of interpretation, including (1) speaking slowly and clearly with frequent pauses, (2) using simple language, (3) avoiding unnecessary professional jargon, and (4) asking cross-checking questions to clarify mutual understanding, especially in situations of doubt.

Besides focusing on engaging participants and making sure there is open communication among the participant, other group participants, and the facilitator, a solution-focused approach to domestic violence offenders also addresses the issue of diversity via the treatment process itself. By respecting and using group participants' cultural construction of solutions, cultural strengths, and resources in the treatment process, the practice orientation of a solution-focused approach naturally addresses the challenges of "multiple worlds" presented by cultural diversity in our society.

Respecting Participants' Culturally Embedded Views of Problems and Solutions

A solution-focused approach views solutions as private, local, meaning-making activities by individual participants. Consequently, in our work with domestic violence offenders from diverse backgrounds, we do not assume having a priori expertise sufficient to objectively categorize and solve their problems. Our focus is on utilizing a "not-knowing" stance and participants' self-determined goals to enter into their subjective experiences of their problem situations and collaboratively engage in a solution-building process that is viable and responsive to their cultural context. In this way, a solution-focused perspective encourages facilitators to fully respect participants' culturally embedded constructions of their life situations in the solution-building process.

Utilizing Cultural Strengths

Our treatment program focuses on what participants can do rather than what they cannot do. Consequently, one key premise of interventions is the principle of utilization, that is, utilizing participants' existing resources, skills, knowledge, beliefs, motivation, behavior, and social network in their cultural context to lead them to their desired outcomes. We avoid teaching participants skills or intervening in their lives in ways that may fit our "model" of what is good but may not be appropriate or viable in their cultural context. Instead, we assist participants in noticing, amplifying, sustaining, and reinforcing the identified cultural strengths and resources regardless of how small or infrequent they may be.

Collaborating with Participants

In our program, we serve as facilitators of a collaborative therapeutic process whereby the participant is the "knower" who owns the resources to achieve change and defines the goal of treatment. We do not rely on formal treatment theories to filter the stories and experiences of participants of diverse backgrounds. In place of a hierarchical facilitator-participant relationship is a more egalitarian and collaborative relationship between participants and facilitators. The facilitator becomes the participants' "community of other" to whom they continuously redefine and codevelop new meanings and new realities through a dialogue of "solutions." In this way, the therapeutic process is collaborative and egalitarian and participants' self-determination is fully respected.

Pragmatic Change: A Focus on Specific, Behavioral, and Small Change

Some cultural minority populations have been described as pragmatic and instrumental in seeking treatment (Ma, 1998). They are likely to expect treatment to be brief and effective, consisting of prompt interventions (Lee, 2000). A solution-focused approach advocates establishing specific, clear, and small goals that can make a difference in participants' lives alongside defining clear indicators of change. Solution-focused facilitators assist the participant in identifying the first small step toward desirable change so as to "tip the first domino" in the process of change (Berg & Miller, 1992). Such practice characteristics prove to be a good match with the instrumental help-seeking orientation in participants of diverse ethnoracial backgrounds.

Accountability for Solutions: A Face-Saving Technique

For cultural groups with a collective outlook, shaming the family name or losing face has been considered a major hindrance in seeking treatment or discussing private troubles with outsiders (Lee, 2000). A confrontational approach might also violate the esteemed cultural value of harmony (Ho, 1993). Because saving face is an important cultural factor in social interaction among many cultural minority populations, helping professionals need to consider face-saving techniques when working with them. We use a nonconfrontational approach that focuses on what people can do versus what they cannot do, on what people can do to contribute to the solution versus who has the problem or who causes the problem. The emphasis on goals, solutions, and compliments naturally harmonizes with the practice of face-saving in many cultural minority groups. Such therapeutic moves are essentially face-saving because they allow people to make beneficial changes in their habitual behaviors that may have contributed to or maintained the problem without having to go through the negative emotional experiences associated with losing face, which often can lead to defensive behaviors and massive denial of the problem.

Do's and Don'ts of Working with Diverse Populations

Do listen, listen, and listen.

Do invite participants to participate.

Do discuss the issue of confidentiality.

Do acknowledge cultural dilemmas regarding seeking treatment.

Do respect culturally embedded perceptions of problems and solutions.

Do clearly impart the structure of treatment.

Do observe and respect cultural modes of communication.

Do clarify communication.

Do pair up participants of diverse backgrounds.

Do utilize cultural strengths.

Do collaborate with participants.

Do focus on specific, observable, and small change.

Do utilize face-saving techniques.

Don't assume understanding.

Don't impose culturally inappropriate and insensitive goals or treatment processes.

Don't become involved in blaming talk.

Don't isolate or single out participants from diverse backgrounds.

Individuals Who Are Illiterate

Illiteracy has not presented any particular difficulty in our approach, but it may require some sensitivity on the part of the facilitators. If it becomes clear during the assessment interview that a prospective group participant cannot read or write, all forms that require a signature are read out loud to the individual. Such participants are told that they will be asked to complete homework assignments by turning in a full-page written answer to certain questions the facilitators will ask during the course of the program. They will be required to have someone else write their answers for them, but the content must be their own.

During the first group session, all the group rules are read out loud. Group participants are asked to volunteer to read the rules, so no one is put in an awkward position by being asked to read. Other than the written homework assignments, no reading or writing is required for the group.

We had one group participant who decided to take literacy classes as his goal. He wanted to be able to write to his children, who lived with his estranged wife. On the last day of the group, he read to the participants from a children's book. The whole group cheered, and some members even had tears in their eyes, including the facilitators.

Do's and Don'ts of Working with Individuals Who Have Literacy Issues

Do read out loud all forms that require signatures.

Do inform participants of the written homework requirement.

Do allow participants to volunteer to read out loud.

Do be sensitive to participants who are illiterate.

10

Evaluation of the Treatment Program

Challenges and Issues of Evaluation of Treatment programs

Since the implementation of court-mandated treatment of domestic violence offenders in the mid-1980s, there has been a dramatic expansion of treatment programs all over the country, as well as an increasing interest in evaluating the effectiveness of these programs (Dunford, 2000). To date, there are approximately 35 published program evaluations (Hanson, 2002). Reviews of domestic violence offender treatment programs generally report recidivism rates ranging from 15% to 50% in the year after completion of the program (e.g., Edleson, 1996; Rosenfeld, 1992; Tolman & Bennett, 1990; Tolman & Edleson, 1995). Several influential outcome studies report their findings. Melanie Shepard (1992) did a 5-year follow-up of 100 men who participated in the Duluth program. She reported a recidivism rate of 40%, with recidivists being defined as those who were convicted of domestic assault, being a subject of an order for protection, or being a police suspect for domestic assault. Daniel Saunders (1996) examined outcomes of 218 men at a community-based domestic violence program who were randomly assigned to either feminist-cognitive-behavioral or process-psychodynamic group treatment. He utilized both partners' reports and arrest records and reported a recidivism rate of 45.9% for the feminist-cognitive-behavioral model and 48.5% for the process-psychodynamic group treatment during a 54-month period. Gondolf and White (2001) conducted a follow-up study of 618 offenders in four U.S. cities. Based on reports of female partners, 41% had reassaulted their partners during the 30-month follow-up period. Dutton and his associates (1997) did an 11-year follow-up study of 446 domestic violence offenders, using arrest records only. He and his associates found an 18% recidivism rate, which was considerably lower than rates in studies that include partners' reports in defining recidivism. Two recent experimental evaluations have found batterer treatment programs to be largely ineffective, with no significant differences between those who received group treatment and those who di⌐ not in terms of their attitudes, beliefs, and behaviors (Feder & Forde, 2000) or victims' reports of new violent incidents (Davis et al., 2000).

Definitional Issues

Evaluation of the effectiveness of domestic violence treatment programs is viewed as important but is beset with significant methodological problems that cloud a conclusive understanding (Gondolf, 1997; Quinsey, Harris, Rice, & Lalumiere, 1993). The measure of "successful outcomes" depends on how success is being defined, what sources of information are used, and how long after the program the follow-up is conducted. Currently, most evaluations of treatment programs for domestic violence offenders adopt an input-output design in measuring outcome (Gondolf, 1997). The focus of evaluation is on fixed behaviors of offenders, usually violence, when they enter and leave the program. For evaluations using an input-output design, nonviolence in program participants for an extended period is the single most commonly used criterion in determining successful outcomes (Tolman & Bennett, 1990). Defining recidivism and/or nonviolence, however, poses challenges for evaluators. Cessation of physical abuse does not mean the cessation of psychological abuse; the latter variable is frequently excluded in defining recidivism in many outcome studies (Edleson & Brygger, 1986; Edleson & Syers, 1990). Offenders may not be "violent" because of the inaccessibility of intimate relationships (Mulvey & Lidz, 1993). The criteria to determine either recidivism or nonviolence also differ from one study to another, ranging from the inclusion of arrest records only to self-reports of offenders and their spouses or partners regarding the occurrence of physically abusive behaviors after treatment.

A Deficit Perspective in Evaluation

Another concern that we have about the conventional definition of successful outcome using recidivism rates is its sole focus on problems and deficits. Cessation of violence is clearly an unambiguous goal of treatment programs for domestic violence offenders. On the other hand, another major goal of most treatment programs is helping offenders to develop positive ways of relating in intimate relationships that exclude violence. Lack of attention to positive changes in offenders, such as relational skills and conflict resolution skills in intimate relationships, can plausibly be attributed to the predominance of a deficits perspective over a strengths perspective in evaluative efforts of treatment programs for domestic violence offenders.

Methodological Issues

Research on treatment programs for domestic violence offenders is also encumbered by numerous methodological limitations such as lack of control or comparison groups; sample bias as a result of low response rate (as low as 20% to 40%, as described in DeMaris & Jackson, 1987; Tolman & Bennett, 1990) and high dropout rates (nearly half of the programs had a dropout rate of over 50% of the participants accepted at intake, as mentioned in Gondolf, 1990); agency staff conducting program evaluation, implying the possibility of self-interest (Rossi & Freeman, 1989); and lack of control for background variables or external factors (Gondolf, 1997).

Obviously, limitations of funding and resources play an important part in the process. Conducting outcome studies may also be difficult because of the nature of the population. The recidivism rate may be underreported for offenders who moved to other communities that do not report such data and for those who moved out of the original state of offense (Shepard, 1992). Keeping track of the offenders and their partners via personal contact is never an easy task given the transient characteristics of this population (Gondolf, 1997). In addition, offenders may no longer be in a relationship after the incident. Ethical issues in conducting research with offenders and their partners constitute other major concerns for researchers (Campbell & Dienemann, 2001; Gondolf 2000; Saunders, 1990). Researchers constantly face the challenge of obtaining impartial consent of respondents and protecting the safety of victims in the data collection process while still enlisting maximum participation from potential respondents.

A Narrow Focus of Evaluation

The input-output model is a useful, straightforward, and expedient research design, although it has been under increasing scrutiny for its narrow focus of evaluation. First, such a model does not examine components within the program that may account for successful outcomes. Second, it possibly oversimplifies the more complicated psychological and social processes that contribute to positive changes in offenders. Cessation of violence in offenders is more likely to involve a process of progress and regression that is difficult, if not impossible, to capture with a linear input-output research design (Valliant, 1982; Fagan, 1989). Third, the sole focus of evaluation on offenders' behavioral change excludes the potential effect of the treatment program on other involved parties such as the victims. Also, it does not examine the interrelationship and collaboration of various organizational components and their contribution to positive outcomes (Gondolf, 1997). In view of the importance of partnership in the treatment of domestic violence offenders, excluding system analysis in evaluation would clearly limit our understanding of factors contributing to successful treatment.

Outcome Study of Plumas Project

Despite the pragmatic difficulties and challenges in evaluating the effectiveness of treatment programs for domestic violence offenders, we believe that it is important to carefully accumulate empirical evidence regarding what works with this population so that treatment is not only determined or guided by ideological preferences but also informed by empirically based knowledge (Gingerich & Eisengart, 2000). In addition, our study is guided by the conviction that research should inform and support the development of programs that improve and empower the lives of program consumers, including participants and their spouses. Research is more than an intellectual exercise and should seriously consider whom we hope will benefit and how they can benefit from our research efforts (Small, 1995).

Our study was developed as an attempt to examine the effectiveness of a solution-focused approach for treating domestic violence offenders. We were not sheltered from resource constraints in the evaluation process, and that inevitably led to compromises in the research design. On the other hand, we expanded our focus of evaluation to include program components that are perceived as beneficial by participants and their partners. We also broadened the definition of success to include both the cessation of violence and improvement in relational skills in intimate relationships as a focus of evaluation. The study also represents a collaborative effort between researchers and practitioners.

The study was a one-group pre- and posttest design with a 6-month follow-up to evaluate the effectiveness of the treatment program based on multiple reporting sources that include program participants, their partners, program facilitators, and official arrest records. We collected both quantitative and qualitative data in the evaluation process. We used quantitative data to measure behavioral changes of program participants in terms of cessation of violent behaviors, and positive changes in relational behaviors in intimate relationships and their self-esteem. We used qualitative data to examine components within the program that contributed to positive changes in participants. We attempted to answer the following questions:

- Is there an improvement in the behaviors of program participants in a relational context as evaluated by the partners and spouses of participants?
- Is there an improvement in the self-esteem of program participants based on their self-reports?
- What are the recidivism rates of program participants as based on arrest records and on self-reports of participants and their partners and spouses?
- What is the relation between participants' profiles and recidivism rates as based on official arrest records?
- What treatment components are helpful as perceived by participants and their partners and spouses?
- What facilitators' behaviors are helpful as perceived by participants?
- What treatment components are unhelpful as perceived by participants?

- What do program participants learn from attending the treatment program?
- What positive changes do program participants accomplish as perceived by themselves and their partners or spouses?

Sample

Study participants were male or female court-mandated domestic violence offenders who were offered the opportunity to avoid prosecution by completing the group treatment program and abstaining from further violent conduct. Some of them pleaded guilty and were ordered to attend the program. The spouses and partners of program participants were also included in evaluating the program's effectiveness. Formal consent was obtained from participants regarding their participation in the study. In addition, one member of the research team contacted the spouses and partners of participants to obtain separate consent from them. It was made clear to program participants and their spouses or partners that participation in the study was voluntary, information would be kept confidential, and their decision regarding participation would not affect the treatment the offenders may receive.

Program Participants

Data analyses were based on participants of 14 groups that were conducted between October 1996 and January 2002. Respondents consisted of 90 program participants: 77 males (85.6%) and 13 females (14.4%). The age of the program participants ranged from 19 to 61 years (mean = 37.2, SD = 9). Program participants were predominantly Caucasian (84.1%), with 10.2% African Americans, 3.4% Native Americans, and 2.3% Hispanic Americans. Participants had attained an average of 12.6 years of education (SD = 1.5, range = 9–19). Regarding the marital status of program participants, 46.7% were currently married or lived with a partner, 42.2% were divorced or separated, and 11.1% had never married. Over half of the participants self-identified as laborers (55.1%), 7.9% were professionals, 6.7% were service workers, 5.6% were students, 2.2% were on welfare or disability, 1.1% owned a business, 1.1% were homemakers, and 20.2% were unemployed (see table 10.1).

A mental status examination was conducted at intake by an experienced, licensed clinical social worker, mainly for research purposes. Using *DSM=IV* criteria, 18.8% of the program participants had an Axis I diagnosis: 6.7% had a diagnosis of intermittent explosive disorder, 2.2% major depression, 2.2% schizoaffective disorder, 2.2% impulse control disorder, 2.2% posttraumatic stress disorder (PTSD), 1.1% bipolar disorder, 1.1% attention-deficit hyperactivity disorder (ADHD), and 1.1% adjustment dis-

Table 10.1
Demographic information of program participants (N = 90)

	Percentage (%)
Gender	
Male	85.6
Female	14.4
Ethnicity	
White Americans	84.1
African Americans	10.2
Native Americans	3.4
Hispanic Americans	2.3
Age	
20 or less	3.3
21–30	16.7
31–40	44.4
41–50	30.0
51 and above	5.6
Years of Education	
< High school	12.6
High school	49.4
College	36.7
Graduate and above	1.3
Occupation	
Unemployed	20.2
Laborers	55.1
Professionals/technicians	7.9
Service	6.7
Students	5.6
Welfare/disability homemakers	2.2
Own business	1.1
Homemakers	1.1
Marital status	
Single	11.1
Married	46.7
Divorced or separated	42.2

order. Among the 90 respondents, 25.5% had personality characteristics that suggested an Axis II diagnosis of personality disorder. Consistent with findings of other studies, a sizable number of participants had a diagnosis of antisocial personality disorder (20%). The other diagnoses included dependent personality disorder (2.2%), narcissistic personality disorder (1.1%), obsessive-compulsive personality disorder (1.1%), and personality disorder not otherwise specified (1.1%). In addition, 4.5% had brain in-

Table 10.2
***DSM-IV* diagnoses of program participants (*N* = 90)**

	Percentage (%)
Axis I	
No diagnosis	81.1
Intermittent explosive disorder	6.7
Major depression	2.2
Schizoaffective disorder	2.2
Impulse control disorder	2.2
Posttraumatic stress disorder	2.2
Bipolar disorder	1.1
Attention-deficit hyperactivity disorder	1.1
Adjustment disorder	1.1
Axis II	
No diagnosis	74.4
Antisocial personality disorder	20.0
Dependent personality disorder	2.2
Narcissistic personality disorder	1.1
Obsessive-compulsive personality disorder	1.1
Personality disorder NOS	1.1
Axis III	
No diagnosis	88.8
Brain injury	4.5
Other medical conditions	6.7
Global Assessment Functioning	
Mean = 61.6, SD = 4.1, range = 50–74	

juries, and 6.7% has an Axis III medical condition (see table 10.2). The Global Assessment Functioning (GAF) scores of participants ranged from 50 to 74 (mean, = 61.6, SD = 4.1), meaning that an average program participant was able to function in social, occupational, or school settings with only mild symptoms.

We had collected information about the participants regarding their involvement in criminal offenses and childhood experiences. Of the 90 participants, 61.4% had substance and/or alcohol abuse problems, and 23.3% had involvement with criminal offenses other than domestic violence. In addition, 39.5% of program participants experienced parental divorce or separation, 56.9% were children of alcoholics, and 44.3% had experienced abuse as children (see table 10.3). This profile is consistent with what is being suggested by existing literature regarding characteristics of domestic violence offenders in that a sizable number of offenders have problems with substance abuse, and/or experienced abuse as children.

Table 10.3
Profiles of program participants (*N* = 90)

	Percentage %
Alcohol and/or substance abuse	61.4
Involvement in other criminal offenses	23.3
Parental divorce or separation	39.5
Alcoholism in parents	56.9
Experienced abuse as a child	44.3

Spouses and Partners

Forty spouses and partners consented to participate in the study and completed the questionnaires before the group treatment program. Such a response rate was extremely favorable, since only 46.7% of participants were married or lived with a partner during the time of the study. Of these 40 respondents, 34 (85%) completed the questionnaires at termination, and 22 (55%) were successfully contacted during the 6-month follow-up telephone interview.

Method of Data Collection

Self-assessment of participants' self-esteem and partners' and spouses' evaluation of participants' relational behaviors in intimate relationships were obtained at pretreatment, at termination, and at the 6-month follow-up. In addition, telephone interviews were conducted 6 months after the completion of the treatment group to collect participants' and partners' and spouses' evaluation of the program and levels of violence in their intimate relationships. The instruments administered were as follows.

Index of Self-Esteem

The Index of Self-Esteem (ISE) is a 25-item scale developed by Hudson (1992) to measure the degree, severity, or magnitude of a problem the client has with self-esteem. This instrument was completed by each program participant, who was asked to rate the statements on a 1 to 7 scale. Some examples of the statements are "I feel ugly" and "I feel that people really like to talk with me." ISE scores range from 0 to 100, with higher scores indicating lower self-esteem. The scale has two cutting scores. Scores below 30 ($\pm$ 5) indicate absence of a clinically significant problems related to self-esteem issues. Scores above 70, on the other hand, indicate that respondents have significant problems related to self-esteem issues. The Index of Self-

Esteem has good reliability and validity (Hudson, 1992). In this study, the scale obtained a satisfactory reliability coefficient of .92 (Cronbach's alpha).

Solution Identification Scale

Inspired by the Solution Identification Scale developed by Ron Kral at the Milwaukee Brief Family Therapy Center and the Solution-Focused Recovery Scale for Survivors of Sexual Abuse developed by Yvonne Dolan (1991), Jeffrey Goldman and Mary Baydanan at Peaceful Alternatives in the Home (PATH) developed a 30-item scale to assess solution-oriented relational behaviors in couples (Goldman & Baydanan, 1990). This instrument was completed by partners and spouses, who were asked to rate the statements on a 1 to 10 scale, with 1 being "never" and 10 being "always." Some examples of the statements are "cooperates with partner/spouse," "expresses feeling other than anger," and "supports spouse's or partner's friendships." The scores of the Solution Identification Scale range from 30 to 300, with higher scores indicating better relational skills in intimate relationships. The instrument was originally developed for therapeutic usage in couple therapy (sometimes with couples who have been involved in spousal violence). As such, no reliability and validity tests have been reported. On the other hand, this instrument is based on a solution-focused orientation—a philosophy that is consistent with the practice orientation of this group. In this study, the scale obtained a highly satisfactory reliability coefficient of .93 (Cronbach's alpha).

Follow-Up Questionnaires

Two self-constructed follow-up questionnaires were developed to investigate participants' and their spouses' or partners' opinions about the group. The questions are adapted from questionnaires used by the Brief Family Therapy Center in Milwaukee (de Shazer et al., 1986) and the C. M. Hincks Institute (Lee, 1997) in conducting their respective outcome studies. The 12-item questionnaire for program participants focuses on their perceptions of goals they had sought to attain through group treatment, goal attainment, the development of new positive changes, and current level of violent behaviors in intimate relationships. Other questions aim to investigate participants' perceptions of their experience of the group process. Program participants were asked about aspects of the group that they had found helpful and about their overall satisfaction with and involvement in the group. The 7-item questionnaire for spouses and partners focuses on their perception of positive changes in participants, program components that had been helpful for participants, and level of violent behaviors, including both physical and verbal abuse, of program participants in intimate relationships. The data were collected through a telephone interview by an independent interviewer 6 months after termination of the group.

In addition, the effectiveness of the treatment program was measured by the recidivism rates and program completion rates of participants.

Recidivism Rate

The recidivism rate measured the rate of participants' recommitting violent behaviors after attending the treatment program. We collected the cumulative recidivism rate of participants, meaning that we collected data on reoffending after participants completed the program and did not limit it to a 6-month period. Data on recidivism were collected from the victim witness office, probation office, and district attorney's office. Definitions of recidivism by each source were different because of the difference in the function of each institution and the reporting venue. For instance, the district attorney's office documented cases of domestic violence that were reported and charged. The victim witness office documented cases of domestic violence whenever a victim was referred for service regardless of whether a charge was pressed against the offender or when there was a request for a restraining order. In this study we used more conservative and inclusive criteria that defined recidivism as (1) a participant was arrested for charges related to domestic violence, (2) a domestic violence charge was pressed against a participant, (3) the spouse or partner of a participant was referred to receive services from the victim witness office, or (4) there was a request for a restraining order against a participant.

In addition, reports from participants and their partners or spouses regarding participants' physical and/or verbal abusive behaviors in intimate relationships were collected in the telephone interviews conducted by independent interviewers 6 months after termination of the group. Program participants and their spouses and partners were asked to rate on a scale of 0 to 10 the level of violence before the participants participated in the treatment program and the current level of violence in intimate relationships.

Completion Rate

The completion rate measured the percentage of program participants who successfully completed the treatment program. It was calculated by comparing the number of participants who enrolled in the program and attended the first group meeting and the number of participants who attended at least seven out of eight group sessions.

The selection of instruments was guided by previous research, as well as theoretical orientation of a solution-focused, strengths-based approach for treatment of domestic violence offenders. Previous literature had identified program completion rates and recidivism rates as relevant and valid measures of treatment effectiveness of programs for domestic violence offenders (e.g., Cadsky et al., 1996; Saunders, 1996; Shepard, 1992). Our study obtained data regarding cessation of violence in offenders by using recidivism rates based on official arrest records and self-reports of participants and their spouses or partners at the 6-month follow-up interviews. Consistent with a solution-focused treatment orientation, the study measured positive changes in domestic violence offenders as a consequence of the treatment. The ISE was used to examine offenders' self-evaluation of improvement in their self-image. It was assumed that accomplishment of a personally meaningful goal would be associated with a positive perception of self. The Solution Identification Scale was used to measure positive changes in offenders' relational behaviors in intimate relationships as perceived by their partners and spouses. The focus of investigation of both instruments was consistent with the solution-focused, strengths-based orientation of such a treatment approach. Two instruments that had been widely used in previous prominent studies to examine the levels of violence in intimate relationships were the Conflict Tactic Scale developed by Straus and Gelles (1990) and the Abusive Behavior Inventory (Shepard & Campbell, 1992). These two instruments were not included in the present study because of the underlying philosophical differences between their problem-focused nature and a solution-focused approach for treatment. Despite an emphasis on strengths and solutions in the evaluation process, cessation of violent behaviors in program participants constitutes an important indicator of the effectiveness of the treatment program. Data on recidivism rates from official records and self-reports of participants and their spouses and partners regarding current levels of verbal and physical violence would provide adequate measurement of the levels of violence in intimate relationships.

Methods of Data Analysis

Data collected from various instruments were checked and coded for data processing and statistical analyses. The Statistical Package for Social Sciences was used for this purpose. A series of paired-sample t-tests were used to compare the pre- and posttreatment of the assessment instruments as completed by program participants and their partners or spouses.

Findings

Index of Self-Esteem

Program participants completed the Index of Self-Esteem at pretreatment, termination, and 6-month follow-up. Among the 90 program participants, 87 completed the questionnaire at pretreatment. Of these 87 participants, 82 participants completed the ISE at termination (94.3%), and 48 did so at the 6-month follow-up telephone interview (55.2%). Eighty-two participants completed the ISE at both pretreatment and termination. The ISE mean score of 22.4 (SD = 11.2) at termination compared favorably with the mean score of 24.5 (SD = 12.8) at pretreatment. Paired-sample t-tests comparing the pretreatment and posttreatment outcomes indicated a significant improvement in participants' evaluation of their self-esteem from pretreatment to posttreatment ($t = -2.2$, $df = 81$, $p < .05$; see table 10.4).

Forty-eight participants were contacted 6 months after they had completed the treatment program. Among those whom we could not contact at the follow-up phone interviews, 3 had no telephone, 25 had had their telephone line disconnected, 2 no longer lived at the same residence, 3 refused to respond to the interview despite earlier consent, and 9 could not be contacted despite repeated attempts. Questionnaires were also mailed to those whom we could not contact. Findings indicated that the ISE mean score of 21.2 (SD = 12.4) at the 6-month follow-up compared favorably with the mean score of 26.8 (SD = 14.1) at pretreatment. Paired-sample t-tests comparing the pretreatment and 6-month follow-up outcomes indicated a significant improvement in participants' self-reports of their self-esteem ($t = -3.1$, $df = 47$, $p < .01$; see table 10.4).

Solution Identification Scale

Participating spouses and partners were requested to complete the Solution Identification Scale (SIS) at pretreatment, termination, and 6-month follow-

Table 10.4
Paired-sample t-tests for comparing mean scores of Index of Self-Esteem and Solution Identification Scale at pretreatment, termination, and follow-up.

Instrument	Pretreatment mean score	Termination mean score	t	df	p
Index of Self-Esteem[1] ($n = 82$)	24.5 (SD = 12.8)	22.4 (SD = 11.2)	−2.2	81	<. 05
Solution Identification Scale ($n = 34$)	197.9 (SD = 64.7)	236.8 (SD = 40.3)	3.6	33	<. 001
	Pretreatment mean score	Follow-up mean score			
Index of Self-Esteem ($n = 48$)	26.8 (SD = 14.1)	21.2 (SD = 12.4)	−3.1	47	< .01
Solution Identification Scale ($n = 22$)	192.0 (SD = 55.3)	236.5 (SD = 37.7)	4.1	21	< .001

[1]In the Index of Self-Esteem, a higher score indicates more problems with self-esteem.

up. Only 46.7% of program participants were currently married or living with a partner at the time of evaluation. Forty spouses and partners consented to participate in the study and completed the SIS at pretreatment. Of these 40 individuals, 34 completed the SIS at termination (85%), and 22 did so at the 6-month follow-up phone interviews (55%).

Reports based on spouses and partners of program participants indicated a significant improvement in the participants' relational skills in intimate relationship since their participation in the program. The SIS mean score of 236.8 (SD = 40.3) at posttreatment compared favorably with the mean score of 197.9 (SD = 64.7) at pretreatment. Based on findings from a paired-sample t-test, there was a significant increase of SIS scores from pretreatment to posttreatment based on the evaluation of the spouses and partners, indicating better relational behaviors of program participants in intimate relationships ($t = 3.6$, $df = 33$, $p < .001$; see table 10.4).

Twenty-two spouses and partners responded to the 6-month follow-up phone interviews. The SIS mean score of 236.5 (SD = 37.7) at the 6-month follow-up compared favorably with the mean score of 192 (SD = 55.3) at pretreatment. Based on findings from a paired-sample t-test, there was a significant increase in SIS scores from pretreatment to follow-up, indicating a significant improvement of program participants' relational behaviors in intimate relationships based on the evaluation of their spouses or partners ($t = 4.1$, $df = 21$, $p < .001$; see table 10.4).

Cessation of Violence

Data on recidivism rates of program participants based on official records were collected from the victim witness office, the probation office, and the district attorney's office. We collected the cumulative recidivism rates of participants, meaning that we collected data on reoffending after participants completed the program and did not limit it to a 6-month period. Data from the district attorney's office indicated a recidivism rate of 6.7% (6), the probation office 4.4% (4), and the victim witness office 15.5% (14). Recidivism rates reported by each source were different because of the difference in the function of each institution and the reporting venues. Using more inclusive criteria, an overall recidivism rate of 16.7% (15) was compiled by counting all reoffending cases that were reported by either the victim witness office, the probation office, or the district attorney's office (see table 10.5).

Besides using official records, we examined the change in the level of violence in intimate relationships as reported by group participants and their spouses and partners. At the 6-month follow-up interview, program participants and their spouses and partners were asked to rate on a scale of 0 to 10 the level of violence before the participants participated in the treatment program and the current level of violence in intimate relationships. Respondents were asked to evaluate both physical violence and verbal

Table 10.5
Recidivism reports

Sources of reports	Recidivism rates (%) (number of reoffenders)
Official records (*n* = 90)	
District attorney	6.7 (6)
Probation office	4.4 (4)
Victim witness office	15.5 (14)
DA, PO, or VW	16.7 (15)
Spouses and partners' reports (*n* = 22)	13.5 (3)
Program participants' reports (*n* = 47)	2.1 (1)

abuse in intimate relationships. Findings indicated a significant decrease in the participants' violent behaviors as perceived by the program participants and their spouses and partners. Of the 47 program participants who responded to the question during the follow-up interviews, all except one participant reported committing some sort of violence in intimate relationships prior to receiving treatment. Only 1 man reported committing a low level of violence (2) in his current relationship (table 10.6). The perceived level of violence decreased significantly from 4.6 (SD = 2.7) at pretreatment to 0 (SD = 0.03) at the 6-month follow-up ($t = 11.3$, $df = 46$, $p < .001$). Such a perception of drastic improvement was shared by spouses and partners. Of the 22 spouses and partners who responded to this question during the follow-up interviews, only 3 (13.5%) reported their spouses committing a low level of violence against them (a score of 1, 2, and 3, respectively). The perceived level of violence decreased significantly from a mean score of 5 at pretreatment (SD = 3.3, ranging from 1 to 10) to 0.3 (SD = 0.8, ranging from 0 to 3) at the 6-month follow-up ($t = 6.7$, $df = 21$, $p < .001$; see table 10.7).

Participant Profiles and Recidivism

We also examined the relationship between participants' profiles and recidivism as based on official arrest records. Findings indicated that having a *DSM-IV* Axis I psychiatric disorder or Axis II diagnosis of personality disorder was not related to recidivism. In addition, participants' recidivism was not related to substance or alcohol abuse problems, involvement with criminal offenses other than domestic violence, experience of parental divorce, or coming from a family with a history of parental alcoholism. Findings from chi-square analyses, however, indicated that participants' self-reports of experiencing abuse as a child had a significant association with

Table 10.6
Recidivism reports by program participants at 6-month follow-up
($N = 47$)

Self-reported level of violence on a 0 to 10 scale	Pretreatment[1] % (number of participants)	6-month follow-up % (number of participants)
0	2.1 (1)	97.9 (46)
1	21.3 (10)	0.0
2	8.5 (4)	2.1 (1)
3	2.1 (1)	0.0
4	8.5 (4)	0.0
5	21.3 (10)	0.0
6	4.3 (2)	0.0
7	17.0 (8)	0.0
8	10.6 (5)	0.0
9	2.1 (1)	0.0
10	2.1 (1)	0.0
Mean	4.6	0.0
SD	2.7	0.3
Range	0–10	0–2

[1]Paired-sample t-tests comparing means of self-reported level of violence between pretreatment and 6-month follow-up ($t = 11.3$, $df = 46$, $p < .001$).

recidivism as based on official arrest records ($\chi^2 = 5.4$ $df = 1$, $p < .05$) (see table 10.8).

Completion Rate

Between October 1996 and January 2002, a total of 97 persons were accepted into the program and attended the first session of the group. Among these 97 persons, 90 completed the program, for a completion rate of 92.8%. For the 7 noncompleters, 3 attended a later group and successfully completed the program.

What Did Group Participants Say About Their Experiences?

Besides using standardized measurements to evaluate outcomes, we believe that group participants' narratives about their experiences of attending the group would reveal valuable information for therapists to learn about group treatment with this population.

Data analyses were based on the responses of 75 group participants

Table 10.7
Recidivism reports by spouses and partners of program participants at 6-month follow-up ($N = 22$)

Reported level of violence of program participants on a 0 to 10 scale	Pretreatment[1] % (number of spouses)	6-month follow-up % (number of spouses)
0	0.0 (0)	86.4 (19)
1	22.7 (5)	4.5 (1)
2	4.5 (1)	4.5 (1)
3	13.6 (3)	4.5 (1)
4	13.6 (3)	0.0
5	4.5 (1)	0.0
6	4.5 (1)	0.0
7	4.5 (1)	0.0
8	9.1 (2)	0.0
9	9.1 (2)	0.0
10	13.6 (3)	0.0
Mean	5.0	0.3
SD	3.3	0.8
Range	1–10	0–3

[1]Paired-sample t-tests comparing means of reported level of violence of program participants by spouses and partners between pretreatment and 6-month follow-up ($t = 6.7$, $df = 21$, $p < .001$).

from several sources. An assignment completed by group participants at the end of the group that asked them to write down one page of what they have learned from the group. In addition, we included answers to three open-ended questions in the follow-up phone interviews in data analysis:

- What things in the group did you find most helpful?
- What did the group facilitators say or do that you found helpful?

Table 10.8
Cross-tabulation of abuse during childhood and domestic violence recidivism during study period ($N = 79$)

	Reoffend ($n = 12$)	No reoffense ($n = 67$)
Abused as child	75%	39%
No abuse as child	25%	61%

Chi-square $= 5.4$, $df = 1$, $p < .05$; Fisher's exact test, $p < .05$; Cramer's V $= .26$, $p < .05$.

- Is there anything I (the interviewer) haven't asked that you would like to comment on or let us know?

Methods of Data Analysis

Content analysis was used to understand program participants' perception of the nature of the group treatment program. An emergent design based on the constant comparison method was used to explore the qualitative data (Glaser & Strauss, 1967; Lincoln & Guba, 1985; Charmaz, 2000). Constant interaction and reciprocal consideration of data and method were conducted at each stage of inquiry. The following procedures were adopted: Participants' responses based on the assignment and the follow-up interview were transcribed and computed. The software for qualitative inquiry, QSR NUD*IST VIVO (Nvivo), was used to assist in the data analysis process. All data were coded using an open process during the initial stage. Each "unit" with a single idea was identified, and a code was developed for each of them. Rules of inclusion were made for each code to standardize the content. Codes that addressed similar themes were later organized under "trees nodes." This process continued until the highest-level conceptualization was attained that best described the characteristics of and connection among individual codes. In other words, we stopped the process of coding, recoding, and making connection at the point of "theoretical saturation," when additional data do not increase our understanding of the issue. Sometimes the rule of inclusion was changed to make it more accurate to describe the properties of the included units. After the first round of analysis on all data, we prepared a revised list of codes, and all data were coded again according to this new scheme.

The narration of group participants was rich and fascinating. Instead of focusing just on their perception of what they had learned from the group, comments covered a wide range of participants' perception of their experiences in the group. Several themes can be identified that can be rephrased as the following questions:

- What did participants say about the nature of the program?
- What did participants say about treatment components that are helpful and/or unhelpful to them?
- What did participants say about facilitators' behaviors that are helpful to them?
- What did participants say about what they had learned from attending the program?
- What did participants say about the benefits they had gained by attending the program?

What Did Participants Say About the Nature of the Program?

I Come to a Class

Most participants addressed the group treatment program as a class instead of a treatment program or a group. The following comments illustrate some of these perceptions:

- "What I learned from anger awareness class is . . ."
- "During the last few months, I have been involved in the domestic violence class."

A common theme in such descriptions is the idea that the program is a class with an educational purpose. Such a perception probably conforms with the widely held societal assumption that domestic violence offenders lack certain skills and therefore need to be reeducated. On the other hand, going to a class and learning something new carries a more positive, learning- and growth-oriented connotation than receiving treatment, which might imply the existence of pathology.

I'm Surprised That This Class Is Different from What I Expected

Some participants changed their perception about the nature of the class after attending, as illustrated by the following comments. These participants originally had a negative perception of the class, viewing it as unhelpful or as something imposed on them by the court. All of them, however, mentioned a positive change in their perception. In addition, their comments illustrated their view of the treatment program as not patronizing and non-problem-focused:

- "This class was very different in a lot of ways. I've been through a class before in Reno, and it seemed more like school all over again, which might be good for the students but unfortunate for the majority of people. I think most of the people in life need to learn by practice instead of by someone telling you what is right or wrong."
- "When I first started this 8-week domestic violence class, I thought the group would be centered around why we were sent to the class. To my surprise, the class had nothing to do with why we were here but about working on personal goals."
- "I started this class against my will. I've never been violent or abusive in my entire life. Although after the second class I did realize that there are times in my life when I get angry, very angry! I thought that I wouldn't learn anything by attending, but I thought wrong. Since attending, I've become aware of changes that need to be taken in my life and that there is always room for improvement."
- "When I first started this class I was very doubtful that it would do

any good for me. Now that I have finished my class I have realized, in some unexplainable way, I'm a lot calmer. I don't blow up at the littlest thing. I'm able to think before I react to the conflict without thinking it through, which causes a lot of problems, now that I think first then react to the situation and usually work things out a lot easier."

What Did Participants Say About Treatment Components That Are Helpful to Them?

The narration of participants revealed a range of perceived positive attributes of the treatment program. Many of these positive attributes are consistent with the nature of the group, that is, a goal-oriented, solution-focused group treatment program that utilizes self-initiated goals to provide a context for change.

Goal-Oriented

Several participants succinctly described the goal-oriented nature of the group:

- "The basic class required setting goals and learning to work through or deal with issues in new ways."
- "I really like the idea of setting a goal in order to make what you might call a 'good' habit."
- "It [the class] makes you think about your life and where you want to be with yourself."
- "This course has helped me to maintain focus on my goal."

One participant used the metaphor of bowling to beautifully describe his perception of the goal-oriented nature of the class:

- "I guess one way for me to describe it, (however corny it may be), is to think of my 'goals' as bowling pins. Instead of individually firing at the pins, (or goals), at random, this class has taught me if I set up my goals in order the momentum from knocking one down can be used to catapult you through the others. Sometimes a strike will roll your way and others a space that you will have to try and pick up."

Focus on Positive and Nonblaming Stance

Another appreciated attribute of the program was its focus on positive changes and a complete avoidance of a blaming stance. Because participants were mostly court-mandated clients who carried the label of "domestic violence offenders," many of them might have expected the program to be punitive, confrontational, and blaming. The positive and nonblaming stance of this treatment program probably comes as a helpful surprise for some participants:

- "Why I think this program has some positive outcomes, is because it is not demeaning you or shaming you. It makes you think about your life and where you want to be with yourself. What I got from the program is that everyone of us for one reason or another has something that we can change or improve in ourselves to become a better person."
- "The people who taught this class made sure that you did the work outside of class. They wanted you to do something positive and very achievable."

Fostering New Beneficial Thinking and Behaviors

Helping people to notice a difference that will make a difference in their lives is a major tenet of the solution-focused approach. Such an effort was recognized by some participants, as revealed in their narration of their group experiences:

- "I think that this class helps you to rethink new ideas and helps you to gain the confidence in yourself to try new things in yourself and for your life to help you to make a better way to cope with things, to make a difference, hopefully a better, happier difference."
- "This class I feel was helpful because it gave me skills on how to deal with situations, or just everyday life."

Small, Attainable Changes That Provide Indicators of Progress

Solution-focused treatment emphasizes helping clients to attain small changes that will make a difference in their situation. Small goals are often perceived as more viable and attainable. A participant summarized such a focus with concrete examples:

- "It is a self-taught class of long-term goal setting, but with simple goals, which can really change our lives. Who would have guessed sharing a TV remote control would bring so much joy to any person, or just doing dishes can enhance your daily life so much."

Because of a focus on small changes, participants were more likely to see positive results of their efforts. Such feedback has a positive impact by reinforcing the motivation to change:

- "I've improved immensely by continuing my goal, and I will continue after the class because I can already see the results."

Solutions Come from Within

Some participants appreciated the focus on the self as the person who has the solution:

- "If we look toward change we will often find we have the answer within, and may see it when we are willing to quit looking at the problem."

Self-Focused Learning, Not Lecturing

Another appreciated attribute of the program was its focus on self-initiated experiential learning:

- "I think most of the people in life need to learn by practice instead of by someone telling you what is right or wrong."

Brevity

One participant commented positively on the duration of the program, noting that it was short but "strong":

- "I really am glad for this course, with its shortness and strength."

The feedback from most group participants was consistent with the nature of solution-focused treatment. Other participants, however, provided feedback that was either unexpected or unrelated to the treatment approaches.

A Mixed Group That Includes Both Males and Females

Some participants appreciated the mixed gender composition of the group, which allowed them to perceive things from a different perspective:

- "I have and had been learning a lot about human behavior from both the male and female view of things. Men and women think differently. To understand this is a great help!"
- "I enjoyed this class because there were a lot of men in it and just listening to them, their frustrations, expressing their feeling, because basically I thought they had a different outlook than women. Made me see them in a different light."

What Did Participants Say About Treatment Components That Are Unhelpful to Them?

Several participants provided useful feedback regarding what they considered unhelpful aspects of the treatment program.

Class Too Large

The group consisted of 4 to 10 participants. There might be times when a group became too large and individual participants felt neglected: "I feel the class was too large to be able to get more of what the class could really offer each individual. I sat and didn't get to share and learn as much as I wanted. We spent too much time trying to see what good someone's goal was going to be for them and not enough individual time on my goal and how it's working. I think that in 8 hours of class I got 30 minutes of individual time."

Class Too Short

While some participants appreciated the brevity of the group treatment program, one participant commented that the program was too short for people to make enough progress: "I also feel that the class was about 7 classes short of making more progress."

Not Including Spouse or Partner

Treating couples together in a domestic violence situation is a controversial practice. Nevertheless, one participant expressed a wish to be treated along with his partner. In fact, several couples attended the Plumas program, although at different times: "I feel my spouse and I would have made more progress if she attended the class with me."

Left Out Alcohol Discussion

"Need more discussion concerning alcohol/drug abuse 'cause it can be strong determinant for some people."

Being Court-Ordered to Attend the Program

The participants in this treatment program were court-mandated clients who might not be personally invested in a change process. Such an attitude might hinder other participants' learning experiences: "I learned that this group format is not beneficial to everyone, because people here are just doing their time and that blocks any true expression by others, since personal growth is not their interest and there were times that I felt my time here was wasted." "Would I recommend this class to anyone, probably not, unless they were willing to want to make a change in their own lives. Ah! Did I step on some toes here? What I am saying is, that a person has to want to change their ways, being forced into a class I don't think will help, especially the format you have."

What Did Participants Say About Facilitators' Behaviors That Are Helpful to Them?

The significance of relationship and interaction between clients and therapists can never be overstated. Voluminous outcome studies repeatedly point to the same findings that the therapeutic relationship counts, in fact, more than the proposed techniques of any specific approaches (Asay & Lambert, 1999). The comments of participants in our programs focused on therapeutic and relational behaviors of the facilitators. Several participants also mentioned the personal characteristics of facilitators, including comments that they were great people and relaxed, friendly, and nice.

Therapeutic Behaviors

Having expectations: "The people who taught this class made sure that you did the work outside of class." "They wanted you to do something positive and very achievable." "Didn't let anyone get away with b.s.; made you prove that you worked on your goal."

Asking good questions that encourage thinking: "They asked questions to make you really think." "I think that this class helps you to rethink new ideas." "They pushed you into explaining yourself." "Opening up my mind, going deeper with questions." "They asked lots of questions which brought things to life."

Giving compliments: "Giving compliments helps increase the trust level, and makes everyone feel better about themselves."

Staying positive: "Using positive language that is really helpful; positive attitude, keep everything focused on what can be improved more in the future; not focusing on the past."

Nonpunitive: "They weren't finger-pointing."

"On top" of the session: "They work together well; both 'on top of it.' "

Effective communication: "Helped me get out what [facilitators] really meant." "They made it so you had to answer their questions (they would rephrase the questions so they were more understandable."

Personal sharing: "Facilitators had similar problems but they could deal with them better (better able to manage emotion)."

Focus on doing: "Helpful to have reporting requirement to check on progress of goals. Helped to put goals into action."

Provide feedback: "Make suggestions, giving their ideas and personal opinions on things." "Give good advice on problems."

Attend individual needs: "Well, because of my circumstances I don't drink, do drugs, and have no partner! It was difficult, but they tried to cater to my needs, also."

Help achieve personal understanding: "They listened and helped me see what the problems were." "Mostly they asked questions that made you look to yourself, and saying things aloud so you can form solution by recognizing problem."

Relational Behaviors

Engaging: "To strive for, reach, grasp, and enjoy every concept of understanding relating to and listen to others."

Encouraging: "Encouragement by words and facial expressions." "Encouraged everyone to think for self and come up with own solutions."

Supportive: "Supportive in taking care of self (getting needs met)."

Listening: "Listened and helped me get out what I really meant." "Listening, didn't cut in." "They listened well."

Giving space: "Didn't pressure people, but everybody's story eventually came out, nobody got upset." "Took time with each person to explore feelings."

Being fair: "Didn't take sides."

Being available: "Just being there, helped when I got upset."

Being sincere: "What they said was from the heart."

What Did Participants Say About What They Had Learned from Attending the Program?

Because participants determined and developed their personal goals, the things they said they learned from the class were as diverse as who they were. Three major themes of learning that were identified were learning focusing on self, learning focusing on relationships, and learning focusing on developing helpful attitudes. In addition, because the described learning is self-initiated by group participants, these self-narrated aspects of learning have implications for understanding helpful components of learning experiences for this population.

Learning Focusing on Self

One important theme under the self-focused learning was participants' increased ability to control and/or handle their anger. Using information available from 75 participants, 55% of respondents identified learning or discovering different ways to control their anger as the main thing they had learned from the class. Two other identified themes were increased self-confidence (33%) and a positive outlook on life (57%).

Learning Focusing on Anger Management

Despite the absence of any educational elements in the present treatment program regarding anger management, participants discovered many diverse, effective ways to control anger. Many of the ways that they had discovered on their own are very similar to the conventional wisdom on this topic.

Think Before Act: Participants used many different ways to describe their personal version of "think before act," such as "And at home, I just go into another room until I think about the situation and can talk about whatever is wrong, without yelling." "With my dad I think more before I talk. I don't yell but if I need to speak I'll tell him, 'Let me speak and you will listen for once.' My old way I would've yelled back and no one would get their point across." "My listening skills have kicked in, instead of my reaction skill."

Ask Before Getting Angry: "That I should ask first before I react." "My goal is to be curious when I feel I'm being attacked." "I also learned to listen to what people say in a calm manner, instead of blowing up when they try to talk to me."

Walk Away: "But maybe to take a walk or do something constructive to help vent any frustrations that may led to anger." "And at home, I just go into another room until I think about the situation and can talk about whatever is wrong, without yelling, I learned to control my anger, if someone says something I don't like I just turn my head and do something else."

Yelling Is Unhelpful: "I've learned that yelling at one another won't get us anywhere. It only makes the problem a lot worse." "I learned that the way I handled my anger was wrong. I should not yell and get mad because things can become out of control, and cause more harm than good."

Express Feeling Without Getting Angry: "I have learned that I don't have to hold my feelings about things back. I only have to not take them out on other people. I can still tell how I feel about things. I just don't get mad about them now."

Not to Get Mad at Little Things: "I have worked hard not to get mad over little things." "I don't blow up at the littlest thing." "It's better for me to not let every little thing get to me."

Strengthening Personal Choice Regarding Reaction: "Emotion can only be controlled to a certain extent, but reaction is up to me."

Recognizing Anger: "When anger occurs, recognize it—the fact that no problem can be dealt with in a positive manner or objectively while under the influence of that emotion." "Any time that a situation becomes diffi-cult, I usually catch myself, if not before, at least after only a few swear words."

Stay Calm: "Some of my friends at work have noticed and made com-ments regarding my newfound ability to remain calm under difficult situa-tions." "And that dealing with my anger in a calmer manner is the better choice for me."

Stop Drinking: "When I stopped drinking and using dope it helped my patience and kept my temper at bay also."

Learning Focusing on Relationship

In our program, 83.5% of participants had relationship problems with their spouses or partners, 3.5% had abused their children, and 2.4% had rela-tionship problems with their own parents. Based on the self-initiated nar-ration of 75 participants, 87% of the participants chose to discuss different aspects of learning pertaining to relationship. Fifty-three percent of partic-ipants mentioned learning related to couple relationships; 9% parent-child relationships; 5% relationship issues with their family of origin; 3% work-related relationships; and 16% social relationships in general. The identified themes of relational learning ranged from learning specific to a relationship (such as listening to one's wife, spending more time with family, helping with chores and kids, and being a better dad) to broad-based relational skills, including respecting other people, showing care, engaging in give-and-take, trusting people, using two-way communication, awareness of other's needs, being nice, giving space to self and others, and looking for good in people.

Identified Themes of Relational Learning

Listen to Spouses or Partners: "I've learned that I should listen to her and give her a chance to talk without interrupting, and I've learned I should try to be more understanding toward her and her feelings." "My goal was to really listen to my wife. She didn't like my jokes, where I touch her. This was a good goal for me because not listening to her had been an old habit. This was a good solid base for me to start with."

Two-Way Communication: "I've found out communication between the both of us, instead of taking it upon myself to do whatever I decided, clears up a lot of problems before they even start." "In a period in my life when I shut most people out, this class opened my eyes to not only share my life with them, but to listen, learn and to better understand other beings."

Awareness of Other's Needs: "The biggest asset I am bringing with me from this group, I feel, is my awareness of my significant other's needs." "It has been helpful in making me aware of her feelings. I stop to think of what I'm saying or doing around her."

Be Nice: "Being nice and saying nice things." "So, yes, I will definitely keep up what I'm doing now, which is spending more time with my daughter and being nicer to her, which I've been doing."

Spend More Time with Family: "I also learned that spending more time with my family isn't as bad as I thought it would be and I've really enjoyed them a lot more because of it." "I've learned to include her in my everyday plans, include her in my life, and it makes her feel I want her around and a part of my life. I've learned to take a little time each day to spend just with her. It makes her feel good and loved, and I've seen how much it means."

Give Space to Self and Others: "How to deal with frustration and anger, by taking time out for oneself and giving others their time and space, too." "My goal was to allow my wife her freedom, so to speak, as in going to her appointments and such by herself. At first it was difficult, as in the feeling is she going to be home or not, or is she being shipped out to another hospital. I was able to shift my mind onto other tasks to keep it occupied. I now work and focus my attention on myself to do a few things that make me feel good, but at the same time maintain a sense of calm but with my guard up as in the responsibilities a husband is to make, and I try to make them in more of a loving manner."

Help with Chores and Kids: "I feel that I have learned that I need to work at my own responsibility around my house and in my relationship rather than helping my friends or doing nothing at all. Doing more work at home has helped my relationship with my wife. We have been arguing less than before." "My wife is most likely to notice a change in me. Me being home more, helping with homework, and getting the kids to bed."

To Be a Better Dad: "I also have become more of a daddy than a father. I was acting like my dad, and I did not want my daughter to have a life like I did."

Look for Good in People: "Where I might otherwise overreact, I learned that giving compliments helps increase the trust level and makes everyone feel better about themselves."

Care: "I learned a lot about caring and respecting others." "I learned that others care about me also."

Respect Others: "I learned to respect people and accept people for who they are."

Give-and-take: "I learned that if you give a little of yourself the return is excellent."

Trust: "I see trust is intertwined with a lot of the emotions I feel. The more I trust, the easier it is to deal with those life situations."

Learning Focusing on Developing Beneficial Attitudes

Based on 75 participants' self-narration, 98% of participants mentioned different learning in terms of a change in their attitude: 43% discussed attitudinal change in terms of staying focused on goals; 60% mentioned looking for change in oneself instead of others; 57% talked about taking more responsibility; 57% spoke about staying positive; 8% mentioned the importance of being accepting; and 11% talked about attitudinal change pertaining to letting go. A minority of respondents described their attitudinal change in terms of being more relaxed, flexible, and open and having more patience and a stronger commitment to change.

Learning Pertaining to the Development of Beneficial Attitudes

Stay Focused on Goals: "I've learned in this class that once you have worked on personal goals, and have the discipline to keep trying to better yourself, things seem to fall into place much easier." "I have found that I can make a difference with easy small steps in self-goal-oriented mind thoughts." "What I learned from this group is that if you set your mind on something you can always accomplish."

Stay Positive: "I found out that you can start a positive cycle in your life almost as simply as a negative one. Everyone knows when something goes wrong, everything goes wrong. What I didn't know is when you change a simple thing for the better, it can snowball into a lot more better things." "I learned that focusing my thought solely on the positive and not the negative allows me to stay calm and respond in a positive manner."

Change in Self and Not Others: "Change is possible, but must come from the heart with intent and meaning. People can't change others. You must change yourself." "If we look toward change we will often find we have the answer within." "I learned that I could do nothing about other people. I cannot change the way anyone thinks, feels, or acts. The only person I can do anything about is myself."

Taking Responsibility: "The most important thing I learned, all due to this class, was I needed to take the initiative and responsibility for my own behavior and life." "What I have learned in this group is to always think of what it is and what is the penalty, try to reason out good and bad."

Accepting: "It has taught me that I can be myself, and express myself." "My goal was to be less rigid, not force my ways and methods down everyone's throat." "The goal I determined to pursue was to look at my wife in a different way, much as when we were young and dating. I also decided to quit having expectations of what she would do or become. If I see or receive anything good, I just need to be thankful and in appreciation."

Relax: "The more relaxed I am and less stressed out I am, the more control I have on myself." "Take a deep breath; go get a drink of water or cup of coffee. Best of all make light of it, joke about it, and laugh." "I learned that life doesn't have to be so serious and stressful all the time."

Patience: "By learning to have more patience, it makes me a mellower person. I can deal with problems big or small more rationally. Therefore, I haven't lost my temper, which means no violence." "I see that improvement takes time, it takes commitment, and patience within one's self."

Open and Flexible: "I learned that flexibility is a plus." "The biggest asset I am bringing with me from this group, I feel, is my awareness of my significant other's needs and my ability to be more open-minded."

Commitment: "I learned that I could set goals and reach them simply by committing myself to the thought." "Yes, there are setbacks. Certain triggers that may cause a reaction put us back to comfortable or learned responses that may not be where we want to be. Yet, with commitment I can jump back into my goal and try again to change and grow." "With all change it does not come easy. It takes thought and determination. It can be hard. It is easy to give up."

What Did Participants Say About the Benefits They Had Gained by Attending the Program?

Forty-two percent of participants described better relationships with other people, 39% mentioned their new determination to do something helpful in their life, 39% spoke about feeling better or more confident about self, 19% mentioned being more hopeful, and 10% mentioned developing new skills. Seventeen percent of participants also mentioned a unique personal accomplishment as a result of the group experience: 7% stopped using drugs or alcohol, 5% got a job, 2% started school, and 3% reunited with their children.

Better Relationship with Others

Family relationship: "I have had more time to spend with my family on a happy note instead of a sour one." "I and my household are a lot nicer." "This goal has certainly improved my home life."

Parent-child relationship: "I've always had a problem being able to talk to my dad about what was bothering me, now I'm able to talk to him, tell him my feeling and thoughts. Since I can sit down and talk to him and my stepmom, we have been able to start to become a family that can sit down and discuss everything. It's made all of us, including my wife, kids, and father, a lot closer together."

Couple relationships: "The organization has also helped in my relationship with my girlfriend." "Listening to my wife and doing as she asked has started our relationship to develop into a stronger relationship."

Social relationships: "I believe that with the help of this class and my classmates and the instructors I have become more easygoing and friendly because of the shared personal stories."

Work-related relationships: "At work I have to work on thinking before I speak. I did with two employees."

Developing Determination

Thirty-nine percent of participants talked about their determination to do something better in their life. While some broadly declared their determination to carry on their goal effort, others described their determination in a clear, specific, and contextualized manner. "Yes, I believe I will keep it up in the future. For instance, why would I go back to the way things were? I never got any positive responses from anyone nevertheless my daughter.

All I ever got from anyone was negative responses. I didn't like that one bit, it made me feel like I wasn't in control at any time. But now that I've learned a new tactic, I get better responses."

Feeling Better and/or More Confident About Self

"It makes me feel a lot better about myself." "I feel better about myself, and my family has even noticed the difference in me." "I feel we are both better people because of it [the class]." "In fact I feel really feel good about myself when I'm able to control my temper and manage to solve the problem at hand without exploding."

Being Hopeful

"This class took a leap of faith in leaving to let go and seeing if it is working. Let it work, things do seem to work out for the best." "My wife and I will hopefully never let the lack of communication invade our relationship again."

New Skills

"The bottom line is that these skills I've been working on seem to have a positive effect, certainly better than before." "I know that my husband and even the baby both notice a large difference in the way I follow through and hold firm to our new beliefs."

What Did the Spouses and Partners of Participants Say About the Treatment program?

Positive Changes in Participants as Perceived by Their Spouses and Partners

We consider the spouses and partners of group participants key informants regarding the effectiveness of the treatment program because they are the ultimate beneficiaries of successful treatment. During the follow-up interview, we asked them an open-ended question: "In your own words, can you tell me any positive changes in your spouse or partner after he or she participated in the program?" Twenty-two spouses and partners shared a wide range of positive changes in the participants that were related mostly to emotional skills, relational skills, involvement in family, and motivation to change.

Emotional Skills

Most spouses and partners focused on the issue of anger control when describing changes in the participants. Some mentioned the cessation or reduction of violence: "I can't remember when he blew up last time," "hasn't hit children," "not violent," "less violent physically." Others talked about their partners as less angry: "Anger issues better," "Less aggressive," "He didn't get upset as much as before." Others emphasized their spouses' newly developed skills for controlling anger: "He controls his temper a lot more." "He learns how to deal with anger in different ways." "He now began to think more about anger." "Takes time to think through things." "Think before acting."

Other comments focused on the specific skills that program participants had learned to control anger: "He recognized when he got angry, would try to control it, and when would get angry would go out to garage." "He learns how to deal with anger in different ways. When he starts to get angry he'll leave me alone and compose himself (go off to garage, a ride, room). Before, he'd yell." "He doesn't get upset, when upset will go by himself and come to me later. He's able to handle better. Before, I used to get scared when he's angry and I don't have that feeling anymore now." "He learned ways to deal with anger other than physically, learned to talk things over."

Some spouses and partners, however, focused on other aspects of emotional skills, including increased ability to express emotion and being more calm: "He's able to show more emotion." "He's able to get things off his chest." "She is easier to get along with, she's easygoing, has slowed down." "He's more mellow, more likable." "He's more calm." "She used to be real violent and now she's a lot more mellow than she was." One respondent commented that her spouse "drives a lot slower, more considerate, and less impulsive."

Relational Skills

Another major area of change in participants as reported by their spouses and partners pertains to relational skills. Many spouses and partners talked about positive changes in participants' communications skills that moved toward increased mutuality and/or expressiveness in the communication process: "He listened, he attended." "Now able to discuss with me." "More willing to talking about things and compromise; out of 10 times stopping off—only does it 4 times now." "He seemed to be able to communicate and get along with others better." "Can talk things out." "More able to communicate better than just shouting. Communications improved." "Better to deal with things in a relationship, more tolerant." Other described positive changes in relational skills included the following:

- More considerate
- Asks for wife's feedback
- Much more respectful
- Less arguing
- More honest
- More tolerant

Positive changes in relational skills were not limited to couple relations; participants also function better in social relationships: "He has learned to reach out to others." "He had social interaction with people now compared to then."

Involvement in Family

Spouses and partners also described the program participants as more involved and engaged in the couple's and/or the family's life. Participants helped around the house and spent more time with spouse and children. "Go for walks, lunch, lot of time just for two of them, going to church, give me flowers." "Spend times with daughters." "Taking care of his six-year-old girl." "Helps me with kids." "Participating in family."

Other Positive Changes in Life

Spouses and partners also described other positive changes in participants' lives. Stopping addiction was one of the most frequently mentioned positive changes: "Not using any substances." "He quit smoking and drinking for a short time after." "Abstaining from alcohol." "Stopped drug use." Other described changes included getting back together, taking medication (started taking medicine, Prozac), and keeping jobs ("He kept his job for more than 1 year").

Helpful Treatment Components as Perceived by Spouses and Partners of Participants

During the follow-up phone interview, we asked the respondents, "What things about the program did you find helpful to your spouse or partner?" Several respondents said that they had little information about the program, since their spouses and partners did not talk about it. Others, however, provided a range of ideas about how the program had helped their spouses and partners:

- Take responsibility: "Pointed out stuff for him to take responsibility for."
- Not blaming: "He doesn't try to blame others for his action."
- Realization of consequence: "That if he hurts me again he will go to prison. It's not OK to hurt people."

- Hope: "Provided hope."
- Insight: "Allowed him to see he wasn't handling problems properly."
- Behavior: "Learn how to keep his mouth shut." "They talk a lot about smoking and drinking problems."
- Homework: "The homework was helpful."
- Positive: "Trying to keep positive instead of negative."

Discussion

The outcome study encountered difficulties, resource constraints, and limitations shared by other studies. The major limitations were modest sample size, lack of a control or comparison group, and lack of control of external factors such as divorce, relocation, or incarceration that might influence outcome. In addition, the response rates of participants and their partners and spouses at follow-up interviews were both around 55%. The considerably higher response rates of our study as compared with some other studies of batterer programs do not reduce the problem of selectivity bias in the follow-up study. Participants who improved or had a positive perception of the program might have a higher response rate than those who did not improve or approve of the program. To find out whether there were significant differences between the group of program participants that responded to the follow-up interviews and the group that did not respond, further analyses were conducted to compare the two groups on recidivism rates based on official arrest records, relevant demographic variables (race, education, age, employment, gender), and other background variables (*DSM-IV* Axis I and Axis II diagnoses, alcohol and/or substance abuse, parental divorce, family alcoholism, criminal offenses, experience of abuse as children). Findings of chi-squares did not indicate significant differences between the two groups on any one of these variables. In other words, there is a lack of empirical evidence for selectivity bias between the respond group and the nonrespond group at the 6-month follow-up interviews.

Recidivism rates reported by participants and their spouses had to be interpreted with caution. As mentioned earlier, the response rates of participants and their spouses at the 6-month follow-up were around 55%. Despite the lack of evidence for selectivity bias, we still did not have complete data on all participants and their spouses at the 6-month follow-up. In addition, only 46.7% of participants were in intimate relationships at the time of evaluation. However, data on recidivism rates based on official arrest records were collected for all program participants. Still, we had concerns about the validity of those recidivism rates because some participants might have moved out of the state after completing the program. Consequently, the recidivism rates compiled from official records may not have reflected the actual occurrence of violent behaviors by the offenders. This problem is common to all outcome studies of batterer programs. Attempts were made to find out whether participants whose telephone lines had been disconnected or could not be contacted at the 6-month follow-up were represented in the reoffending group as based on official arrest records. Findings indicated that participants whose telephone lines had been disconnected or could not be contacted were represented in the reoffending group. Among the 42 participants we failed to contact during the follow-up interview, 10 had reoffending records at the victim witness office, the probation office, and/or the district attorney's office. Although such information did not constitute valid proof of local residence of participants, it did imply that some of the participants we failed to interview during the 6-month period still resided within the local judicial system.

Despite limitations, we addressed some existing issues of evaluation of offender programs in our study. We expanded our definition of effectiveness to include both behavioral factors (cessation of violence, changes in relational behavior in intimate relationships and self-esteem of participants) and process factors (components within the treatment program) by utilizing quantitative and qualitative data in the evaluation process. In addition, we utilized multiple reporting sources in the data collection process that included program participants, spouses and partners of participants, program facilitators, and official arrest records (district attorney, probation office, and victim witness officer). The use of strength-based instruments also expanded the conventional evaluation focus of behavioral change in terms of cessation of violence to include positive changes or learning in relational behaviors in intimate relationships.

Utilizing quantitative data, findings of the outcome study provided initial empirical evidence of the effectiveness of a solution-focused approach for treating domestic violence offenders. The recidivism rate of 16.7% for our program, as based on official records, is considerably lower than that for most other treatment programs for domestic violence offenders. It was comparable to the recidivism rate of 13.5% reported by spouses and partners at the 6-month follow-up interviews. Similarly, the program completion rate of 92.8% was impressive compared with rates for most other programs. We believe that the extremely low program dropout rate of 7.2% can largely be attributed to the program's short duration and the clear group rule regarding attendance that was set early on in the treatment process. Among program participants who were involved in intimate relationships (around half of the original sample), findings indicated a significant improvement in their relational skills in intimate relationships as evaluated by their spouses and partners. The improvement in participants' relational skills from pretreatment to posttreatment was maintained 6 months after completion of the program. In addition, participants and their spouses and partners perceived a significant decrease in participants' verbal and physical violent behavior 6 months after participants' completion of the program. Based on self-reports of participants, findings indicated a significant increase in their self-esteem from pretreatment to posttreatment. The increase in participants' self-esteem was maintained 6 months after their completion of the treatment program. In addition, findings indicated that participants' recidivism was not related to their profiles, including *DSM-IV* diagnoses, substance and/or alcohol abuse problems, involvement with criminal offenses, parental divorce, and parental alcoholism. However, experience of childhood abuse was found to be associated with recidivism in participants.

Content analysis of qualitative data elucidates helpful treatment components and therapeutic factors perceived by program participants and their spouses and partners. The helpful components of the treatment program include being goal oriented, focusing on the positive, being nonblaming, fostering new beneficial thinking and behaviors, emphasizing self-focused learning but not lecturing, looking for small changes with clear indicators of progress, emphasizing solutions and strengths from within, and including both genders in the treatment program. Spouses and partners of participants shared similar perceptions of the helpful nature of our program. The cited beneficial components of the program were being nonblaming, focusing on the positive, providing hope, and assisting participants in developing insight and attaining behavioral changes. A major helpful component that was mentioned only by spouses was helping participants to take responsibility and understand consequences of violence.

Beneficial therapeutic behaviors of group facilitators include having expectations, asking good questions that encourage reflection, giving compliments, staying positive, being nonpunitive, staying "on top" of the session, having effective communication skills, focusing on doing, providing feedback, attending to individual needs, and assisting participants in achieving personal understanding. Program participants described beneficial relational behaviors of group facilitators as engaging, encouraging, being supportive, listening, giving space, being fair, being available, and being sincere. Findings of the qualitative data also illuminate participants' self-narrated descriptions of learning and benefits that they attained as a result of coming to the treatment program, as well as their spouses and partners' descriptions of positive changes in participants as a consequence of attending the program.

An understanding of participants' and spouses' and partners' perception of helpful treatment components and beneficial therapist behaviors provides valuable information for therapists to learn about effective group treatment with this population. Examining self-narrated positive changes, benefits, and learning of participants also helps us understand the personal and social impact of treatment programs on participants and their significant others.

Conclusion

The described outcome study is part of a broader effort to examine the effectiveness of offender programs. The dual purposes of our study are (1) to establish empirical evidence of a solution-focused, strength-based approach for treating domestic violence offenders and (2) to examine helpful program components that can effectively inform practice. We sincerely believe that research should inform practice and vice versa.

Despite efforts to evaluate the effectiveness of batterer programs, Gondolf (1997) suggested, "In a social science court, most of the batterer program evaluations would be dismissed on technicalities or as circumstantial evidence" (p. 208). Such scrutiny probably applies to our study. Despite initial empirical evidence that indicates comparatively lower recidivism rates, higher program completion rates, and positive feedback from participants and their spouses of a solution-focused approach for treating domestic violence offenders, we cannot conclude in any decisive manner that our program is more effective than other treatment approaches because of a lack of comparison groups and the use of nonrandomized samples in our present study. Limitations of research methodology, on the other hand, present both challenges and opportunities for practitioners and researchers to further examine the effectiveness of treatment programs using a solution-focused approach in treating domestic violence offenders. In addition, there is a clear and unambiguous need to search for methodological rigor, a clear conceptualization of effectiveness, an expanded focus of evaluation, and the inclusion of a strengths perspective in the field of domestic violence treatment.

Specific recommendations for future investigations include employing control groups that include conventional treatment modalities such as feminist-cognitive-behavioral models, psychodynamic approaches, and so forth; using a larger sample for more precise and refined statistical analysis; developing multisites that include both urban and rural locations, well-off and deprived communities, and localities with more ethnic and racial diversity; developing strategies to improve response rates for follow-up interviews; using multiple reporting sources; developing strengths-oriented instruments and frameworks in the process of evaluation; expanding the focus of evaluation to include offenders' behaviors, social impact on consumers including the victims, and organizational components that contribute to positive outcomes. In addition, it is imperative to include qualitative methods in addition to quantitative methods in the process of evaluation. Qualitative methods can better assist researchers in understanding the subtle process of change in domestic violence offenders.

11

Afterword

Potential Modifications of the Program

When we discover effective approaches to change, we naturally want to identify the potential applications and limits of the approach. We have been asked whether this model can be used in significantly longer treatment models and whether it can be used with other populations with different types of problems.

The current model has evolved through many minor modifications and adjustments, yet the core structure has remained the same. The aspects that we believe are necessary are related to three critical elements: (1) the active belief that people can create their own solutions, (2) the belief that the element of choice in treatment creates a powerful force for change, and (3) the belief that focusing on small, goal-related behaviors can provide a powerful catalyst for developing meaningful and lasting change in a relatively short time. We believe that utilization of this model must include at a minimum these basic elements.

These elements present certain advantages as well as limitations. For example, we feel strongly that it would be counterproductive to combine this approach with one that assumes that participants require expert-driven, long-term treatment. We believe that when participants must focus on goal-related behavior over a short period and are expected to make significant life changes, a powerful and compelling self-fulfilling prophecy is created. Conversely, when the message is that change is unlikely to occur in the immediate future or can occur only under preset conditions, we believe that the results will reflect these expectations. Needless to say, we are skeptical of adding a solution-focused component to a lengthy and otherwise problem-focused treatment program, and we believe that doing so would negatively affect outcomes. Consistent beliefs and expectations are important, as well as critical, conditions of this approach.

Two important questions, then, are how long is too long, and do some people require more group sessions then others? Our use of an

8-week format was originally a result of limited resources and dissatisfaction with earlier efforts. Later we continued using the 8-week format because it worked and it was part of our research design. Our current thinking is that it is possible, if not probable, that more group sessions may have some benefits. Our subjective observation is that some individuals simply need a few more contacts to solidify the changes that they are becoming committed to.

We believe the upper limit should not exceed 12 group sessions, and the lower range is the current format of 8 group sessions. We have come to this conclusion because a small number of participants appear to need additional groups beyond the currently required 8 sessions; some participants have informed us that a few more sessions would be of benefit to them. At the same time, many individuals would be demoralized and less focused if required to attend any number of sessions beyond 12 groups. This implies that there is actually a potentially negative treatment effect when groups last longer then 12 sessions.

An alternative to adding sessions directly on to succeeding sessions is to add "booster" sessions at set intervals after a core of 8 to 12 sessions. We have experimented with this arrangement on a voluntary basis and found that participants had significant interest on the front end but in general found it difficult to follow through. If this alternative was utilized, we believe it would have to be mandatory. We have not studied the impact of this alteration but feel it may expand the benefits of the program by encouraging longer term investment in goal-related behavior and better focus on behaviors that the participant has discovered to be helpful. There is, of course, the possibility of a negative outcome if participants feel that the facilitators don't have confidence in the changes they have already achieved. Because of this potential, we recommend this modification with reservation.

We have often discussed the length of group sessions and continue to believe that 60- to 70-minute sessions are optimal. Like most people, the individuals we work with find it difficult to maintain attention after an hour of focused effort. Additionally, the time constraint of 1 hour has the added bonus of pressing everyone, including the treatment team, to work hard to do as much as possible within the limited time. Pressure to use time effectively increases efficiency and productivity.

For many years we have conducted groups with various numbers of participants and have concluded that the optimal number of participants is approximately 8. As groups increase in size up to 12 participants, the quality of the group process can be maintained at acceptable levels with most groups, but not without some risk of losing focus with some participants. Working with groups larger then 12 is almost always unsatisfactory because it is difficult to give enough attention to the goal development and utilization processes of all participants. When this occurs, the risk of dropouts and poorly focused goal work is increased.

Alternative Applications: Expanding Possibilities

We have applied this program with other populations, including groups for parents who have children placed outside the home by the court and/or social services. In this application, the court orders parents to attend eight group sessions prior to having their children return home. The goal is to improve the likelihood of successful reunification while decreasing return placements. Initially the parents, much like domestic violence offenders, were somewhat angry, yet they quickly became advocates of the group because they felt supported and challenged by the process. When providing feedback on this group, most participants felt the groups should have had more sessions. We believe this may be because many parents felt isolated and unsupported in their attempts to get their children back. Prior to working with this population we had predicted that it would be very difficult to engage them in the process, but this proved to not be the case. In fact, most parents wanted to talk about solutions and appreciated hearing others talk about solutions as well. We have not been able to conduct research regarding this project but believe it holds much promise.

With modifications we have used a group-based, solution-focused approach in working with teens in wilderness and activity-based treatment programs. The teens in this program were not mandated to attend or successfully complete the program. Initial efforts to implement individual goals were marginally successful and somewhat difficult within the group process. As a result of over 10 years of evolution, we shifted to a format that emphasizes helping adolescents actively search for solutions as problems arise in real-life situations. The staff models solution-based responses and searches, combined with compliments that we refer to as appreciations. We have recently implemented research to evaluate this project.

Colleagues have successfully applied a modified format of our program to treat adolescents identified as substance abusers. In this mandated program, teens were required to develop goals and discuss them in much the same manner as in our domestic violence treatment program. Local judges attended the final sessions to hear firsthand about participants' progress and to compliment their efforts.

We believe the solution-focused group format with, or in some cases without, modifications has many potential applications. One of the strengths of solution-focused models is that they do not require the facilitators to develop different treatments for each problem because the participants are respected as capable of creating their own unique solutions.

Domestic Violence System of Response

This book is not intended to develop a comprehensive system of care for domestic violence. On the other hand, we would be remiss if we failed to address some of the basic system response requirements that we have found important for addressing the issue of domestic violence. The discussion also includes our broader thoughts about treatment programs for domestic violence offenders.

Multimodal and Multiperspective System Responses to Domestic Violence

The existing literature indicates that domestic violence offenders are not a homogeneous group of people who can be easily characterized by any single profile. Some offenders may have experienced or witnessed abuse as children (Straus, 1996; Saunders, 1995); others may have problems with alcohol abuse (Kaufman, 1993). Some are violent outside of their homes and have criminal records, while others are violent only in their "havens" (Holtzworth-Munroe & Stuart, 1994). Some have a *DSM-IV* diagnosis, whereas others do not. Some offenders suffer from the effects of poverty, while others are the "haves" in our society. In other words, treatment programs deal with a wide range of people who come to violence through a variety of pathways. In addition, domestic violence is a highly complex social-cultural-political issue with a deep-rooted history. The ethnoracial diversity of our society adds to the complexity of the picture, since different cultures engender diverse beliefs and practices about gender, marriage, power, and authority.

Consequently, we believe that solutions to end domestic violence are likely to be diverse and multifaceted, involving more than any one type of treatment that a single institution can offer. After reviewing different perspectives and approaches to intervening in domestic violence, Eisikovits, Enosh, and Edleson (1996) conclude that the current scene implies a both-and attitude (Goldner, 1992) that tends to lean toward pragmatism—a pragmatism focusing on immediate, urgent needs of battered women without losing sight of the need for long-term, deep-rooted structural and cultural changes in gender relations. Schwandt (1994) further describes the current social movement as pluralistic and plastic, in with a variety of symbols and language systems that have been used to address the subject of domestic violence. From our perspective, our approach for treating domestic violence offenders is part of the pluralistic, societal effort to develop pragmatic solutions to end the more immediate, visible violence in intimate relationships. A solution-focused approach, however, distinguishes itself from other conventional approaches by utilizing the language and symbols of "solution and strengths" as opposed to the language of "deficits and blame."

Developing Supportive Connections

The complex and diverse nature of domestic violence requires the involvement of different players in its cessation. Many systems are immediately involved, such as law enforcement, probation departments, district attorneys, judges, treatment providers, health care professionals, women's shelters, and researchers. In the background are institutions such as family, marriage, church, media, and schools systems that play a central role in transmitting or educating people about values and practices regarding gender roles, power, and relationships.

We believe that coordinated efforts of different social-political-cultural systems are crucial in eradicating domestic violence. The development of a highly structured coordination among the vast number of institutions is difficult, if not counterproductive, because of the complexity of networks involved. Consistent with the philosophy of our program, however, it is important to look for common goals, small changes, and connections among institutions that can create a positive difference in the process. We have found it very useful to develop cooperative relationships with certain players in the broader system. Empirical evidence indicates that combined interventions of arrest, incarceration, legal advocates, victim services, the court's criteria for batterer programs, as well as the court's responses to noncompliant participants contribute to the reduction of recidivism and/or program effectiveness (Edleson, 1991; Kaci & Tarrant, 1988; Steinman, 1988). In our work, we maintain connections with the district attorney, probation departments, and judges, since all these people play important roles in seeing that offenders are held accountable for their behavior. We suspect that most group participants will never voluntarily seek treatment for their problems; they come to our program only because they are mandated to do so. In this way, the "positive therapeutic impact" of our group treatment program is made possible only by the strong backup of legal power. In other situations, we recognize that punishment, including limited incarceration, sends an important message that in some cases reduces or prevents further violent behavior, not just with offenders but perhaps with otherwise potential offenders.

Besides making connections with the legal agencies, we find it very important to develop supportive relationships with people who are providing services for victims (Gondolf, 1991). An implicit and ultimate concern of most treatment programs for domestic violence offenders is the safety of victims. We want feedback from providers serving the victims because they have types of information on the results of treatment that we could not attain through other means. They also can affect outcomes by how they address victims, and thus we take every opportunity to inform and help them understand what we do. Collaboration with other involved service providers for offenders is also beneficial. Our emphasis on collaboration is supported by existing literature that indicates a positive impact of collaboration with other services such as mental health programs and victim services on the effectiveness of treatment programs for offenders (Eisikovits & Edleson, 1989).

Another crucial connection is between researchers and service providers (Edleson & Bible, 2001; Gondolf, Yllö, & Campbell, 1997). We strongly believe that it is very productive for service providers and researchers to work directly together to answer questions that are of interest to each other and the population they serve. Many service providers who attempt to create new avenues and approaches to addressing problems do so with little or no research support, making it difficult to tell whether or not meaningful change is occurring. Similarly, most service providers want to be effective and want to know which parts of what they are doing are effective, yet they do not have the effective means or resources to evaluate what they do. For researchers, the benefits of collaboration include enhanced legitimacy and utilization of research, development of improved and relevant research questions, enhanced research implementation, increased cooperation with agencies, and connection to the field, making the research efforts relevant to meaningful social purposes (Edleson & Bible, 2001). By sharing expertise and pulling resources together, partnership between researchers and service providers enhances society's ability to improve treatment programs and expand knowledge regarding these programs.

We have found certain strategies or components particularly relevant in developing and maintaining connections with different partners. These components include establishing clear roles and expectations of collaboration early on in the process, maintaining ongoing communication and sharing of useful information, developing attitudes that fosters trust and cooperation, maintaining nonhierarchical relationships, remaining flexible in problem solving, and spending time in each other's domain to foster increased understanding. These are fundamental and ordinary components of relationship building, although their impact on collaboration can be far-reaching and significant.

Separation of Social Control and Treatment

Despite our strong belief in concerted efforts, we believe that efforts of different systems should be coordinated but not confused. There must be a clear separation of punishment, legal decision making, and facilitation of change responsibilities. Each system has its own mandate and purpose. Confusion of responsibilities is problematic for both the participant and the provider. For instance, judges want to make the best decisions based on an informed position that addresses the issue of justice; attorneys want to provide the best defense for their clients; and prosecutors want to hold people accountable for breaking the law; and treatment providers emphasize positive changes and growth in individual participants. Conflicting roles of professionals of different domains may serve to confuse rather than benefit participants.

The separation of social control and treatment functions is relevant to service providers of treatment programs for domestic violence offenders. We avoid taking a social control stance that focuses on holding offenders accountable for their problems, educating them about what is right or wrong. Treatment cannot effectively serve a social control function for the simple reason that therapists are not legitimized by society to punish and control people. We can do only what we are professionally trained to do, that is, to assist people in a self-initiated process of change. Other advantages of separating punishment from treatment include the following: (1) It is easier for a group facilitator to engage and develop a working relationship with group participants because the facilitator does not play a role in determining who gets what punishment but simply provides treatment to the participant who is mandated or required by the courts to receive treatment; (2) it is more likely that participants will talk about issues they feel are relevant to changes they need to make, rather then simply wanting to present themselves in a good light so that they can get the court off their backs; and (3) the group facilitator is relieved from the dilemma of having to provide treatment and at the same time be a social control agent.

Focusing on Strengths

Community responses to domestic violence have largely been dominated by a deficits perspective. Most batterer programs utilizing cognitive-behavioral-feminist frameworks focus on addressing cognitive and behavioral deficits of domestic violence offenders (Saunders, 1996). The focus is on confronting batterers to take responsibility for the problem of violence and reeducation. Most evaluations of batterer programs have used recidivism as the sole criterion for measuring success of treatment. Again, the focus is on a deficit, that is, violent behaviors of offenders. The questions that are raised appear to revolve around why a person is violent, how a person acts violently, how severe the violence is, and so forth. Asking questions based on a deficits perspective has greatly contributed to our understanding of the phenomenon of domestic violence, such as the violence cycle (Walker, 1984), psychological and social characteristics of offenders, and risk factors that contribute to violence

Advocating the use of a strengths-based approach for treating domestic violence offenders is not without controversy. Some service providers may find it unsettling to adopt a nonconfrontational approach that builds on the strengths of offenders in treatment instead of focusing on their weaknesses and deficits. Such an approach appears to be antithetical to the conventional wisdom of using punishment to extinguish negative behaviors. On the other hand, inquiry that operates from a strengths perspective explores a different set of questions that may potentiate new knowledge and new understanding about treating domestic violence offenders (Bennett & Williams, 2001). Relevant treatment questions can be: How does, and what makes, a person learn to negotiate, respect, communicate, listen, mutually resolve conflict, and fight without being violent in an intimate relationships? What are the strengths of an offender that can be utilized in assisting him or her to develop alternative beneficial behavior? Relevant research questions may include: What are the protective factors in the environment of people who have witnessed and/or experienced violence as children but do not use violence to resolve conflict? How do people stop being violent? What are the decision-making processes that are associated with mutual conflict resolution? The list of questions is endless, although addressing a different set of questions will lead us to uncharted territory that is likely to offer new knowledge and perspectives regarding treatment of offenders and responses to domestic violence.

Addressing Diversity as an Integral Part of Community Responses

Cultural diversity presents important challenges for treating domestic violence offenders. Whereas minority males are overrepresented among men arrested and prosecuted for domestic violence, they complete treatment programs at much lower rates than white offenders (Bennett & Williams, 2001). Race is a significant factor that has influence on trust, comfort, willingness to discuss critical issues, and participation in treatment groups for domestic violence offenders (Williams, 1995). People from diverse cultural backgrounds engender diverse beliefs regarding gender, marriage, power, and relationships and also exhibit different conflict resolution skills and help-seeking behaviors. A national study of domestic violence treatment programs (Williams & Becker, 1994) indicated that being color-blind was the most common approach adopted by domestic violence treatment programs to address (or not address) issues of cultural diversity that might contribute to the ineffectiveness of domestic violence treatment programs.

Developing cultural competence is a constantly discussed but mostly unresolved challenge for treatment providers. The existing literature usually describes cultural competence training as consisting of developing cultural awareness, culture-specific knowledge, and skills (Green, 1995). The emphasis on the components of cultivating awareness, imparting knowledge, and developing skills focuses on the "content" level of the training effort. We believe that providers should also engage in an ongoing reflexive process in which they can continuously examine, challenge, question, and expand their cultural assumptions in working with offenders from diverse backgrounds. It is through such a reflexive process that providers can go beyond being culturally sensitive or competent and fundamentally change their practice cognitively, affectively, and behaviorally in a respectful, responsive, and effective manner (Lee & Greene, 2002).

Diversity is not limited to race, ethnicity, or culture. Diversity also includes sexual orientation, religious beliefs, disabilities, and so on. In addition, despite commonly held views of domestic violence as being perpetrated by males upon females, domestic violence takes many forms, including females assaulting males, and both genders attacking each other. It also occurs in same-sex relationships. Eradication of domestic violence ultimately requires an awareness and understanding of the many and varied forms violence takes.

Conclusion

There is much diversity and great differences in how the problem of domestic violence is or should be approached. A solution-focused approach that uses the language and symbols of "solution and strengths" for treating domestic violence offenders is part of the pluralistic, societal effort to develop pragmatic solutions to end the more immediate, visible violence in intimate relationships. From our perspective, effective community-wide change cannot occur without the development of effective partnerships among different systems in which roles and responsibilities are clearly defined. These partnerships ideally should result in a seamless system that prevents individuals from slipping through the cracks. An orchestrated system assures that offenders get to treatment and complete it in a timely manner; offers effective choices, support, advocacy and intervention for victims; and evaluates its effectiveness and modifies its approaches accordingly. While doing so, it is imperative not to lose sight of offenders from diverse backgrounds and the varied forms that domestic violence can take. In order for treatment programs to be effective, they have to address the issue of diversity as an integral part of the treatment process instead of perceiving it as just another dimension competing for the group's time and attention.

The use of the language and symbols of "solution and strengths" for treating domestic violence offenders is not without controversy. On the other hand, we strongly value diversity and multiple voices in the search for effective treatment of domestic violence offenders. A single voice or a single vision can only replicate the dynamic in abusive relationships. While valuing multiple voices, it is important to evaluate the effectiveness of a particular treatment program and carefully examine the associated mechanisms and processes that contribute to its effectiveness so that treatment is based on an informed position in addition to ethical choices or ideological preferences.

The following story concludes our thoughts about our work with domestic violence offenders. A number of years ago, while camping and climbing in the High Sierra, I sat near a mountain lake surrounded by steep, walled granite cliffs. The cliffs formed a natural amphitheater that allowed me to hear the sounds of two climbers ascending the rock walls in the early morning light. I tuned my ears to their conversation and focused my eyes on their ascent.

It was clear that the older, more experienced climber was asking questions and complimenting the younger climber, who was in the lead. At times the younger climber would say, "I don't think I can do this" or "There really is no place to go, no holds here." The older climber would say, "You're doing great, I'm impressed by what you've accomplished." This was followed by, "Is that a crack above your head?" The younger climber, reaching up, stretching, feeling for the crack, responded, "It's too far, but there's a little knob up there I might be able to use . . . yea!" "That's great. You're doing wonderfully. What do think about having lunch on that shelf above you?" "Sounds like a good goal. I think I can do that."

As the young climber approached the overhanging shelf, it was apparent that he was anxious. Watching and listening, my hands became slippery with sweat. The older climber's voice rang out calm and clear, "Of course you're scared. This is a very challenging spot. What can you do to calm yourself?" The young climber responded tersely, *You're the expert. You tell me!* The older climber waited, looking up, opening his mouth as if to speak but thinking better of it. The young climber finally said, "I just need to take a breath and look at this rock." The older climber responded, "You're the man. Take in some air and look around." This statement clearly conveyed the reality that the young climber would have to be the expert regarding his current dilemma and that the older climber respected his ability to "get the job done."

The young climber asked, "Do you think I can jam my foot in that crack and swing around the shelf?" The older climber paused, "Can't really tell from here. It looks possible. What do you think?" "I'm going to try it . . . keep tension in the ropes . . . Oh yea!! I'm up and over. That was easier than I thought." The older climber yelled, "That was incredible! What a great move. That was a major move. You're becoming a real fine climber."

As I lay back on the smooth slabs of rock, I thought back to a comment made by Steve de Shazer during training at the Brief Therapy Center in Milwaukee. In summary, Steve said that much of the world is focused on constructing problem descriptions rather than solutions. When climbing a mountain, as in most of life's adventures, it is often much more useful to focus on the solutions.

Appendix 1

Theoretical Perspectives
of Domestic Violence

Domestic violence is a prominent issue in our society. It has pervasive and harmful consequences for victims, mostly women and children, and for the society as a whole. Many theories have been put forward to explain the etiology of domestic violence that include micro-oriented theories, macro-oriented theories, and multidimensional theories.

Micro-oriented Theories

Micro-oriented theories understand and explain the etiology and dynamic of domestic violence from an individual perspective. Characteristics of individuals constitute the focus of examination.

Social Learning Theory

Social learning theory utilizes the concept of modeling (Bandura, 1973) and classical and operant conditioning (Skinner, 1953) to explain how individuals acquire violent behaviors in intimate relationships. Social learning theory proposes that individuals learn how to behave through experience of and/or exposure to violence. Oftentimes, this theory is termed the "intergenerational transmission of violence" when applied to situations of domestic violence. Individuals who experience or witness violence in their family of origin learn that violence is an appropriate tactic or acceptable means for getting what they want (Doumas, Margolin, & John, 1994; Arias & O'Leary, 1988; Straus, Gelles, & Steinmetz, 1980). Critics of the theory, however, argue that this explanation is insufficient because not everyone who witnesses or experiences violence as a child grows up to be violent. A review conducted by Kaufman and Ziegler (1987) suggested that the rate of intergenerational transmission of violence was only 30%. In addition, not all violent individuals have been exposed to violence as children (Arias & O'Leary, 1984). Still, social learning theory remains one of the most popular theories for explaining domestic violence; it suggests that victimization and witnessing of violence are among the most consistent risk markers for adult violence (Hotaling & Sugarman, 1986; Saunders, 1995).

Psychopathology and/or Personality Characteristics

A psychopathogical explanation suggests that individuals are violent because of various types of personality styles, psychopathologies, and psychological characteristics, including borderline personality organization (Dutton & Starzomski, 1993); aggressive or hostile personality styles (Heyman et al., 1995); narcissistic personality styles (Dutton, 1994a; Gondolf, 1999; Hamberger & Hastings, 1990); extreme jealousy and anxiety about abandonment (Holtzworth-Munroe, Stuart, & Hutchinson, 1997); elevated levels of depressive symptoms (Vivian & Malone, 1997) mediated by a higher level of self-reported anger (Feldbau-Kohn, Heyman, & O'Leary, 1998); low self-esteem (Gondolf, 1988); and high need for power (Dutton & Strachan, 1987). From such a perspective, violent acts are carried out by sick individuals who might not have control over their behaviors. Critics of the psychopathological explanation for domestic violence argue that such an approach reduces offenders' responsibility for their actions and minimizes the role of social structure in perpetuating violence in our society (D. O'Leary, 1993).

Biological and Physiological Explanations

Biological and physiological explanations focus on the contribution of individual biological and neurological factors in producing violent behaviors. Rosenbaum and his associates (1994) found than more than 90% of men in their sample had experienced head injury prior to the first instance of aggression, and men with head injuries were almost six times more likely to be batterers than men without head injuries. Other factors such as childhood attention deficit disorder (Elliot, 1988) and biochemical factors such as testosterone and serotonin (Johnson, 1996) have been identified as risk markers for relationship violence. Such an explanatory theory, however, eliminates responsibility on the part of the offender for his actions.

Alcohol and Violence

Substance abuse, especially alcohol consumption, is commonly associated with intimate violence (Fagan, 1993). Studies have also found a significant association between a family history of violence, current alcohol use, and the incidence of spouse abuse (Kaufman, 1993).

Micro-oriented theories focus on individuals' characteristics for explaining violent behaviors. These theories have made significant contributions to our understanding of the etiology of domestic violence, although they either reduce responsibility of or blame the offenders for their actions. Such approaches also minimize the role of social structure in contributing to and maintaining violence in intimate relationships.

Macro-oriented Theories

Macro-oriented theories focus on the social and cultural conditions that contribute to the occurrence of domestic violence. Domestic violence is no longer being viewed as an individual pathology. Instead, it is embedded in broader sociocultural conditions that reinforce and support violent behaviors. The more prominent theories include the feminist perspective, family violence perspective, and the subculture of violence.

Feminist Perspective

Feminist theory focuses primarily on violence of men against women. From such a perspective, violence against women is a manifestation of a system of male dominance and female submission supported by the concept of patriarchy (Chornesky, 2000; Dobash & Dobash, 1979) and maintained by various societal institutions, including male-dominated social structure and socialization practices that teach men and women gender-specific roles (Yllö & Straus, 1990). In particular, family represents one of the most powerful social institutions that reinforces the submission of women to men and patriarchal values. Violence becomes a means to maintain social control and male power over women (Levinson, 1989). Feminist explanations of violence also focus on the relationship between the cultural ideology of male dominance and structural forces that limit women's access to resources. Critics of the feminist perspective question its explanatory power regarding domestic violence. For instance, only a small percentage of men use violence against women, despite strong patriarchal beliefs and structure in the society. In addition, Dutton (1994b) suggest that a broad focus on male privilege and dominance cannot predict individual thoughts and actions and is too simplistic because it ignores differences among men. Also, such a framework cannot account for violence by women in both lesbian and heterosexual relationships (Straus & Gelles, 1990). Still, the feminist perspective remains a predominant macrostructural theory for explaining domestic violence, since 90% to 95% of domestic violence victims are women (Kurz, 1997).

Family Systems Perspective

The family systems perspective views domestic violence from an interactive and relational perspective (Lloyd, 1999; Margolin, 1979). It focuses on the nature of family structure to understand the origin of domestic violence, and gender does not constitute a major focus of examination because women are found to be as violent, as men (Stets & Straus, 1990). Violent behaviors are usually part of a pattern of escalating retributive strategies used by the couple to resolve differences. Characteristics that make a family prone to violence include legitimizing violence by using corporal punishment, accepting violence as one solution to family conflict, providing basic training in the use of violence through physical punishment, and creating a link between love and violence (Straus, 1990). The semi-involuntary nature of family membership makes family socialization a powerful force in shaping individuals' behaviors. Because a family violence perspective emphasizes the mechanisms that maintain domestic violence in general and does not focus on violence against women, it has been heavily criticized by feminists as neglecting the role of patriarchal beliefs and structures in maintaining violence against women, discarding empirical evidence that 90% to 95% of victims in domestic violence are women (Kurz, 1997), and diverting resources from assisting women victims.

Subculture of Violence

The subculture of violence perspective suggests that in certain subcultures violence is viewed as acceptable and is even encouraged. These groups are more likely to accept the use of violence to achieve what people want. For instance, individuals from a lower social class are more likely to accept and use violence than are individuals from a higher class (Wolfgang & Ferracuti, 1982). Schwartz and DeKeseredy (1997) developed the male peer support group model and suggested that violence against women is supported among male peer subgroups that reinforce values that condone violent behavior as a legitimate means to dominate and control women.

Integrative Frameworks

Integrative frameworks attempt to integrate micro factors (such as psychological or personality characteristics, relationship dynamics, substance abuse) and macro factors (such as gender, class, culture, and race) in explaining domestic violence. These frameworks are multidimensional. For example, Gelles (1983) used principles of both exchange theory and social control theory in explaining violence. Exchange theory assumes that human behaviors are guided by a calculation of rewards and punishments (Homans, 1967). Social control theory postulates that deviant behaviors will occur in the absence or inadequacy of social sanction against the behavior. In other words, offenders use violence because the reward of violence is greater than the cost (i.e., social sanction and/or other negative consequences). Anderson (1997) integrates elements of feminist and family violence perspectives in examining domestic violence. Patriarchal beliefs and structures serve to increase the risk for violence against women because they influence the power structure within the family or intimate relationships. Heron, Javier, McDonald-Gomez, and Adlerstein (1994) developed the social etiological model to explain domestic violence. This multidimensional interactive model of violence and aggression incorporates both structural and personal factors in understanding domestic violence. Violence against women is a result of structural inequalities in our social system and in particular the organization of family. At the personal level, an individual may have a distortion of reality and morality to justify the use of violence to resolve conflicts and gain control in intimate relationships.

Appendix 2

Written Assignment

Participants are requested to write a one-page assignment on one of the following topics. If they hand in less than one page, it is returned to them, and they are told to write at least a complete page. We are not interested in English composition, just their thoughts on the topic. The number of assignments we give is dependent on the time available in the group; sometimes we give only two during the 8-week group. We always give assignment six at the seventh session and request that it be returned by the eighth session. The topics of the assignment are as follows.

Assignment 1

What are the small things that make a relationship work?

Assignment 2

What do you do to let your partner know you care about him or her, and what does he or she do to let you know you are cared about? Do both of you know how the other shows caring?

Assignment 3

If a miracle happened so the problem that brought you here were resolved, describe what your life would look like.

Assignment 4

Describe a person in your life who had a powerful positive impact on you and why.

Assignment 5

What would you like your life to look life 6 months from now?

Assignment 6

What have you learned from this group? What do you intend to keep working on even after the group is over? How confident are you on a scale of 1 to 10 that you will keep working on your goal after the group is completed?

Appendix 3

Group Rules

Rule 1. Attendance

There will be eight group sessions. You must inform us prior to a session if you will not be able to attend. You will still be responsible for any assignments due for the session you missed. If you miss more than one session, you will be terminated from the program. We are required to report your attendance to the probation office. We expect you to be on time. Arriving after the sign-in sheet has been passed around will constitute one miss.

Rule 2. Violence

Violence of any sort is unacceptable. Any use of violence will result in termination from the program.

Rule 3. Confidentiality

Everything discussed in this group is confidential. If you break this rule, you will be terminated from the group.

Rule 4. Alcohol and Drugs

You will be asked to leave the group if you are thought to be under the influence of drugs or alcohol. This means any use of alcohol or drugs on the day of the group will lead to your being discharged from the group.

Rule 5. Assignments

You will be expected to read and complete all written assignments. If for some reason you find it difficult to complete a task, it is your responsibility to ask for help.

Rule 6. Group Discussion

Participants are expected to discuss and share their ideas and thoughts during the group. If you disagree with the facilitators or other participants, you are encouraged to express that disagreement. However, all disagreements are to be handled with respect for other person's opinions, ideas, and feelings.

Rule 7. No Blaming Talk

We will not directly focus on the behavior of others, and we will discourage you from doing so. It has been our experience that the only person's behavior that you can change is your own.

Rule 8. Goals

You must have a goal by the end of the third session. The goal must be something you choose to do different that improves your life that other people can notice and can be positively affected by. If you don't have a goal by the third session, you will not be able to continue.

References

Adams, D. (1988). Treatment models of men who batter: A pro-feminist analysis. In K. Yllö & M. Bograd (Eds.), *Feminist perspectives on wife abuse* (pp. 176–199). Newbury Park, CA: Sage.

Anderson, K. L. (1997). Gender, status, and domestic violence: An integration of feminist and family violence approaches. *Journal of Marriage and the Family, 59,* 655–669.

Arias, I., & O'Leary, K. D. (1984, November). *Factors moderating the intergenerational transmission of marital aggression.* Paper presented at the 18th annual meeting of the Association for the Advancement of Behavior Therapy, Philadelphia.

Arias, I., & O'Leary, K. D. (1988). Cognitive-behavioral treatment of physical aggression in marriage. In N. Epstein, W. Dryden, & S. Schlesinger (Eds.), *Cognitive-behavioral therapy with families* (pp. 118–150). New York: Brunner/Mazel.

Aronsson, K., & Cederborg, A. C. (1996). Coming of age in family therapy talk: Perspective setting in multiparty problem formulations. *Discourse Processes, 21,* 191–212.

Asay, T. P., & Lambert, M. J. (1999). The empirical case for the common factors in therapy: Quantitative findings. In M. A. Hubble, B. L. Duncan, & S. Miller (Eds.), *The heart and soul of change: What works in therapy.* Washington, DC: American Psychological Association.

Bandura, A. (1973). *Aggression: A social learning analysis.* Englewood Cliffs, NJ: Prentice Hall.

Bateson, G. (1972). *Steps to an ecology of mind.* New York: Ballantine.

Bateson, G. (1979). *Mind and nature: A necessary unity.* New York: Dutton.

Becvar, D. S., & Becvar, R. J. (1996). *Family therapy: A systemic integration.* Boston: Allyn and Bacon.

Belenky, M. F., Clinchy, B. McV., Goldberger, N. R., & Tarule, J. M. (1997). *Women's ways of knowing: The development of self, voice, and mind.* New York: Basic Books.

Bennett, L. W., & Williams, O. J. (2001). Intervention programs for men who batter. In C. M. Renzetti, J. L. Edleson, & R. K. Bergen (Eds.), *Sourcebook on violence against women* (pp. 261–277). Thousand Oaks, CA: Sage.

Berg, I. K. (1990). *Goal negotiation with mandated clients*. Milwaukee: WI: Brief Family Therapy Center.

Berg, I. K. (1994). *Family-based services: A solution-focused approach*. New York: Norton.

Berg, I. K., & DeJong, P. (1996). Solution-building conversations: Co-constructing a sense of competence with clients. *Families in Society, 77*, 376–391.

Berg, I. K., & Dolan, Y. M. (2001). *Tales of solutions: A collection of hope-inspiring stories*. New York: Norton.

Berg, I. K., & Kelly, S. (2000). *Building solutions in child protective services*. New York: Norton.

Berg, I. K., & Miller, S. (1992). *Working with the problem drinker: A solution-focused approach*. New York: Norton.

Berg, I. K., & Reuss, N. (1998). *Solutions step by step: A substance abuse treatment manual*. New York: Norton.

Berger, P. L., & Luckmann, T. (1966). *The social construction of reality: A treatise in the sociology of knowledge*. New York: Doubleday.

Blount, R. W., Silverman, I. J., Sellers, C. S., & Seese, R. A. (1994). Alcohol and drug use among abused women who kill, abused women who don't and their abusers. *Journal of Drug Issues, 24*, 165–177.

Bograd, M., & Mederos, F. (1999). Battering and couple therapy: Universal screening and selection of treatment modality. *Journal of Marital and Family Therapy, 25*, 291–312.

Cadsky, O., Hanson, R. K., Crawford, M., & Lalonde, C. (1996). Attrition from a male batterer treatment program: Client-treatment congruence and lifestyle instability. *Violence and Victims, 11*, 51–64.

Campbell, J. C. (1986). Nursing assessment for risk of homicide with battered women. *Advances in Nursing Science, 8*, 36–51.

Campbell, J. C., & Dienemann, J. D. (2001). Ethical issues in research on violence against women. In C. M. Renzetti, J. L. Edleson, & R. K. Bergen (Eds.), *Sourcebook on violence against women* (pp. 57–72). Thousand Oaks, CA: Sage.

Cantwell, P., & Holmes, S. (1994). Social construction: A paradigm shift for systemic therapy and training. *Australian and New Zealand Journal of Family Therapy, 15*, 17–26.

Charmaz, K. (2000). Grounded theory: Objectivist and constructivist methods. In N. K. Denzin & Y. S. Lincoln (Eds.), *Handbook of qualitative research* (2nd ed., pp. 509–535). Thousand Oaks, CA: Sage.

Chornesky, A. (2000). The dynamics of battering revisited. *Affilia: Journal of Women and Social Work, 15*, 480–501.

Chung, D. K. (1992). Asian cultural commonalities: A comparison with mainstream American culture. In S. M. Furuto, R. Biswas, D. K. Chung, K. Murase, & F. Ross-Sheiff (Eds.), *Social work practice with Asian Americans* (p. 27–44). Newbury Park, CA: Sage.

Davis, R. C., Taylor, B. G., & Maxwell, C. D. (2000, January). *Does batterer treatment reduce violence? A randomized experiment in Broolyn*. New York: Victim Services.

de Becker, G. (1997). *The gift of fear: Survival signals that protects us from violence*. Boston: Little, Brown.

de Shazer, S. (1994). *Words were originally magic*. New York: Norton.

de Shazer, S. (1991). *Putting difference to work.* New York: Norton.

de Shazer, S. (1988). *Clues: Investigating solutions in brief therapy.* New York: Norton.

de Shazer, S. (1985). *Keys to solutions in brief therapy.* New York: Norton.

de Shazer, S., Berg, I. K., Lipchik, E., Nunnally, E., Molnar, A., Gingerich, W., & Weiner-Davis, M. (1986). Brief therapy: Focused solution development. *Family Process, 25,* 207–221.

DeJong, P & Berg, I. K. (1999, March). *Co-constructing cooperation with mandated clients.* 45th annual program meeting, Council on Social Work Education, San Francisco.

DeJong, P., & Berg, I. K. (2002). *Interviewing for solutions* (2nd ed.). Pacific Grove, CA: Brooks/Cole.

DeMaris, A., & Jackson, J. (1987). Batterers' reports of recidivism after counseling. *Social Casework, 68,* 142–154.

Dobash, R. E., & Dobash R. P. (1979). *Violence against wives: A case against the patriarchy.* New York: Free Press.

Dolan, Y. M. (1991). *Resolving sexual abuse: Solution-focused therapy and Ericksonian hypnosis for adult survivors.* New York: Norton.

Doumas, D., Margolin, G., & John, R. S. (1994). The intergenerational transmission of aggression across three generations. *Journal of Family Violence, 9,* 157–175.

Dunford, F. (2000). The San Diego Navy Experiment: An assessment of interventions for men who assault their wives. *Journal of Consulting and Clinical Psychology, 68,* 468–476.

Dutton, D. G. (1994a). The origin and structure of the abusive personality. *Journal of Personality Disorders, 8,* 181–191.

Dutton, D. G. (1994b). Patriarchy and wife assault: The ecological fallacy. *Violence and Victims, 9,* 167–182.

Dutton, D. G. (1995). Intimate abusiveness. *Clinical Psychology: Science and Practice, 2,* 207–224.

Dutton, D. G. (1998). *The abusive personality: Violence and control in intimate relationships.* New York: Guilford.

Dutton, D. G., Bodnarchuk, M., Kropp, R., Hart, S., & Ogloff, J. (1997). Wife assault treatment and criminal recidivism: An 11-year follow-up. *International Journal of Offender Therapy and Comparative Criminology, 41,* 9–23.

Dutton, D. G., & Starzomski, A. J. (1993). Borderline personality in perpetrators of psychological and physical abuse. *Violence and Victims, 8,* 327–337.

Dutton, D. G., & Strachan, C. E. (1987). Motivational needs for power and spouse-specific assertiveness in assaultive and nonassaultive men. *Violence and Victims, 2,* 145–156.

Edleson, J. L. (1991). Coordinated community responses to women battering. In M. Steinman (Ed.), *Woman battering: Policy responses* (pp. 203–220). Cincinnati, OH: Anderson.

Edleson, J. L. (1996). Controversy and change in batterers' programs. In J. L. Edleson & Z. C. Eisikovits (Eds.), *Future interventions with battered women and their families* (pp. 154–169). Thousand Oaks, CA: Sage.

Edleson, J. L., & Bible, A. L. (2001). Collaboration for women's safety. In C. M. Renzetti, J. L. Edleson, & R. K. Bergen (Eds.), *Sourcebook on violence against women* (pp. 73–95). Thousand Oaks, CA: Sage.

Edleson, J., & Brygger, M. (1986). Gender differences in self-reporting of batter-ing incidents. *Family Relations, 35,* 377–382.

Edleson, J. L., & Syers, M. (1990). Relative effectiveness of group treatments for men who batter. *Social Work Research Abstracts, 26,* 10–17.

Eisikovits, Z. C., & Edleson, J. L. (1989). Interviewing with men who batter: A critical review of the literature. *Social Service Review, 37,* 385–414.

Eisikovits, Z. C., Enosh, G., & Edleson, J. L. (1996). The future of intervention in woman battering. In J. L. Edleson & Z. C. Eisikovits (Eds.), *Future interven-tions with battered women and their families* (pp. 216–223). Thousand Oaks, CA: Sage.

Elliot, F. A. (1988). Neurological factors. In V. B. Van Hasselt, R. L. Morrison, A. S. Bellack, & M. Herson (Eds.), *Handbook of family violence* (pp. 359–382). New York: Plenum.

Erickson, M. H. (1980). *The collected papers of Milton H. Erickson on hypnosis* (Vol. 4, Ernest L. Ross, Ed.). New York: Irvington.

Fagan, J. (1989). Cessation of family violence: Deterrence and dissuasion. In L. Ohlin & M. Tonry (Eds.), *Family violence* (pp. 377–425). Chicago: Univer-sity of Chicago Press.

Fagan, J. (1993). *Set and setting revisited: Influences of alcohol and illicit drugs on the social context of violent events.* Rockville, MD: National Institute on Alcohol Abuse and Alcoholism Research.

Feder, L., & Forde, D. R. (2000, June). *A test of the efficacy of court-mandated counseling for domestic violence offenders: The Broward Experiment.* Executive summary of final report. Washington, DC: National Institute of Justice.

Feldbau-Kohn, S., Heyman, R. E., & O'Leary, K. D. (1998). Major depressive dis-order and depressive symptomatology as predictors of husband to wife physical aggression. *Violence and Victims, 13,* 347–360.

Geffner, R., & Mantooth, C. (1999). *Ending spouse/partner abuse: A psychoeduca-tional approach for individuals and couples.* New York: Springer.

Gelles, R. J. (1983). An exchange/social control theory. In D. Finkelhor, R. J. Gel-les, G. T. Hotaling, & M. A. Straus (Eds.), *The dark side of families: Current family violence research* (pp. 151–165). Beverly Hills, CA: Sage.

Gingerich, W. J., & Eisengart, S. (2000). Solution-focused brief therapy: A review of the outcome research. *Family Process, 39,* 477–498.

Glaser, B., & Strauss, A. L. (1967). *The discovery of grounded theory: Strategies for qualitative research.* Chicago: Aldine.

Goldman, J., & Baydanan, M. (1990). *Solution Identification Scale.* Denver, CO: Peaceful Alternatives in the Home.

Goldner, V. (1992, March/April). Making room for both/and. *The Family Therapy Networker,* 55–61.

Gondolf, E. W. (1988). Who are those guys? Toward a behavioral typology of bat-terers. *Violence and Victims, 3,* 187–203.

Gondolf, E. W. (1990). An exploratory survey of court-mandated batterer pro-grams. *Response, 13,* 7–11.

Gondolf, E. W. (1991). A victim-based assessment of court-mandated counseling for batterers. *Criminal Justice Review, 16,* 214–226.

Gondolf, E. W. (1997). Expanding batterer program evaluation. In G. Kaufman Kantor & J. L. Jasinski (Eds.), *Out of the darkness: Contemporary perspectives on family violence* (pp. 208–218). Thousand Oaks: CA: Sage.

Gondolf, E. W. (1999). MCMI-III results for batterer program participants in four cities: Less "pathological" than expected. *Journal of Family Violence, 14*, 1–17.

Gondolf, E. W. (2000). Human subject issues in batterer program evaluation. In S. W. Ward & D. Finkelhor (Eds.), *Program evaluation and family violence research* (pp. 273–297). Binghamton, NY: Haworth.

Gondolf, E. W., & White, R. J. (2001). Batterer program participants who repeatedly reassault: Psychopathic tendencies and other disorders. *Journal of Interpersonal Violence, 16*, 361–380.

Gondolf, E. W., Yllö, K., & Campbell, J. (1997). Collaboration between researchers and advocates. In G. Kaufman Kantor & J. L. Jasinski (Eds.), *Out of the darkness: Contemporary perspectives on family violence* (pp. 255–267). Thousand Oaks: CA: Sage.

Green, J. W. (1995). *Cultural awareness in the human services.* Needham Heights, MA: Allyn and Bacon.

Hamberger, L. K., & Hastings, J. E. (1990). Recidivism following spouse abuse abatement counseling: Treatment implications. *Violence and Victims, 5*, 157–170.

Hanson, B. (2002). Interventions for batterers: Program approaches, program tensions. In A. R. Roberts (Ed.), *Handbook of domestic violence intervention strategies: Policies, programs, and legal remedies* (pp. 419–448). New York: Oxford University Press.

Harris, G., Rice, M., & Quinsey, V. (1993). Violent recidivism of mentally disordered offenders: The development of a statistical prediction instrument. *Criminal Justice and Behavior, 20*, 315–335.

Hart, B. (1994). Lethality and dangerousness assessments. *Violence Update, 4*, 7–8.

Hastings, J. E., & Hamberger, L. K. (1988). Personality characteristics of spouse abusers: A controlled comparison. *Violence and Victims, 3*, 31–47.

Heron, W. G., Javier, R. A., McDonald-Gomez, M., & Adlerstein, L. K. (1994). Sources of family violence. *Journal of Social Distress and the Homeless, 3*, 213–228.

Heyman, R. E., O'Leary, K. D., & Jouriles, E. N. (1995). Alcohol and aggressive personality styles: Potentiators of serious physical aggression against wives? *Journal of Family Psychology, 9*, 44–57.

Ho, M. K. (1993). *Family therapy with ethnic minorities.* Newbury Park, CA: Sage.

Holtzworth-Munroe, A., & Stuart, G. L. (1994). Typologies of male batterers: Three subtypes and the differences among them. *Psychological Bulletin, 116*, 476–497.

Holtzworth-Munroe, A., Stuart, G. L., & Hutchinson, G. (1997). Violent versus nonviolent husbands: Differences in attachment patterns, dependency, and jealousy. *Journal of Family Psychology, 11*, 314–331.

Homans, G. C. (1967). Fundamental social processes. In N. Smelser (Ed.), *Sociology* (pp. 549–593). New York: Wiley.

Hotaling, G. T., & Sugarman, D. B. (1986). An analysis of risk markers in husband to wife violence: The current state of knowledge. *Violence and Victims, 1*, 101–124.

Hudson, W. W. (1992). *The WALMYR Assessment Scales Scoring Manual.* Tempe, AZ: WALMYR.

Jacobson, N. J., & Gottman, J. (1998). *When men batter women: New insights into ending abusive relationships.* New York: Simon and Schuster.

Jenkins, A. (1990). *Invitations to responsibility: The therapeutic engagement of men who are violent and abusive.* Adelaide, South Australia: Dulwich Centre Publications.

Johnson, H. C. (1996). Violence and biology: A review of literature. *Families in Society: The Journal of Contemporary Human Services, 77,* 3–18.

Kaci, J. H., & Tarrant, S. (1988). Attitudes of prosecutors and probation departments toward diversion in domestic violence cases in California. *Journal of Contemporary Criminal Justice, 4,* 187–200.

Kantor, G., & Straus, M. A. (1987). The "drunken bum" theory of wife beating. *Social Problems, 34,* 213–230.

Katz, J. (1985). The sociopolitical nature of counseling. *Counseling Psychologist, 13,* 615–624.

Kaufman, J., & Ziegle, E. (1987). Do abused children become abusive parents? *American Journal of Orthopsychiatry, 57,* 186–192.

Kaufman, G. Kantor. (1993). Refining the brush strokes in portraits of alcohol and wife assaults. In *Alcohol and interpersonal violence: Fostering multidisciplinary perspectives* (NIH Research Monograph No. 24, pp. 281–290). Rockville, MD: U.S. Department of Health and Human Services.

Keeney, B. P., & Thomas, F. N. (1986). Cybernetic foundations of family therapy. In F. P. Piercy & D. H. Sprenkle (Eds.), *Family therapy sourcebook* (pp. 262–287). New York: Guilford.

Kernis, M. H., & Sun, C.-R. (1994). Narcissism and reactions to interpersonal feedback. *Journal of Research in Personality, 28,* 4–13.

Kropp., P. R., Hart, S. D., Webster, C. D., & Eaves, D. (1999). *Spousal assault risk assessment guide: User's manual.* North Tonawanda, NY: Multi-Health Systems.

Kurz, D. (1997). Violence against women or family violence? Current debates and future directions. In L. L. O'Toole & J. Schiffman (Eds.), *Gender violence: Interdisciplinary perspectives* (pp. 443–453). New York: New York University Press.

Lax, W. D. (1996). Narrative, social constructivism, and Buddhism. In H. Rosen & K. T. Kuehlwein (Eds.), *Constructing realities; Meaning-making perspectives for psychotherapists* (pp. 195–220). San Francisco: Jossey-Bass.

Lee, M. Y. (1997). A study of solution-focused brief family therapy: Outcome and issues. *American Journal of Family Therapy, 25,* 3–17.

Lee, M. Y. (2000). Understanding Chinese battered women in North America: A review of the literature and practice implications. *Journal of Ethnic and Cultural Diversity in Social Work, 8,* 215–241.

Lee, M. Y., & Greene, G. J. (2002, February). *A teaching framework of transformative multicultural social work education.* Paper presented at the 48th annual conference of the Council of Social Work Education, Nashville, TN.

Lee, M. Y., Greene, G. J., & Rheinscheld, J. (1999). A model for short-term solution-focused group treatment of male domestic violence offenders. *Journal of Family Social Work, 3,* 39–57.

Lee, M. Y., Greene, G. J., Uken, A., Sebold, J., & Rheinscheld, J. (1997, July). *Solution-focused brief group treatment: A viable modality for treating domestic violence offenders?* Paper presented at the 5th International Family Violence Research Conference, Durham, NH.

Levinson, D. (1989). *Family violence in cross-cultural perspective* (Vol. 1). Newbury Park, CA: Sage.

Lincoln, Y. S. & Guba, E. G. (1985). *Naturalistic inquiry.* Thousand Oaks, CA: Sage.

Lindsey, M., McBride, R. W., and Platt, C. M. (1993). *AMEND: Philosophy and curriculum for treating batterers.* Littleton, CO: Gylantic.

Lipchik, E., Kubicki, A. D. (1996). Solution-focused domestic violence views: Bridges toward a new reality in couples therapy. In S. D. Miller, M. A. Hubble, & B. L. Duncan (Eds.), *Handbook of solution-focused brief therapy* (pp. 65–98). San Francisco, CA: Jossey-Bass.

Lloyd, S. A. (1999). The interpersonal and communication dynamics of wife battering. In X. B. Arriagapa & S. Oskamp (Eds.), *Violence in intimate relationships* (pp. 91–111). Thousand Oaks, CA: Sage.

Ma, J.L.C. (1998, October). *Cultural construction of the roles and functions of family therapists: The Hong Kong experience.* Paper presented at the Second Pan Asia-Pacific Conference on Mental Health, Beijing.

Margolin, G. (1979). Conjoint marital therapy to enhance anger management and reduce spouse abuse. *American Journal of Family Therapy, 7,* 13–23.

Martin, D. (1976). *Battered wives.* San Francisco, CA: Glide.

McNeill, M. (1987). Domestic violence: The skeleton in Tarasoff's closet. In D. J. Sonkin (Ed.), *Domestic violence on trial: Psychological and legal dimensions of family violence* (pp. 197–217). New York: Springer.

Mederos, F. (1999). Batterer intervention programs: The past and future prospects. In M. F. Shepard & E. L. Pence (Eds.), *Coordinating community responses to domestic violence: Lessons from Duluth and beyond* (pp. 127–150). Thousand Oaks, CA: Sage.

Miller, G. (1997). *Becoming miracle workers: Language and meaning in brief therapy.* New York: Aldine de Gruyter.

Milner, J. S., & Campbell, J. C. (1995). Prediction issues for practitioners. In J. C. Campbell (Ed.), *Assessing dangerousness: Violence by sexual offenders, batterers, and child abusers* (pp. 20–40). Thousand Oaks, CA: Sage.

Monahan, J. (1996). Violence prediction: The past twenty and the next twenty years. *Criminal Justice and Behavior, 23,* 107–119.

Mulvey, E. P., & Lidz, C. W. (1993). Measuring patient violence in dangerousness research. *Law and Human Behavior, 17,* 277–278.

Murphy, C. M., & Baxter, V. A. (1997). Motivating batterers to change in the treatment context. *Journal of Interpersonal Violence, 12,* 607–619.

Nardone, G., & Watzlawick, P. (1993). *The art of change.* San Francisco: Jossey-Bass.

Neimeyer, R. A., & Mahoney, M. J. (1993). *Constructivism in psychotherapy.* Washington, DC: American Psychological Association.

O'Hanlon, W., & Wilk, J. (1987). *Shifting contexts: The generation of effective psychotherapy.* New York: Guilford.

O'Leary, K. D. (1993). Through psychological lens: Personality traits, personality disorders, and level of violence. In R. Gelles & D. Loseke (Eds.), *Current controversies on family violence* (pp. 7–30). Newbury Park, CA: Sage.

O'Leary, K. D. (1988). Physical aggression between spouses: A social learning theory perspective. In V. B. Van Hasselt, R. L. Morrison, A. S. Bellack, & M. Hersen (Eds.), *Handbook of family violence* (pp. 31–56). New York: Plenum.

Pence, E., & Paymar, M. (1993). *Education groups for men who batter: The Duluth model.* New York: Springer.

Quinsey, V., Harris, G., Rice, M., & Lalumiere, M. (1993). Assessing treatment efficacy in outcome studies of sex offenders. *Journal of Interpersonal Violence, 8,* 512–523.

Rappaport, J. (1985, fall). The power of empowerment language. *Social Policy, 15–* 21.

Rees, S. (1998). Empowerment of youth. In L. M. Gutierrez, R. J. Parsons, & E. O. Cox (Eds.), *Empowerment in social work practice: A sourcebook* (pp. 130–145). Pacific Grove, CA: Brooks/Cole.

Rice, M. E. (1997). Violent offender research and implications for the criminal justice system. *American Psychologist, 52,* 414–423.

Roberts, A. R., & Kurst-Swanger, K. (2002). Court responses to battered women and their children. In A. R. Roberts (Ed.), *Handbook of domestic violence intervention strategies: Policies, programs, and legal remedies* (pp. 127–146). New York: Oxford University Press.

Rosen, H., & Kuehlwein, K. T. (Eds.). (1996). *Constructing realities: Meaning-making perspectives for psychotherapists.* San Francisco: Jossey-Bass.

Rosenbaum, A., Hoge, S. K., Adelman, S. A., Warnken, W. J., Fletcher, K. E., & Kane, R. L. (1994). Head injury in partner-abusive men. *Journal of Consulting and Clinical Psychology, 62,* 1187–1193.

Rosenbaum, A., & O'Leary, K. D. (1986). The treatment of marital violence. In N. S. Jacobson & A. S. Gurman (Eds.), *Clinical handbook of marital therapy* (pp. 385–405). New York: Guilford.

Rosenfeld, B. (1992). Court-ordered treatment of spouse abuse. *Clinical Psychology Review, 12,* 205–226.

Rossi, P., & Freeman, H. (1989). *Evaluation: A systematic approach.* Newbury Park, CA: Sage.

Russell, M. N. (1995). *Confronting abusive beliefs: Group treatment for abusive men.* Thousand Oaks, CA: Sage.

Saleebey, D. (1997). Introduction: Power in the people. In D. Saleebey (Ed.), *The strengths perspective in social work practice* (2nd ed., pp. 3–19). New York: Longman.

Saunders, D. G. (1990). Issues in conducting treatment research with men who batter. In G. T. Hotaling, D. Finkelhor, J. T. Kirkpatrick, & M. A. Straus (Eds.), *Coping with family violence: Research and policy perspectives* (pp. 145–156). Newbury Park, CA: Sage.

Saunders, D. G. (1995). Prediction of wife assault. In J. C. Campbell (Ed.), *Assessing dangerousness: Violence by sexual offenders, batterers, and child abusers* (pp. 68–95). Thousand Oaks, CA: Sage.

Saunders, D. G. (1996). Feminist-cognitive-behavioral and process-psycho-dynamic treatments for men who batter: Interaction of abuser traits and treatment models. *Violence and Victims, 11,* 393–413.

Saunders, D. G., & Azar, S. T. (1989). Treatment programs for family violence. In L. Ohlin & M. Tonry (Eds.), *Family violence: Crime and justice: A review of research* (Vol. 11, pp. 481–545). Chicago: University of Chicago Press.

Schechter, S. (1982). *Women and male violence: The vision and struggles of the battered women's movement.* Boston, MA: South End Press.

Schwandt, T. A. (1994). Constructivist, interpretivist approaches to human inquiry. In N. K. Denzin & Y. S. Lincoln (Eds.), *Handbook of qualitative research* (pp. 118–137). Thousand Oaks, CA: Sage.

Schwartz, M. D., & DeKeseredy, W. S. (1997). *Sexual assault on the college campus: The role of male peer support.* Thousand Oaks, CA: Sage.

Shepard, M. F. (1992). Predicting batterer recidivism five years after community intervention. *Journal of Family Violence, 7,* 167–178.

Shepard, M. F., & Campbell, J. A. (1992). The abusive behavior inventory: A measure of psychological and physical abuse. *Journal of Interpersonal Violence, 7,* 291–305.

Skinner, B. F. (1953). *Science and human behavior.* New York: Macmillan.

Small, S. A. (1995). Action-oriented research: Models and methods. *Journal of Marriage and the Family, 57,* 941–955.

Sonkin, D. J. (1995). *The counselor's guide to learning to live without violence.* Volcano, CA: Volcano Press.

Steinman, M. (1988). Evaluating a system-wide response to domestic violence: Some initial findings. *Journal of Contemporary Criminal Justice, 4,* 172–186.

Stets, J. E., & Straus, M. A. (1990). Gender differences in reporting marital violence and its medical and psychological consequences. In M. A. Straus & R. J. Gelles (Eds.), *Physical violence in American families: Risk factors and adaptations to violence in 8,145 families* (pp. 151– 165). New Brunswick, NJ: Transaction.

Straus, M. A. (1990). Social stress and marital violence in a national sample of American families. In M. A. Straus & R. J. Gelles (Eds.), *Physical violence in American families: Risk factors and adaptations to violence in 8,145 families* (pp. 181–201). New Brunswick, NJ: Transaction.

Straus, M. A. (1996). Identifying offenders in criminal justice research on domestic assault. In E. S. Buzawa & C. G. Buzawa (Eds.), *Do arrests and restraining orders work?* (pp. 14–29). Thousand Oaks, CA: Sage.

Straus, M. A., & Gelles, R. J. (Eds.). (1990). *Physical violence in American families: Risk factors and adaptations to violence in 8,145 families.* New Brunswick, NJ: Transaction.

Straus, M. A., Gelles, R. J., & Steinmetz, S. (1980). *Behind closed doors: Violence in the American family.* Garden City, NY: Anchor.

Sue, D. W., & Sue, D. (1990). *Counseling the culturally different: Theory and practice.* New York: Wiley.

Tolman, R. M. (1989). The development of a measure of psychological maltreatment of women by their male partners. *Violence and Victims, 4,* 159–177.

Tolman, R. M., & Bennett, L. W. (1990). A review of quantitative research on men who batter. *Journal of Interpersonal Violence, 5,* 87–118.

Tolman, R. M., & Edleson, J. L. (1995). Intervention for men who batter: A review of research. In S. Stith & M. A. Straus (Eds.), *Understanding partner violence: Prevalence, causes, consequences, and solutions* (pp. 262–274). Minneapolis, MN: National Council on Family Relations.

Troemel-Ploetz, S. (1977). "She is just not an open person": A linguistic analysis of a restructuring intervention in family therapy. *Family Process, 16,* 339–352.

Uken, A., & Sebold, J. (1996). The Plumas Project: A solution-focused goal-directed domestic violence diversion program. *Journal of Collaborative Therapies, 4,* 10–17.

Valliant, G. (1982). *The natural history of alcoholism.* Cambridge, MA: Harvard University Press.

Vivian, D., & Malone, J. (1997). Relationship factors and depressive symptomatology associated with mild and severe husband-to-wife physical aggression. *Violence and Victims, 12,* 3–18.

Walker, L. (1984). *The battered woman syndrome.* New York: Springer.

Wallace, J., Vitale, J., & Newman, J. (1999). Response modulation deficits: Implications for the diagnosis and treatment of psychopathy. *Journal of Cognitive Psychotherapy, 13,* 55–70.

Walter, J. L., & Peller, J. E. (1992). *Becoming solution-focused in brief therapy.* New York: Brunner/Mazel.

Warrior, B. (1976). *Wifebeating.* Somerville, MA: New England Free Press.

Watzlawick, P., Weakland, J. H., & Fisch, R. (1974). *Change, principles of problem formulation and problem resolution.* New York: Norton.

Weisz, A. N., Tolman, R. M., & Saunders, D. G. (2000). Assessing the risk of severe domestic violence: The importance of survivors' predictions. *Journal of Interpersonal Violence, 15,* 75–90.

Wesner, D., Patel, C., & Allen, J. (1991). A study of explosive rage in male spouses counseled in an Appalachian mental health clinic. *Journal of Counseling and Development, 70,* 235–241.

Wexler, D. B. (1999). *Domestic Violence 2000: An integrated skills program for men. Group leader's manual and resources for men.* New York: Norton.

Williams, O. J. (1995). Treatment for African American men who batter. *CURA Reporter, 25,* 610.

Williams, O. J., & Becker, L. R. (1994). Partner abuse programs and cultural competence: The results of a national study. *Violence and Victims, 9,* 287–295.

Wilson, M., & Daly, M. (1993). Spousal homicide risk and estrangement. *Violence and Victims, 8,* 3–17.

Wittgenstein, L. (1958). *Philosophical investigation* (G.E.M. Anscombe, Trans.). New York: Macmillan.

Wolfgang, M., & Ferracuti, F. (1982). *The subculture of violence* (2nd ed.). London: Tavistock.

Yalom, I. D. (1995). The theory and practice of group psychotherapy. New York: Basic Books.

Yllö, K., & Straus, M. A. (1990). Patriarchy and violence against wives: The impact of structural and normative factors. In M. A. Straus & R. J. Gelles (Eds.), *Physical violence in American families: Risk factors and adaptations in 8,145 families* (pp. 383–399). New Brunswick, NJ: Transaction.

Zeig, J. K. (1985). *Ericksonian psychotherapy: Vol. 1. Structures.* New York: Brunner/Mazel.

Index